INCENDIARY

Handwritten annotations:

I want it, babe

I want to have an orgasm later

Dude this is bad

I'm trying to talk about my sexual preferences Am I really !

oh my I have no shame

Sometimes vs

easier

Even though you're so vulnerable right now

Will

& vs any one trying to break in

At least your super cute

eck stuff

Not that, I like it but you wald

Satanists

I know a few and they're nice folks

You're surprisly rough, I really like it

ALSO BY MICHAEL CANNELL

I. M. Pei: Mandarin of Modernism
The Limit: Life and Death on the 1961 Grand Prix Circuit

INCENDIARY

THE PSYCHIATRIST,
THE MAD BOMBER,
AND THE INVENTION OF
CRIMINAL PROFILING

MICHAEL CANNELL

 MINOTAUR BOOKS 🙢 NEW YORK

www.minotaurbooks.com

Frontispiece: *The New York Times*/Redux

Designed by Steven Seighman

The Library of Congress has cataloged the hardcover edition as follows:

Names: Cannell, Michael T., author.
Title: Incendiary : the psychiatrist, the mad bomber, and the invention of criminal profiling / Michael Cannell.
Description: New York : Minotaur Books, [2017] | Includes bibliographical references and index.
Identifiers: LCCN 2017000713 | ISBN 9781250048943 (hardcover) | ISBN 9781250048936 (ebook)
Subjects: LCSH: Brussel, James A. (James Arnold), 1905–1982. | Bombings—New York (State)—New York—Case studies. | Criminal behavior, Prediction of—Case studies. | Criminal psychology—Case studies.
Classification: LCC HV6640 .C36 2017 | DDC 363.325092 [B]—dc23
LC record available at https://lccn.loc.gov/2017000713

ISBN 978-1-250-18236-4 (trade paperback)

Our books may be purchased in bulk for promotional, educational, or business use. Please contact your local bookseller or the Macmillan Corporate and Premium Sales Department at 1-800-221-7945, extension 5442, or by email at Macmillan SpecialMarkets@macmillan.com.

First Minotaur Books Paperback Edition: August 2018

10 9 8 7 6 5 4 3 2 1

CONTENTS

PREFACE

THIS IS A BOOK ABOUT MADNESS—MADNESS AND GUNPOWDER.

In these pages lives a serial bomber, a paranoid schizophrenic who, for a long, harrowing stretch of the 1950s, convulsed New York with dread. The nearly three dozen homemade explosives he set off in public places brought into being a culture of fear more than four decades before terrorism became an American fixation. He embodied everything unnerving about the years W. H. Auden called "the age of anxiety." Whatever cruelty they inflicted, the century's two great wars were at least fathomable. The bomber was not. He was like a dream distortion of postwar disquiet—unhinged, unrelenting, perpetually hidden in city shadows.

The bomber had a rightful grievance against an uncaring employer. His resentment transmogrified into a consuming rage. The venom spouted from a dark psychic hole where logic does not go. I correct myself: where normal logic does not go. Schizophrenics follow their own logic. We just don't understand it.

The NYPD certainly didn't understand it. The famously tough-minded New York detectives stumbled and fumbled, as a harassing band of newspaper reporters detailed at every turn. For more than a century the police had relied on muscle and shoe leather to collar bad guys. The street corner respected the billy club, and that was that. But the reliable strong-arm methods proved useless in the face of a schizophrenic serial bomber.

"Seldom in the history of New York," wrote the Associated Press, "has a case proved such a torment to police."

The bomber's rampage came at a time when science was transforming the way Americans thought about the world around them. Jonas Salk came up with the polio vaccine, eradicating a disease that had crippled hundreds of thousands. Bell Labs paved the way for modern electronics, and all that came with it, by inventing the silicon transistor. Physicist Edward Teller created the hydrogen bomb.

Scientific advancements, however, did not elevate policing, at least not in New York. The NYPD's corrupt precinct captains and stubborn commanders resisted new methods promoted by college-educated criminologists—until the serial bomber forced them to adapt. With the manhunt reaching critical urgency, the police took the unprecedented step of asking a psychiatrist what the forensic evidence revealed about the bomber's troubled inner life. What strange sort of person was he, and what wounding life experience led to his murderous avocation? In other words, they asked the psychiatrist to invent a new criminal science, one that would peer into the mind of the bomber. The term *profiling* would not be coined for another two decades.

Until then the only investigators who had drawn portraits of a criminal's emotional history existed in the stories of Edgar Allan Poe and Sir Arthur Conan Doyle. Sherlock Holmes could size up the evidence and bring blackmailers and assassins to mind with photographic precision. Could a psychiatrist do the same in real life? Could life imitate a murder mystery?

Today art mostly imitates life. Television and movies have so inundated us with fictional accounts of profiling that we easily lose sight of what a breakthrough it was in 1957. Every one of today's profilers, real or televised, traces his or her lineage back to the psychiatrist who depicted the serial bomber with uncanny accuracy.

What follows is an account of profiling's beginnings. Everything in these pages is true, including the quotations (though the bomber's thoughts are speculation). Like any resonant story it contains at its heart an unanswerable question: Can science alone grasp the intricacies of the human mind, or does true understanding require the reverberative powers of intuition? How does one apprehend the wits of a madman?

These questions gripped me as I worked on this book over the past three years. Along the way I came to understand that to write about madness is to write about one's self, however obliquely.

The virtuous man is content to dream what
a wicked man really does.
—Plato

Everybody has a hunch occasionally.
—Dr. James Brussel

INCENDIARY

PROLOGUE

December 1956

SHORTLY AFTER LUNCH ON A COLD DECEMBER MORNING IN 1956, A TRIO of New York City detectives stepped out the back door of the copper-domed police headquarters looming like a dirty gray temple above the tenements and trattorias of Little Italy. Across the street, half-shrouded in winter shadow, a revolver-shaped sign hung outside John Jovino's, the oldest gun store in the city, if not the country, where patrolmen bought the .38 Specials slung on their hips. Directly above Jovino's hung a fire escape where Weegee, the dean of tabloid photographers, perched with his boxy black Graflex flashbulb camera for choice views of handcuffed mobsters and murderers dragged in for booking. Down the block, on the corner of Grand Street, was a German restaurant called Headquarters. Under its carved mahogany ceiling, at a lengthy oak bar, the top brass took their off-duty rye and beer. Officers requiring discretion could enter the bar through an underground tunnel.

Today the three detectives had no time for such distractions. Led by a veteran captain, Howard Finney, they walked briskly to an unmarked police cruiser, a big green-and-white Plymouth, idling at the curb, and drove south through the winding downtown streets on an urgent errand.

Four days earlier a bomb had exploded during a showing of *War and Peace* at the Paramount movie palace on Flatbush Avenue, in Brooklyn.

At 7:55 p.m., as an audience of fifteen hundred gazed up at a St. Petersburg drawing room rendered in saturated Technicolor reds and blues, a thundering detonation flashed from orchestra row GG, followed by billows of ashen smoke. For an instant the air rang with shock, like the hushed moment after a window shatters. Then screams filled the theater—screams of pain, panic, and fright as moviegoers glimpsed faces and scalps scythed open by shrapnel. The audience sprang to its feet, like worshippers rising in unison for a hymn, and pressed hard for exits, leaving behind six injured. Above them the glimmering loveliness of Audrey Hepburn in ball gown and tiara waltzed on under the soft blue eyes of Henry Fonda.

The Paramount blast was not an isolated event. Any New Yorker who read newspapers knew that for sixteen years the police had searched for a serial bomber who identified himself only as F.P. He had planted thirty-two homemade explosives in the city's most crowded public spaces—theaters, terminals, subway stations, a bus depot, and a library—injuring fifteen. He timed most of the devices to go off shortly after 5:00 p.m., the height of rush hour.

F.P. had yet to kill, but it was only a matter of time. The *New York Journal-American,* an afternoon newspaper of scrappy disposition, called him "the greatest individual menace New York City ever faced." The capture of a bomb-building psycho with an insatiable, unreasoned grievance, the newspaper said, was "the most agonizing challenge of modern times."

In all those years, a period stretching back to 1940, the largest, most formidable police force in the world had failed to hustle up any worthy leads. Its failings were easily excusable as long as the bomber crafted crude and ineffective ordnance. But by 1956 his handiwork showed a lethal new proficiency. He declared his intent to kill in letters sent to newspaper editors. Each rambling, raging letter was cryptically signed "F.P."

The New York mood, already clouded by Cold War anxiety, darkened by the day. With each bomb the police looked more hapless. The mayor spoke of lawlessness. On the morning after the Paramount explo-

sion the newly installed police commissioner, Stephen P. Kennedy, ordered the "greatest manhunt in the history of the Police Department."

Desperation drove the police to pursue a course they had never before
considered in the department's 111-year history. On that late fall afternoon
Captain Finney and his two bomb squad sidekicks left headquarters to call
on Dr. James A. Brussel, a psychiatrist with expertise in the workings of
the criminal mind. If physical evidence could not lead the police to F.P.,
maybe emotional insights could.

A wiry figure with a droll smile and a pencil mustache dyed to match
his dark, combed-back hair greeted Captain Finney in the downtown
Broadway offices of the New York State Department of Mental Hygiene,
where Dr. Brussel served as deputy commissioner. He split time between
the department offices and a private psychiatric practice conducted in his
home on the grounds of a Queens psychiatric hospital. If Captain Finney
was circumspect and grave, Dr. Brussel was the opposite: loud of opinion, quick-witted, and manically animated.

Captain Finney emptied a satchel of evidence on Dr. Brussel's desk.
Out spilled photographs of unexploded bombs and theater seats ripped
open with pocketknives, along with photostats of strangely worded letters and crime scene reports amassed over sixteen years. "The bombs and
the letters: these were all the police had," Dr. Brussel would write. "The
rest was a mystery."

The three detectives barely stirred as Dr. Brussel picked through the
evidence, pausing to write notes in a pad. His mind assembled the possibilities as the information accrued. Captain Finney "was a short, stocky
man of many accomplishments and few words," Dr. Brussel later wrote.
"He was looking at me, waiting for me to say something. I was looking
at the pile of photographs and letters he had tossed on my desk."

Dr. Brussel sensed that Captain Finney, a quiet, deep-thinking type,
was prepared to listen, no matter how far-fetched the psychiatric feedback
might be. The two other bomb-squad detectives, on the other hand, barely
disguised their skepticism. They looked like caricatures of hardened

cops—square shouldered and thick chested with hard-set jaws clouded by five o'clock shadow. They rolled their eyes and smirked sideways at each other, like ill-behaved boys dragged to evening prayer. "They fidgeted, they sighed, they exchanged glances of alternating amusement and impatience," Dr. Brussel would write. "Catching criminals was police work. What could a psychiatrist know about it?"

To street-hardened detectives a psychiatrist carried no more weight than a psychic or a fortune-teller. Dr. Brussel knew that by venturing a psychiatric assessment of the bomber—what we now call a profile—he would be putting his profession's credibility on the line. And his own.

After two hours Dr. Brussel rose from his desk and stood at a window overlooking City Hall. The lowering sun cast weak winter rays on the dour municipal buildings standing against a blue-gray dusk. Twelve stories below, the first surge of rush-hour traffic thickened with long-finned sedans and Checker cabs clogging Broadway. Streetlights winked on. Chambers Street filled with men in trench coats and brimmed hats, heads down and shoulders slouched against the cold. They moved with haste, as New Yorkers do. "Any one of the people I saw below could have been the Mad Bomber," Dr. Brussel would write. "There was a man standing next to a car. Another man was lounging in a doorway. Another was strolling along, looking up intently at the buildings. Each of them was on these streets at that hour for some reason. Perhaps a legitimate reason, perhaps not. . . . So little was known about the Mad Bomber that virtually anyone in the city could be picked at random as a suspect. Anyone—and no one."

The manhunt had lasted so long and had engendered so much frustration that Captain Finney and his men had come to feel as if they were chasing a specter loose in the streets. "He seemed like a ghost," Dr. Brussel later recalled, "but he had to be made of flesh and blood. He had been born, he had a mother and father, he ate and slept and walked and talked. Somewhere people knew him, saw his face, heard his voice. . . . Probably thousands of people in and around New York had some fleeting contact with him at one time or another. He sat next to people on the subways and busses. He strolled past them on sidewalks He rubbed elbows with them in stores. Though he sometimes seemed to be made of night stuff, unsolid, bodiless, he patently did exist."

For a long moment Dr. Brussel looked as if he had slipped into a trance, as if he were straining to hear a signal in the white noise of the city—a psychic tap tap tap—that would lead him to the bomber.

While he was staring out at the strangers aswarm in the street, something clarified in Dr. Brussel's mind, like pixels cohering to form a picture. A detailed image of a living, breathing man took shape. He turned to Captain Finney and described his fugitive, right down to the cut of his jacket.

PART ONE

THE MANHUNT

CHAPTER ONE

ANGEL OF JUSTICE

October 1951

FIVE YEARS EARLIER, ON THE AFTERNOON OF OCTOBER 22, 1951, F.P. DROVE his Daimler sedan ninety miles down the Taconic Parkway, carefully minding the speed limits. If a highway patrolman stopped him, he might have cause for suspicion. The patrolman might frisk F.P., and he might discover the heavy object F.P. carried in his coat pocket.

In the earliest days of his bombing campaign F.P. rode the train to Manhattan, but he felt unbearably conspicuous. He was one of the few male passengers boarding in the hours after the morning commute. The women dressed for city luncheons or matinees shot him suspicious looks. The conductor paused a little too long while punching his ticket, as if to memorize his features. Or so F.P. imagined.

He parked the Daimler on Riverside Drive near Ninety-Sixth Street, as he always did, lingering in the driver's seat to slowly, deliberately pour gunpowder from a bottle into a length of pipe steadied between his leather lace-ups. By waiting to arm the bomb, he reduced the chance of an accidental explosion during his drive to the city.

He was on foot now, walking among the sober-faced office buildings standing shoulder to shoulder in midtown. A wealth of goods filled store windows—shined-up oxford shoes and woolen suits, Danish living room sets, DuMont televisions in dark wood cabinets. F.P. admired it all, as one covets things one will never have. The sidewalk crowds brushed by F.P., heightening his sense of invisibility. All the while the live bomb buried deep in the pocket of his overcoat ticked away like a mechanical heartbeat.

Soon the first wave of commuters would march east to Grand Central Terminal and board trains to outlying towns—Bedford, Rye, Darien. Clinking ice buckets and the hugs of pajama-soft children awaited them in ranch homes set back among the russet leaves of October. No such comforts would greet F.P. He had no job. No real home of his own. No familial warmth. He had none of the consolations he saw depicted on television or in *Life* magazine ads. What he nurtured instead was a grievance and a growing conviction that he—and he alone—was chosen to be a great avenger, an angel of justice.

Standing on the corner of Forty-Third Street and Broadway, F.P. could see the full neon honky-tonk shine of Times Square pulsating above him. Camel cigarettes. Admiral appliances. Chevrolet. The billboards glimmered and blinked with the wattage of a thousand lightbulbs, as if to compensate for the gloom of a dying afternoon.

On the west side of Times Square stood an ornate old movie palace called the Paramount, fronted by an oversize marquee with a gaudy highboy swoop. Four years later the Paramount would host one of the first rock-and-roll parties with Chuck Berry and other acts produced by radio DJ Alan Freed, but in 1951 it was still an old-fashioned movie theater equipped with a Wurlitzer that droned out popular standards before the newsreels and previews.

The lobby would be empty, or nearly so, when F.P. stepped inside among the white marble columns and crystal chandeliers to buy a ticket for *The Mob,* a gangster movie about a cop who infiltrates the waterfront rackets. The movie was the latest installment in a noir genre portraying tough guys and foul play on the city docks. A poster in the lobby portrayed three men with meaty gangster faces above the tagline "Cruel, Cunning, Cold as Ice."

F.P. looked anything but cruel or cunning. Nothing about him would have aroused the ticket taker's suspicion, dressed as he was in a forgetta-ble suit and tie. He was an almost perfectly nondescript forty-eight-year-old, stocky but not fat, with gold-rimmed eyeglasses, a slight pudge of double chin, and thinning colorless hair combed to a polite pompadour. He looked unremarkable in every way, as if life had failed to make a dis-tinguishing mark on him.

"He's the perfect example of a man you'd never recognize the second time you saw him," an acquaintance said. Nothing in his manner suggested what hung over him. He betrayed no hint of the murderous thoughts he carried.

He seated himself in an empty section of the center orchestra some distance from other moviegoers in the sparse late-afternoon crowd. The houselights dimmed, commanding the audience to silence. Up on the big screen, the story began. Rain pours hard on West Sixty-Third Street. In-side a pawnshop, Detective Johnny Damico haggles over earrings he wants to buy for his girlfriend. Walking home, he hears gunfire. A body lies facedown in the wet, empty street. A man in a trench coat stands over the victim with a gun. The shooter produces a shiny badge. He identifies himself as Lieutenant Henderson from the Twenty-First Precinct. Hen-derson says he'll go over to a nearby diner to phone in a report of the shoot-out to headquarters. Instead he slips out the back door.

It was time for F.P. to make his own escape. He stood up and shuffled down the aisle, as if leaving to use the men's room. The bomb stayed behind. He walked away unnoticed under the throbbing shine of Times Square lights.

CHAPTER TWO

BOMB SQUAD

October 1951

THE BOMB SQUAD SETTLED IN FOR ITS EVENING SHIFT JUST AS F.P. LEFT the Paramount Theater on October 22. The detectives killed time in an open squad room on the top floor of a three-story brick-and-brownstone building on Poplar Street, hard against the long downslope of the Brooklyn Bridge off-ramp in a nearly deserted backwater of the Brooklyn Heights neighborhood. Miniature models of a dozen bomb types hung from the ceiling, like hobby aircraft in a boy's bedroom.

The detectives sat around drab metal desks in their cheap G-man suits, narrow ties loosened and hats pushed back, shuffling paperwork and kidding around. If things got really quiet, they might deal a hand of rummy. The green lights strung along the bridge cables twinkled outside their windows. One might reasonably assume that they talked about the New York Giants, who had two days earlier surged from a 17–0 halftime deficit to beat the Philadelphia Eagles at the Polo Grounds. Whatever the subject, the banter would have been loose and light-hearted, despite the evasive serial bomber causing them anxious days. By custom, bomb squad detectives affected the deliberately relaxed manner found among those who work in close contact with dangerous possibilities, as if reserving their acuity for when they needed it most.

The squad consisted of ten detectives drawn from a waiting list. Most were former military-ordnance officers or commercial blasters who, by quirk of personality, chose to earn a living handling combustibles. All volunteered. All were married with children. The bomb squad was known within police circles as the world's most dangerous assignment. The men's bravery earned them no hazard pay, no special benefits. The turnover rate was among the lowest in the police department.

The job entailed stretches of boredom relieved by moments of trembling dread. The knowledge of what could happen went unspoken, but it was always with them. "It is a little flirtation we play with the unknown," said Captain Finney, the commanding officer of the bomb squad and the affiliated crime lab.

There was little in the way of preparation for the excruciating job of handling and defusing live explosives. Captain Finney conducted no formal training, with no protocols or procedures to impart, only a series of prohibitions handed down from squad veterans. Never submit to curiosity. Never smoke near explosives. Never handle suspicious packages unless told to do so. Never tilt them or turn them. Never carry them into a precinct house or an inhabited public space. Never cut a string or lift a cover. Never submerge a bomb in water. Never open a suitcase the conventional way; open it by removing the pins in its hinges. These were hard-earned lessons.

Americans have a short memory for violence, but the bomb squad never forgot. All ten detectives were aware that forty-three years earlier, in January 1908, a bomb blew out the façade of Pasquali Pati & Sons, a bank on Elizabeth Street serving the swelling population of poor, hardworking Italians settling in the grimy tenement blocks of Little Italy, where children played in streets clumped with residual horse dung and laundry fluttered on lines strung between windows. Seventeen years after arriving from Calabria, Pati had fattened himself up as the J. P. Morgan of Little

Italy. He proved his solvency in terms his depositors could understand: $40,000 worth of gold coins and paper bills displayed in the bank window for passersby to admire.

In the moments after the blast, Pati's son, Salvatore, ran about the glass-covered street leaping and grasping for the fluttering bills while blood dripped from a cut over his left eye. The bomb throwers slipped off among the shoppers and pushcarts. They had no designs on the swirling cash; they had thrown the bomb as retribution. Days earlier Pati had opened an envelope in his bank office. It contained an extortion threat: pay tribute to the Black Hand or face the penalty. The stationery bore the dark ink outline of a hand holding a dagger. Pati had refused.

More than 3 million Italians disembarked from steamships in the first fifteen years of the twentieth century. Most, like Pati, arrived as peasant folk—*paesani*—from poor rural towns. Calabrians, Sicilians, Puglieses, in threadbare vests and bowler hats queued up on Ellis Island. The great resettlement carried with it hidden foot soldiers for the ancient crime syndicates based in Sicily and Naples. They had come to America to escape prosecution for murder and other violent crimes. The Black Hand met the fugitives on the piers and put them to work. One by one the shopkeepers on Mulberry and Mott Streets received extortion letters with the black imprint of smoking bombs and other menacing symbols. "Woe upon you if you do not resolve to buy your future happiness," they warned. "Bring the money if you do not wish to die."

Merchants who refused to pay the fee—usually between $50 and $100—could expect a bomb in their mailbox or tossed into the parlor where their toddlers played, or some other grim payback. In 1909, the body of a holdout was found crammed in a barrel with his genitals stuffed in his mouth.

The Black Hand confirmed the opinion of many New Yorkers that the Italians pouring down the gangways were a dirty, quarrelsome breed infected with violent European habits. They had carried disorder to America, just as imported fruit can carry contagion.

The decent, law-abiding citizens of Little Italy feared that the Black

Hand threatened their hard-earned standing. *Bollettino della Sera,* an Italian-language newspaper published in lower Manhattan, warned that the "doors of this country would be closed to Italians if the Black Hand atrocities continued."

In December 1908, a group of Italian-born detectives met secretly above a Centre Street saloon. A lieutenant with a heavyset face named Joe Petrosino rose to address his colleagues. At just five feet three inches and two hundred pounds, he was soft bellied and barrel shaped. The police department had waived the height requirement when he joined the force at age twenty-three. Petrosino proved skilled with his fists, despite his size, and he racked up spectacular arrest records. His colleagues in the predominantly Irish ranks called him the Dago, but they addressed him with respect. In 1895 Teddy Roosevelt, then police commissioner, made Petrosino head of the homicide division.

Now Petrosino proposed to form a secret police corps, the original bomb squad, to fight the Black Hand. The corps had to be staffed by Italian detectives, he said. The merchants of Little Italy would never trust the Irish cops.

Petrosino exceeded all expectations, arresting five hundred and halving the number of bombings. He went undercover in the saloons and spaghetti kitchens of Prince Street, picking up bits of information while disguised in a long-brimmed felt hat, fake whiskers, and a red bandanna tied around his neck. By infiltrating among the Black Hand's operatives he learned of its conspiracies and secret plans with an ease his Irish colleagues could not fathom—all of which he recorded in a journal he called "the library of crime."

"He knew every manner and custom of the Sicilian and Calabrian murderer," *The Washington Post* wrote at the time, "and it was only necessary for him to glance at the wounds on a victim's body to know what inspired the murder and what branch of the mafia was responsible."

Arrests alone would not eradicate the Black Hand. Petrosino would have to kill the network at its roots. Fortunately for him, a newly enacted law allowed the police to deport immigrants convicted of a crime in another country within three years of their arrival in the United States. To make use of it, Petrosino would have to travel back to the land of his birth to obtain the criminal records of suspected mobsters operating on the New York streets. "The United States has become the dumping ground for all the criminals and banditti of Italy, Sicily, Sardinia, and Calabria," Petrosino said.

In February 1909 Petrosino kissed his wife, Adelina, and their one-year-old daughter good-bye and boarded a steamship bound for Genoa. His luggage contained a .38 revolver and a notebook with a list of potential informants. Petrosino had planned to travel undercover as a businessman seeking treatment in Italy for an intestinal infection until, days before his departure, *The New York Herald* printed a story detailing his mission. He knew that its publication put him at risk. Monsignor John F. Kearney, his pastor at St. Patrick's Old Cathedral in Little Italy, had warned that he might not return. "Probably not," Petrosino said with a smile, "but it is my duty to go, and I am going."

At 9:00 p.m. on March 12, Petrosino left a restaurant in Palermo to meet informants in Piazza Marina. It was a trap. Two men approached as Petrosino stood beneath an overhanging fig tree. They fired four shots. He drew his revolver and returned fire, then collapsed. His shots missed, but their report alerted a sailor strolling nearby. He knelt at Petrosino's side as his eyes went still.

The Black Hand expired shortly after Petrosino did, but the fledgling bomb squad, renamed the Bomb and Radical Squad, continued to handle sporadic bombings, most planted by foreigners. In the Red Scare years after World War I the bombers were more likely to be anarchists or Bolsheviks than extortionists. Bomb-making manuals were handed out along with radical manifestos. The targets, then as now, were the symbols of American power and profit.

Shortly before noon on September 16, 1920, a warm Thursday morning, a rickety horse-drawn covered wagon, the kind used to deliver milk and eggs, rattled east along Wall Street. The driver reined the bay mare to a halt across the street from the domed J. P. Morgan bank rising like a stone citadel at the corner of Wall and Broad—an intersection known in financial circles simply as the Corner. Across the street was the New York Stock Exchange. On the opposing corner a bronze statue of George Washington stood above the granite steps of the sub-Treasury, marking the site of his inauguration and the place where Congress first convened.

Seven months earlier, men and women had stood on these streets to cheer twenty-five thousand high-stepping soldiers returning from the Great War. The banners and rousing Sousa marches gave way to a postwar swoon—unemployment, shuttered factories, homeless families—and the unpleasant privations of Prohibition. Hard times hit, followed by dissent. Bolsheviks had murdered the Russian royals in 1918; there was reason to believe that revolt would spread to America. A series of bombs exploded in 1918 and 1919, including two designed to assassinate Attorney General A. Mitchell Palmer. President Woodrow Wilson, fearing insurrection, struck back. On January 2, 1920, more than three thousand suspected leftists, most of them immigrants, were arrested in thirty cities. Hundreds were deported on suspicion of "force and violence."

Eight months after the arrests, the wagon came to a halt on Wall Street, blocking traffic. Rather than pull out of the way, the driver stepped down to the footboard and slipped away. For some minutes the carriage stood still, the mare bowing and raising her head against the halter and shooing flies with her tail. Across the street, the Morgan partners assembled for their daily conference in a second-floor meeting room. Noon bells clanged from the spire of Trinity Church a few blocks to the west. A crowd of messenger boys, clerks, and brokers streamed onto the street for lunch hour, unaware of the ticking muffled by a burlap tarp thrown across the wagon. Then, without warning, Wall Street erupted. A hundred pounds of dynamite shredded the horse and wagon. Window sash weights, sawed in half, were packed with the explosives. They sprayed pedestrians with jagged slugs, killing thirty. (Eight more would die in the hospital.) A concussive wave of flame rolled down Wall Street, knocking hundreds of pedestrians off their feet.

The smoke cleared to reveal windows shattered as high as the twelfth floor. Horse flesh and human limbs lay in blood pools. A woman's severed head, hat and all, hung plastered to a wall. A Morgan banker in charge of gold shipments was struck by a metal slug and slumped dead at his desk. Shards of jostled glass rained down on the scene below. Panicked survivors stampeded down Wall Street, trampling the wounded. Women who stayed behind to help tore their underwear into bandages and tourniquets. Bodies lay under white sheets at George Washington's bronze feet. Brokers wept. For a few hours the wealthiest intersection in the world looked like the bombed-out European cities New Yorkers had read about during World War I.

The country came together with an upswell of patriotism and vowed revenge on the foreign perpetrators, just as it would in the aftermath of another September attack, just blocks away, eighty-one years later. Some warned that President Wilson was using the event as an excuse to strip away civil rights. They feared that retaliation would only provoke further violence and tarnish America's reputation abroad.

For the first time the word *terrorism* gained currency in the American vocabulary. Investigators spent months probing anarchists as far away as Russia and Poland, without resolution. The Wall Street bombing helped confirm American suspicions of Europe as an incorrigible incubator of uncontrolled hatreds and lawlessness.

The same misgivings hung over the preparations for the World's Fair in Flushing Meadows, Queens, two decades later. It was an awkward year to celebrate global togetherness. By the time the fair opened its gates, in April 1939, Hitler had seized Czechoslovakia and Italy was trampling Albania. The fair nonetheless persisted with its sunny promise of a better life. Forty-four million visitors pushed through the turnstiles to admire "the world of tomorrow," which showcased on-the-cusp gadgetry including black-and-white television, escalators, color photography, nylon, fluorescent lights, and air-conditioning. The fair spoke in earnest tones of a world where machines washed your laundry and nations marched together in peace. The future would be "as harmonious as the stars in their courses overhead."

The optimism didn't prevent the NYPD from standing heavy guard. By the time the fair reopened for a second season in the spring of 1940, France had fallen and London was evacuating its children. The British Pavilion looked directly across the Court of Peace at the Italian Pavilion. The two countries were at war.

At 3:30 p.m. on July the Fourth an electrician found a suspicious canvas satchel in an electrical utility room on the second floor of the British Pavilion. He put his ear to the bag; a dull ticking sounded from its depths. Might a worker have left a radio or alarm clock in an overnight bag? The electrician carried the bag downstairs and through a crowd of about fifteen hundred visitors assembled for afternoon tea. He gave the bag to his supervisor who, in turn, carried it back through the crowd to a security office. A guard thought to call the police. Two plainclothes detectives carried the satchel to a vacant stretch near a service road that ran behind the Polish Pavilion. They placed the bag on the ground and backed away; it was still ticking. Nearby "many people were having drinks in an open court under gay umbrellas," *The New York Times* reported.

Bomb squad detective Joseph Lynch was in his small Bronx apartment playing bridge with his wife, Easter, and her mother when the phone rang. He and Easter had planned to visit their ten-year-old daughter, Essie, who was in St. Joseph Hospital in Yonkers with a painful bone infection. When the call came, Lynch scrambled. On his way out the apartment door Lynch told Easter to expect him home for dinner. He picked up his partner, Freddie Socha, in a car borrowed from his sister. "It was his day off," Socha's brother Henry said later. "If it had been a nicer day, he probably would have been out on a trip with his wife and he never would have been home when his partner called."

The two men drove—drove fast—to Flushing Meadows. They approached the bag, cautiously, without protective gear, wearing only the dark suits favored by detectives. After some nervous consultation, Socha turned the bag on its side and snipped a two-inch hole from a corner so Lynch could peer inside. With eye fixed to the hole he spied a few of the sixteen sticks of dynamite bundled with nails to act as shrapnel. In a hushed voice Lynch said, "It's the business"—meaning the real thing. Before Socha could respond, the bomb exploded in their faces. The blast gouged a five-foot-wide crater and stripped a nearby maple tree of bark. Its leaves fluttered to the ground. Socha's body flew ten feet from the blast site. Lynch's mangled body landed thirty-five feet away. The explosion echoed like artillery fire through the Westinghouse time capsule, the racetrack on the roof of the Ford Pavilion, and the parachute jump. Most visitors assumed it was fireworks.

A nail inserted in a strip of flesh believed to be part of Lynch's nose was found four hundred feet away. The metal shard was collected for laboratory analysis, which was still a relatively new process. Detectives also found a fragment of a clock made by the Connecticut Clock Company, which, they determined, had counted down to detonate at the moment the two men happened to be examining the satchel. The Irish Republican Army was suspected, but, as with the Wall Street blast, the bomber was never caught. It is hard not to think of that bundle of dynamite hidden in a satchel as a prelude to war, exploding as it did five months before Pearl Harbor.

The dread of that fairground afternoon lingered for a generation, like a nightmare that refuses to relinquish its hold. The sudden obliterating shock wave. The unguarded detectives pitched like rag dolls. The festive music droning in the background as orderlies carted off the dismembered bodies, or what was left of them.

The apprehension echoed down the years to the bomb squad rooms on Poplar Street where detectives pulled their shift on the evening of October 22, 1951, hours after F.P. had departed the Paramount Theater. Just above a table where the detectives played rummy hung a sign warning against reckless heroics. Affixed to the sign were shards of zinc, carbon, and wire removed from the body of Joseph Lynch.

Bomb squad detectives accepted obliteration as an occupational risk. Lynch's fate could befall any of them, on any day. Even by that standard the squad was enduring a particularly harrowing stretch as it chased F.P.

through the streets of New York. For the police, F.P.'s spree constituted a frightening new frontier. The extortionists and anarchists of the early century were at least understandable. Their methods might be bloodthirsty, but their objectives were clear. Now, in the 1950s, the bomb squad chased a different kind of bomber—a shadowy figure driven by madness.

What scared the detectives on Poplar Street most was F.P.'s uncanny elusiveness. His derangement had not made him easier to catch. On the contrary, he seemed to possess great reservoirs of calculation. Seven months earlier, on March 29, 1951, he had walked down a heavily traveled ramp to a vaulted lower concourse in Grand Central Terminal, a tiled space known as the whispering gallery. He had paused and, unnoticed by passersby, dropped a pipe bomb into a sand-filled cigarette urn outside the entrance to the Oyster Bar. The bomb exploded with an earsplitting reverberation at the height of rush hour, spraying sand and metal bolts. The smoke was still billowing across the walkway when the phone rang in the Oyster Bar. "Was there much damage?" a man asked. His voice had a hint of foreign timbre. The bomb could have killed commuters had F.P. situated it with that intention. It appeared that he deliberately chose an out-of-the-way location, as if aiming a shot across the bow.

It wasn't the location of F.P.'s bombs that concerned detectives so much as his persistence. In the following months F.P. set off bombs in the New York Public Library at Fifth Avenue, in the West Concourse of Grand Central, and in a telephone booth and in the lobby of Con Ed headquarters. He blew a hole in a concrete wall in the Port Authority bus station, filling the concourse with swirling waves of smoke during rush hour. His tempo was quickening.

The bomb squad responded to each alert with fireman haste—day and night—in a fleet of white-topped police cruisers and an old green Chevrolet station wagon with walnut panels packed with the elaborate bomb gear developed for the men's protection, and the public's, after the World's Fair blast. (Never again would a detective advance on a bomb unprotected, as Lynch and Socha had.) The squad had done everything asked of them—everything but make an arrest.

Just a week earlier F.P. had called Grand Central to warn of a live bomb in a storage locker. "Get this straight," he said in a voice shaking with agitation. "There is a bomb planted in a locker on the main floor of Grand Central Terminal." He didn't say which locker.

The bomb squad sealed off the main waiting room and conducted a tedious three-hour search of all three thousand lockers. Half were in use. The manager of the parcel room worked his way down the rows, opening each locker with a deft clockwise flip of his wrist using a master key attached to his belt loop with a long braided cord.

Sergeant Peter Dale, the rangy, well-constructed head of the bomb squad, inspected the contents, one by one, with a flashlight. He brought with him a fluoroscope, an X-ray device used to screen the contents of bags and packages. At 3:30 p.m. the squad came to the last locker. Inside they found a battered yellow suitcase. Dale peered through a hole in its corner and shook his head. There was no bomb. They had encountered only an endless series of duffels, shopping bags, and briefcases. The whole enervating exercise had been a trick designed to waste their time.

F.P. had not yet killed, but it was assumed to be a matter of time. Dale's boss, Captain Finney, needed to dig up some quick leads or his men would be carrying body bags from the bomb sites under the popping flashbulbs of tabloid photographers. Meanwhile the bomber's siege was beginning to unnerve a populace already agitated by rising crime rates. The newspapers filled columns with accounts of larceny, muggings, and gang skirmishes. But the random violent act, stranger on stranger, had a singularly chilling effect. The bomber was a phantom, a bogeyman, who gathered the suppressed anxieties of the mushroom-cloud era.

By the evening of October 22, F.P. had returned home from the Paramount Theater. The bomb squad was killing time on Poplar Street. On West Forty-First Street the city editor of the *Herald Tribune* sat pale faced under the crude radium-blue fluorescent lights in the open newsroom editing an article about a longshoremen's strike paralyzing the New York waterfront and halting rail freight. It was a pressing night for news. The Soviets had tested a nuclear weapon that day, and the editors debated which story should lead the next morning's front page.

At 10:15 p.m. a copyboy handed the city editor a special-delivery envelope postmarked from Mount Kisco, a commuter town in Westchester County. Letters arrived by the hundreds, but special delivery called for immediate attention. The editor cut short a quarrelsome reporter and tore open the envelope. The writer warned that a bomb had been placed in the restroom of the Paramount Theater in Times Square, two blocks north of the *Herald Tribune* office:

> BOMBS WILL CONTINUE UNTIL THE CONSOLIDATED EDISON COMPANY IS BROUGHT TO JUSTICE FOR THEIR DASTARDLY ACTS AGAINST ME. I HAVE EXHAUSTED ALL OTHER MEANS. I INTEND WITH BOMBS TO CAUSE OTHERS TO CRY OUT FOR JUSTICE FOR ME. IF I DON'T GET JUSTICE I WILL CONTINUE BUT WITH BIGGER BOMBS.

As always, it was signed "F.P."

The bomb squad arrived at the Paramount in a procession of unmarked police cruisers trailed by the green station wagon. Fire trucks and ambulances waited nearby. The final curtain had just fallen at a dozen theaters, flooding the streets with fast-walking pedestrians waving down cabs or beelining to the Times Square subway. The sidewalk crowds parted for the detectives. They pushed open the double doors leading into the art deco Paramount lobby, where F.P. had bought his ticket less than five hours earlier. Police from the Midtown South Precinct had already roped off the downstairs restrooms without alerting the audience. Better not to incite panic. While the fictional detective on the screen upstairs chased tough-talking gangsters on the waterfront, the real-life detectives swarmed the downstairs bathrooms, looking under sinks and toilets for the hidden bomb. Nothing. Then a detective removed a grille from a ventilation shaft in the men's room. There it lay, a length of pipe capped at both ends.

Now came the delicate job of determining the nature of the bomb and safely removing it. "Every infernal machine is different," said William Schmitt, a veteran bomb-squad detective with heavyset jowls. "The ones that work on acid, the ones that work on a watch, the ones that work on position. We get the people away and then figure out what we're going to do."

The job would fall to Peter Dale, the sergeant Captain Finney had appointed to run the hands-on operations of the bomb squad while Finney supervised it and its affiliate, the crime lab. Captain Finney was the quiet, cerebral director, set apart from the ranks by his graduate degrees and his mastery of forensic theory. Dale was the opposite, a husky, gregarious blue-collar sergeant with a twinkly demeanor undimmed by the dangers at hand.

In the downstairs restroom of the Paramount, Sergeant Dale pulled a bucket-shaped steel helmet with ghoulish eye slits, like an executioner's hood, over his gray crew cut. He pushed stout arms into bulletproof gloves. Around his torso he strapped interlocking metal plates wrapped in green canvas cinched with a belt. A dangling band protected his crotch. His face was moist with apprehension as he prepared to stand alone over the bomb. After the World's Fair disaster, the bomb squad had adopted a rule that only one detective at a time could stand in harm's way.

"There's plenty of tension anytime you're doing this kind of work," said Dale. "Your body is a bunch of nerves. Anybody tells you, 'I don't care,' he's just a whackeroo."

Sergeant Dale joined the bomb squad in 1940, replacing Detective Lynch three months after he died in the World's Fair bombing. Over the following eleven years Dale had worked his way up to squad leader. His father and grandfather had worked as powder men—licensed blasters who dynamited building foundations and tunnels. For most of Dale's young life he expected to follow their path. He left school before finishing eighth grade to apprentice as a drill runner and powder monkey on his father's jobs. He was awaiting his blaster's license when his father fell ill. As his father lay dying, he urged Dale to quit the dynamite life. "It's hard, dangerous work," his father said, "and after a certain age you can't take it anymore, and there's no retirement or pension right." Dale joined the police department for security, an irony not lost on him.

He was now fifty-one. He had qualified for retirement seven years earlier. That might have been the prudent course, given the worry his wife and seven children expended on him back at their simple two-story home in the Bronx. But Dale intended to stay on until age sixty-three, the mandatory retirement age. He was content in the company of bombs, despite the harrowing possibilities. If anything, he was too brave. "One of these days I'm going to be scraping you off a wall with a putty knife," Dale's boss, Captain Finney, had warned.

Like a conspicuous number of his colleagues, Sergeant Dale reported to Poplar Street each day with the reassurance of a devout faith. He found it easier to lay his expert hands on a bomb knowing that no man meets death before the time God appoints for him. "The good man upstairs has been very good to me," Dale said.

Divine reassurance could not entirely eliminate Dale's fears. He knew that he had to either defuse the bomb in the restroom or remove it. He was slick with sweat inside his thick protective suit as he slow-stepped toward the bomb behind a shield of bulletproof glass that he had confiscated from a Lincoln town car belonging to Dutch Schultz, the gangster, and mounted with an iron stand-up frame. He advanced on the bomb half-crouched, half-lying down. His face was protected, or so he hoped, but his hands and arms were exposed. His squad mates watched from a distance. Dale's solar plexus tightened. For detectives, these five or six steps to the bomb were known as the longest walk in the world. It was the only time when the inviolable chain of command did not apply. The man in the protective suit was always in charge. He made the decisions, regardless of rank.

Dale now stood a stride's distance from the bomb, fully exposed save for his padding, prodding it with a pole equipped with a rubber gripping mechanism, the kind of utensil used by grocers to fetch cereal boxes from high shelves. He jostled the bomb with the grocery grippers again and again, this way and that, pausing each time for a long dreadful moment.

If the bomb were built with a so-called mercury switch, then a tilt or knock would send a bead of mercury sliding down a glass tube to touch a set of contacts. Or the contact points may have been placed a small distance apart. Either way, a knock or jiggle would complete the electrical circuit and activate the bomb. If Dale believed the bomb might be triggered by movement, he and his squad mates would be forced to detonate it where it lay, regardless the damage it might cause to the theater.

Fortunately for Dale, nothing happened. When he felt satisfied that the bomb was not one triggered by movement—known in the taxonomy of bombs as a position-control device—the question became how to remove it. He slowly, gingerly, lowered it into an eighty-pound steel mesh bag, called the envelope. It looked like a purse made of chain mail. Two detectives slipped a fifteen-foot pole through rings rigged to the envelope and, hoisting the pole by its ends, carried the envelope upstairs like a roasted pig. A simple stumble could kill them both. So they walked as slowly as pallbearers, making their way to the street where passersby, their hands clapped to their mouths, watched with macabre fascination from behind a line of blue police barricades.

Caution required the bomb squad to move the bomb to a safe location before they handled it further. So the detectives deposited the envelope in the back of Big Bertha, a flatbed truck rigged with an arched enclosure, like a covered wagon, made of five-eights-inch-thick woven steel cable left over from the construction of the Brooklyn Bridge. The bomb squad designed and built Big Bertha two months after the World's Fair blast to ensure that live bombs could be transported through crowded streets without endangering the public. "Everybody along the street would be in danger if we transported a bomb in a police radio car," Dale said.

Big Bertha could, in theory, withstand the explosive force of twenty-four sticks of dynamite, though the bomb squad had never had cause to test its resilience. Its reinforced steel door pivoted up on a block and tackle. The word DANGER ran across its side in big letters, a code-red warning to spectators as Big Bertha pulled away escorted by motorcycle cops and the urgent wail of sirens.

The detectives operated on the assumption that a bomb can inflict damage in a circumference of about three hundred feet. As a precaution, Dale and his crew drove to an empty lot on the far West Side. Dale dusted the bomb for fingerprints, then laid it to rest, as heedfully as resting a baby in its cradle, in a fifty-gallon iron tank filled with No. 10 grade motor oil to slow or stop its timing mechanism and deaden an explosion. He then knelt to touch a stethoscope to the bomb. He listened: no hint of ticking, just sweet silence.

To confirm that the oil had arrested the bomb's beating heart, Dale now peeked at its insides with the fluoroscope, a device the bomb squad carried, along with other gear, in the old green Chevrolet station wagon. The fluoroscope, which was about the size of an old-fashioned black-and-white television set, X-rayed the bomb's internal mechanics with a time lapse of thirty seconds or so. If the resulting image contained a blur, it meant the clock hand of a timing mechanism was still rotating. Dale pressed his eyes to the viewer. He wore lead gloves and a lead coverall to protect himself from the radiation. Within the cloudy dark image he could pick out the wires running from the clock to a battery. But there was no blur: he was in the clear.

Bomb handlers commonly suffered racking shakes on the downslope of the adrenaline ride, and they heaved deep breaths of relief. "I really sweated on that one," Dale said. "I knew it was the real thing, and even though I thought I knew how it operated, you never can tell for sure."

Until now F.P. had planted his homemade devices in phone booths and other out-of-the-way spots where they would provoke sensations, but inflict limited damage. All that would change now. The Paramount bombing signaled a dangerous new phase in his campaign. As he warned in his letter to the *Herald Tribune,* F.P. intended to build bigger bombs and place them in theaters and other densely populated locations. Police officials at headquarters called Whitelaw Reid, the editor of the *Herald Tribune,* and asked him not to print the bomber's letter. Publicity would only encourage the bomber, they said, and likely spawn a raft of imitators.

Weeks later, after years of frustrations and setbacks, dead ends and reversals, Captain Finney and his team finally had a breakthrough: after searching the files of hundreds of aggrieved Con Ed employees, they found a handwriting sample that seemed to match the block characters in F.P.'s letters. The next day, accompanied by state police, they arrested a short, white-haired fifty-six-year-old named Frederick Eberhardt in North Stonington, Connecticut. He had worked for Con Ed for more than twenty years splicing cables and doing other outdoor maintenance work. The company had fired him for stealing from job sites. A jury trial acquitted him of wrongdoing. Since then he had filed a civil suit against the company for damages. The suit apparently wasn't revenge enough. During police interrogation he admitted to sending Con Ed threatening mail. He also confessed to mailing a phony pipe bomb filled with sugar to the company's personnel director.

"This defendant is a particular source of annoyance to the New York City police," an assistant district attorney told the judge at Eberhardt's arraignment. "We are firmly convinced that he is not of sound mind." Eberhardt's wife, Louise, sobbed as guards led him in handcuffs to the notorious psychiatric ward at Bellevue Hospital for a month of observation. "This arrest is an outrage," she told reporters. "He never sent those things. He couldn't hurt a fly." The police had arrested Eberhardt on a thin margin of evidence, but they felt confident that a damning preponderance of proof would materialize now that they had him in custody.

New Yorkers reacted with relief that a suspect had finally been taken into custody. They assumed that the police wouldn't have arrested Eberhardt without some certainty of his guilt. In the following days, Captain Finney sat in his Poplar Street office hoping that with Eberhardt confined, the bombings would end. Every day without a bombing further verified Eberhardt's guilt.

It would be an enormous comfort to end the bomb terror. The fall of 1951 had been a time of growing alarm over his random acts, and concurrent apprehension about a more dangerous world. In October, President Truman signed a pact guaranteeing military protection to "free peoples." From Hanoi to Havana, the United States was poised to intervene if the

Communists made a move. Nuclear war was no longer an abstract possibility. At 10:33 a.m. on November 28, a damp and dreary day, New York conducted its first postwar air-raid drill. Sirens rang through the chill morning air, bringing the usual clamor to a standstill. Traffic halted. Drivers, taxi passengers, and pedestrians filed into shelters. A ghostly quiet settled on the streets, like a scene from a science-fiction movie. The millions were all under cover, except for police and civil-defense wardens uniformed in white helmets. Ten minutes later the all clear sounded and the bustle resumed.

That evening an explosion blasted from a pair of coin-operated storage lockers in a mezzanine above the train tracks in the Union Square subway stop, a hectic stretch of corridor cluttered with shoeshine stands, florists, and newsstands. The discharge sent locker doors flying like Frisbees. Earl Scott, an off-duty fire department lieutenant passing by in street clothes, said it sounded like "a stick of dynamite."

Scott did what any civilian would do: he called the cops. Police headquarters relayed his alert to the bomb squad's Poplar Street office, where Detective William Foley, just starting the night shift, answered the phone. "Is it him again?" he thought to himself. Amazingly, nobody was hurt, but F.P. had operated with insidious effect by timing his detonation at the end of New York's most anxious day.

The blast exonerated Eberhardt, but officials held him until his monthlong sentence ended. On May 15, 1952, he stepped through the wrought-iron gates of Bellevue onto First Avenue. He would later call his incarceration "the most harrowing days of my life."

In the coming months F.P. would drop a series of letters into Westchester mailboxes—never the same mailbox twice lest he give some indication of his true location and habits. In each case he carefully wiped the envelope with a rag for fingerprints before sliding it through the mail slot. In the enclosed letters he taunted the police for their bungling failures and vowed to place more bombs—bigger bombs—in densely packed public places, where they were likely to maim, mangle, and kill.

The bomber identified himself as F.P., but the tabloids, in their way, were calling him the Mad Bomber of New York. He had a name, but not a face. New York's case-hardened detectives sometimes said that they built a mental picture of a suspect as bits of information accumulated, the way a jigsaw puzzle of a New England farm or a field of poppies gains coherence as the pieces fall into place. The detectives would typically imagine the suspect striding toward them on the street. But not now. Not this time. The bomb squad detectives agreed that that when they thought of F.P., when they tried to picture him in their mind's eye, they saw a figure with his back turned—unrecognizable and unknowable.

CHAPTER THREE

MR. THINK

October 1951

F.P. WAS A MAN OF ROUTINES. IN THE DAYS AFTER HE PLANTED HIS BOMB in the Paramount Theater, in late October, he paged, column by column, through a stack of New York newspapers—the *Post, Daily Mirror, Herald Tribune, World-Telegram and Sun,* the *Times,* and the rest.

His mood darkened by increments as the tabloids and broadsheets failed to proclaim the obvious truth. They swelled with news of Chinese troops massed in the Korean hills and complaints of street gangs facing off in Corona and Cobble Hill, Harlem and Hell's Kitchen. There were reports, as well, of the Soviets testing a nuclear device over a steppe in northeast Kazakhstan, and the US military detonating a mushroom cloud of its own in the Nevada desert.

F.P. had to sort through all of it—the foreboding Cold War arms reports, the avuncular doings of Dwight Eisenhower, Charlie Conerly and the New York Football Giants rounding into late-season form—before finding the Paramount bomb scare relegated to a modest mention tucked in the back pages alongside two-paragraph accounts of car accidents and ads for department store sales.

F.P. could feel an oncoming flood of hot anger. The bomb he'd planted in the Paramount had earned no more coverage than the one he'd placed in the same theater six months earlier, or, for that matter, the one in a

Port Authority telephone booth three months before that. He had expected the newspapers to take up for him, to convey the news of injustices done to him by a cabal of malevolent political and corporate forces, starting with the Con Edison utility company. Instead the newspapers ignored him—or worse, dismissed him as a crackpot.

The slight fit cruelly into the pattern of his life. It wasn't the first time he had felt invisible. To qualify as a true American in the 1950s one had to be a white Protestant. Eastern Europeans were suspect. In the Cold War era—the dark McCarthy years tinged with suspicion—questions about allegiance and loyalty would linger about those with funny-sounding names.

As a Slav, F.P. was sure that he would always stand on the outside looking in. Unless he could wake up the public, shock them into seeing the injustices. It hadn't worked so far, maybe because the bombs were too small. F.P. had designed and built them with the explosive charge of a hand grenade. Incendiary power had not been his main goal. He was not trying to kill people, not yet anyway. He was simply trying to make a point. He believed that terror would gradually gather from the unpredictable nature of his bombing campaign, and from its persistence. The resulting fearfulness would naturally lead the public to see the misdeeds and disgrace. Terror would open their eyes. "I've read that a man with a hammer can wreck a sixteen-inch naval gun, just by hitting it until it shatters," he would say. "It's the same with bombs."

F.P. was not like serial arsonists. He got no sexual charge from seeing his devices explode or witnessing the panic they incited. Instead his inclination was to coldly observe the damage from the remove of his private world. He had known racking pain in his life, but he looked impassively on the fear and suffering of others. He coolly observed the mayhem inflicted by his own hand, as a god would.

F.P. made a point of searching the papers while drinking coffee in a diner or seated on a park bench—anywhere but the sagging family house halfway up a short, steep hill where his two unmarried older sisters might see them and wonder. His sisters had no inkling of what he was up to.

And why would they? His hands did not rend his clothes. He did not listen obediently to voices in his head whispering demonic dictates. On the contrary, he maintained a studiously normal bearing—in most ways.

In any case, he barely saw his sisters. They had already left for their jobs at a brass mill and buckle factory by the time he rose for toast and coffee in the morning. Most days he ate an early dinner of soup or sausage with a glass of milk, then retired to his room before they got home.

On Sundays F.P. faithfully attended 9:00 a.m. mass at St. Joseph's, but when he knelt in the darkened confession booth, some things, many things, he did not mention to the priest. He did not admit what he had done, and he did not ask for penance. He had recently decided to forgo the confession booth altogether. "I just couldn't go in and confess, knowing that I had to go on with what I was doing," he would say. "I just couldn't do that."

In the afternoons, after a sandwich and a sip of port, he strolled the neighborhood, always alone, with head bowed in thought and hands clasped behind his back. The local kids called him Mr. Think. He always wore a business suit, fedora, and dark overcoat. If a passerby said good morning, he replied politely enough. The passerby might detect a raspiness in Mr. Think's shallow breaths, or a faint gurgle sounding from deep within his gorge. They might see him bend over with a coughing fit. When he recovered, he smiled as people do among strangers. It was a distant smile, a smile without warmth. He walked on before they could engage him in further pleasantries.

F.P. wasn't alone in harboring secret daydreams of murder and violent revenge. Many of us, in the privacy of our thoughts, imagine the satisfaction of sweet retribution for some slight or insult. Johann Wolfgang von Goethe, the German poet, said, "There is no crime of which I do not deem myself capable." The difference is this: Goethe never acted on his impulses. He might have contemplated violent acts—acts of revenge and rage—but he withheld himself. Layers of restraints, both emotional and societal, prevent us from going through with these urges. Most of us, anyway. Those checks somehow failed F.P. He hovered between decorum and derangement. Violent thoughts colonized his mind. He exchanged smiles with neighbors, then waged imaginary arguments with his adversaries, repeating them over and over. So he plunged on, following his malignant stars.

As he walked the streets, F.P. was aware of the ways in which his life departed from the normal run of things. No wife. No children. No job. No friends. He hadn't met anybody worthy of his friendship in years. Besides, friends only complicated matters. Friendship was messy. No, F.P. pursued something far nobler than companionship. His solitude freed him to pursue his mission. He had a vision of himself as a shining paragon, like a comic-book superhero, who, transformed from normalcy, rises to defend justice—mankind's lonely champion in a grand struggle against the evil-minded. The world was tarnished, and only he could make it right.

The solitary neighborhood rambles usually led F.P. back to a corrugated-tin garage behind the family home. He carefully wiped his shoes with a rag hung specifically for that purpose on a hook outside the garage door. However troubled his mind might be, he could always think clearly and creatively at the workbench tucked in a far corner of the garage. He didn't need friends or the intimacy of a normal family. He was happiest surrounded by short sections of pipe, bits of copper wire, cheap wristwatches, and black gunpowder siphoned from shotgun shells—the basic ingredients of bomb making. Whether F.P. was aware of it or not, he had chosen to work with many of the same materials used in the nearby mills, the mills where mishaps had disfigured or killed scores of workers during his childhood.

F.P. had a gift for the scrupulous, small-scale chores of bomb making— soldering wires to flashlight bulbs, machining threads in lead pipes, cutting the ends off of .22 caliber bullets and neatly pouring the gunpowder into canisters. The bomb maker's handiwork came naturally to him. He focused on these details without overly concerning himself with what happened when they ignited.

In the winter of 1952 he set to work on a new bomb design triggered by a watch mechanism capable of a much larger charge. He had moved beyond his first crude devices. He was now prepared to make bombs too big for newspaper editors to ignore. Though he knew that with bigger bombs came a greater risk of capture.

Folklore says that lightning never strikes the same spot twice. The same myth applied to F.P.'s targets. On June 30, 1952, he blasted a hole in a row of seats at a frowsy old midtown movie palace called the Lexington Theatre, built as an opera house in 1910. The manager could reasonably assume that F.P. would not return. He was wrong. The repeat visit would become a standard part of F.P.'s repertoire, and it would contribute to the creeping unease he cast over public places. Six months later he once again stepped beneath the Lexington Theatre marquee, blazing like a star over Fifty-First Street, and bought a ticket for *Everything I Have Is Yours,* a second-rate musical about a young couple struggling to establish dancing careers. An hour later, just as the wife finds that she's pregnant and must give up dancing, a searing white flash lit up the paneled ceiling and private boxes stacked on either side of the proscenium. Scraps of upholstery and other charred debris swirled in the air, then rained down like confetti on ash-powdered seats. The audience stood and looked around in high alarm, unsure of what happened. Their ears clanged like fire alarms. A woman in mid-orchestra called out. A gush of blood ran down her leg.

CHAPTER FOUR

_____

REVERSE PSYCHIATRY

March 1953

FROM THE KITCHEN OF THEIR MODEST BRICK HOME, AUDREY BRUSSEL could hear her husband haranguing patients in his upstairs office in his rapid-fire voice. He was too demonstrative—too hopped up with urgent intuitions and exhortations—to play the reserved psychoanalyst jotting notes in dour detachment.

Sigmund Freud was still working in Vienna when Dr. James A. Brussel earned his medical degree at the University of Pennsylvania in 1929. Dr. Brussel was close enough to the great man's prime that he subscribed to basic Freudian orthodoxies, but was young enough to discard some of the profession's Old World customs. For example, he had no use for the classic Freudian couch. Patients in his private practice sat upright in a beat-up leather chair facing Dr. Brussel's lean face with its thin mustache and combed-back hair. "It is an ordinary human face," he would later write, "marked by tracks of many years." His bulging eyes accentuated his frenetic manner. A pipe smoldered at his elbow but rarely touched his lips. He was too busy talking. He was a performer, not a listener.

If patients' attention flagged during Dr. Brussel's perorations, they could distract themselves by glancing out the window at the dozens of brick buildings with barred windows at Creedmoor State Hospital, a sprawling three-hundred-acre mental hospital in the borough of Queens.

Dr. Brussel saw private patients in his home office on the hospital grounds. As assistant commissioner of the New York State Department of Mental Hygiene, his day job was supervising the treatment of more than six thousand anguished souls at Creedmoor and other public asylums in and around New York City.

To walk Creedmoor's endless wards was to plummet into a black world where sunken-eyed men rocked themselves to and fro while openly masturbating or pitching feces against a wall. Giggling girls, pretty as prom queens, urinated on linoleum floors, then kneeled to spread the puddles with their hands. Boys cocked their ears to voices directing them to stab their fathers to death. Old men sat quietly for hours, then, without warning, rose to bang violently on a radio or throw a cigarette urn at an attendant. Matrons who appeared perfectly poised and prim casually mentioned that they've been dead for a decade. Middle-aged men swatted swarms of invisible bugs and explained that their doctors were really assassins.

Creedmoor modeled itself on pastoral nineteenth-century asylums. The self-controlled patients tilled the soil in vegetable gardens and tended livestock on the expansive grounds outside Dr. Brussel's window. They acted in theater productions, played in an eighteen-piece orchestra, and labored in giant kitchens and laundries. Work was therapy. Honest labor bestowed on the troubled mind a modicum of dignity and self-sufficiency. It cured nobody, but it grounded patients in real life and distracted them from imagined terrors.

Many patients, however, were too loony or catatonic to weed carrot patches or play concerti. It was common for white-coated orderlies to restrain schizophrenics in straitjackets, sedate them with lithium, or pacify them at bedtime with doses of an odorous brown liquid called paraldehyde. Doctors also routinely induced hypoglycemic comas with insulin injections. The patients lay insensate until awoken by a strong hit of glucose. When they regained consciousness, they were usually calmer and cleansed of madness, at least temporarily. (Though not all patients woke from the comas.)

Dr. Brussel sanctioned the use of lobotomies in 1952; its originator, the Portuguese neurologist Egas Moniz, won the Nobel Prize for the procedure in 1949. It was believed that schizophrenia, depression, and acute anxiety resulted from a gang up of emotions. Doctors observed that they could pacify a patient's moods by destroying nerve tissue in the prefrontal lobes. They would drill a pair of holes into the skull and push a spike into the brain. Creedmoor's annual report stated its use of the lobotomy was "further evidence of the desire to keep up with the modern trend in the care of patients."

These procedures may sound barbaric, but they were all Dr. Brussel had—until drugs came along to revolutionize treatment. By the mid-1950s, Dr. Brussel and his colleagues working in state hospitals were beginning to inject schizophrenics in their care with a new drug called chlorpromazine—better known by its brand name, Thorazine. Nobody quite understood how Thorazine worked, or why. What mattered to Dr. Brussel was that under its influence patients grew less agitated, less combative. It was a way out of the asylum, a sliver of possibility in a world of darkness.

Thorazine was the first in a wave of new psychopharmacological drugs—tranquilizers, antianxiety medications, and mood stabilizers. Though not cure-alls, these did in many cases bring relief from the hallucinations and the ghostly voices hissing to the afflicted. Patients who had by necessity been restrained no longer felt the urge to throw chairs or hang themselves. Doctors stopped strapping them down for shock treatment or lobotomies. For the first time they could shave and light cigarettes on their own. They were free to walk hospital grounds unsupervised. The drugs restored hope of a normal life.

Years later reports would come of overcrowding and abuse in the squalid wards of Creedmoor, as at other public asylums, but in the mid-1950s Creedmoor was a proud example of how psychiatry was thought to be ridding the world of darkness and despair.

Dr. Brussel was in charge of it all. He and Audrey lived in a compound of simple brick cottages clustered on the hospital grounds where doctors, administrators, and their families dwelled in close acquaintance-ship, as faculty do on a campus. Dr. Brussel was the top man at Creed-moor, and at the city's other psychiatric hospitals. He was a dominant presence off duty as well. At parties thrown by fellow doctors and ad-ministrators, he was the fastest talker, the first with a one-liner, the guest most likely to seat himself at the piano for a round of show tunes. "He was a man who was not happy unless he was at the center of attention," said his stepson John Israel. "He dominated the room. He dominated con-versation."

Dr. Brussel's was always the most assured voice in the room, and pos-sibly the craziest. A new acquaintance might be forgiven for confusing him with a mental patient, as if Dr. Brussel had been exposed to a con-tagious madness in the wards. While seated with guests at the dining table, he fed a pair of squawking parakeets by clenching food scraps between his teeth for them to pluck with thrusting beaks. These odd feedings were a moment of wing-flapping chaos in an otherwise neurotically ordered household. Dr. Brussel obsessively arranged sharpened pencils in cups ac-cording to size, and he dictated his wife's hairstyle, her taste in clothing, and her choice of friends.

Dr. Brussel imagined dangers threatening his carefully ordered world. He protected himself by carrying a loaded snub-nosed revolver at all times. The revolver was in his briefcase when he rode the train to his Broadway office. It was there when he made the rounds of mental hospitals to in-terview the manic and the melancholy. Dr. Brussel never indicated who he imagined might attack him, aside from mentioning methadone ad-dicts who sometimes hit him up for prescriptions.

"I've never fired my .32 Iver Johnson at anyone," he would say. "But it's never far from reach while I attend patients in my mid-Manhattan office or on outside calls. And, believe me, if I ever need to shoot—I will."

He was not above using the pistol for dramatic effect. While teaching a survey course on the psychology of crime at Yeshiva University, he stood on a desk and waved the pistol in the air to get students' attention. His balance of mind could not have been helped by his addiction. In his briefcase and desk drawers he kept vials of Demerol, an addictive opiate, which he injected in his thigh with a startling disregard for privacy.

Dr. Brussel was a creature of the 1950s, a decade known for restive artists such as Jack Kerouac and Jackson Pollock. Dr. Brussel, too, was keyed up and restlessly prolific. In the evenings, when he was finished supervising the treatment of psychotics and manic depressives, he sat in the upstairs office of his brick cottage and composed reams of crossword puzzles for *The New York Times* and *Herald Tribune* on graph paper he made himself by compulsively drawing grids on blank pages. Hour after hour he darkened the pages with words and lists of clues: goddess of peace. Neck muscle. Clusters of spores. Pipe material. Roman road. Honey drink. Mañana men. Glacial ridges. Hemingway epithet. Aesop's race.

Dr. Brussel had an uncommonly quick mind and a facility for interlocking clues. He produced so many puzzles that he was obliged to publish under three names, lest his byline become awkwardly pervasive. His inventiveness, always eccentric and irrepressible, spilled forth in songs, cartoons, and offbeat writings. He composed an operetta called *Dr. Faustus of Flatbush,* which met a riotous reception at a psychiatric convention, and he published his psychoanalyses of Dickens and van Gogh. He saw in Tchaikovsky signs of an Oedipus complex. His analysis of Mary Todd Lincoln found her to be "psychotic with symptoms of hallucinations, delusion, terror, depression and suicidal intentions."

Psychiatrists usually presented themselves as solemn scientists. Brussel was more like a vaudeville lyricist. Amid the sober disquisitions on transference and dissociative disorder found in *Psychiatric Quarterly,* he published a ditty on psychosomatic illness:

The wild epileptic,
The grouchy dyspeptic, the child with the croup or the pox,
the bilious hepatic . . .
They're psychosomatic, they can't stand reality shocks.
Hurray for this ism

That sews up the schisms 'twixt body and mind—yes, it's hot!
Must all things erratic
Be psychosomatic? Gee, whiz! Ain't there something that's not?

Brussel was mostly occupied with the thankless and endlessly complicated task of caring for the thousands of chronically ill housed in state mental hospitals. "There are hazards involving other patients," he wrote by way of complaint in *Psychiatric Quarterly.* "There are dissatisfied relatives who, seeing no improvement—or perhaps a worsening—in a patient's condition, carry unfavorable reports back to the community; there are matters of administration and economy; and considerations of distracted and harassed personnel, constantly menaced by physical harm."

Not surprisingly, Dr. Brussel supplemented the dreary supervisory grind, and his bureaucrat's salary, with a private practice in psychoanalysis. The field was booming, especially in New York, where it was newly fashionable to recline on the Freudian couch for as many as five sessions a week. Goateed analysts with Austrian accents had fled Vienna amid the Nazi invasion of 1938. The émigrés were welcomed like European royalty. They took up prestigious academic posts, founded psychoanalytic foundations, and bestowed their insights on admiring patients from Waverly Place to Park Avenue. "For those in the movement, it was as if the Vatican and its cardinals had shifted the site of the Holy See from Rome to Manhattan," wrote Dr. Jeffrey A. Lieberman, a psychiatry professor at Columbia University.

Freudian theory stressed personal fulfillment and the significance of sex—a pitch-perfect message for progressive-minded New Yorkers of the 1950s. Intellectuals in particular were in the thrall of psychoanalysis. Celebrities, including Marilyn Monroe and Vincente Minnelli, were in analysis. At Upper West Side dinner parties guests spoke openly of their dream analysis and projection.

The subtext was this: Roosevelt and Eisenhower had conquered fascism. Analysts were the new heroes, taking on the mind's dark demons.

"Psychoanalysis was in the air, like humidity, or smoke," Anatole Broyard wrote in his memoir of New York in the 1950s. "You could almost smell it. The whole establishment had moved to New York in a counter invasion, a German Marshall Plan."

Dr. Brussel occupied a position of low prestige compared to the accented analysts on Park Avenue. A Brooklyn-born mental health administrator, he had an undistinguished practice on the side. Some patients saw him simply because they needed his signature for disability claims. He never trained as an analyst, relying instead on his own eccentric methods. He was in his fifties, and what did he have to show for it?

Whatever his frustrations, Dr. Brussel was nonetheless whip smart and ambitious. "When you sat down with him," his stepson John Israel said, "you could feel the energy." Dr. Brussel was shrewd enough, and ambitious enough, to recognize that psychiatry could potentially do more than subdue the troubled souls huddled in the Creedmoor wards and minister to Upper West Side neurotics. Why couldn't doctors apply the new understandings of the mind to help solve societal and political problems?

In Dr. Brussel's view, psychiatry had already shown that it could contribute to the pressing issues of the day. In the early stages of World War II, "Wild Bill" Donovan, buccaneering director of the Office of Strategic Services, the wartime intelligence agency, struck up a friendship with Walter C. Langer, a psychiatrist in Cambridge, Massachusetts, who studied under Freud's daughter Dr. Anna Freud, in Vienna during the initial Nazi incursion of the 1930s. Donovan and Langer discussed the possibilities of psychiatric warfare over clubby breakfasts at Donovan's Georgetown home. As the war turned toward its endgame, Donovan issued a specific request: Could Langer determine how Hitler might react as Americans and Russians troops closed on Berlin?

Over the following months Langer and three researchers looked for clues in the Führer's speeches and writings. They interviewed a dozen Hitler acquaintances, including Princess Stephanie Julianne von Hohenlohe, of Austria, who was arrested in the United States as a suspected spy, and a disaffected Nazi official named Otto Strasser. The researchers studied Hitler's fear of horses, moonlight, and syphilis, his aversion to physical contact with women, his fixation on wolves, severed heads, and pornographic movies. By drawing on his knowledge of patients with similar pathologies, Langer forecast what Hitler's behavior might be as his mindset deteriorated. Langer personally delivered his 135-page report to Donovan's home in late 1943. He considered it too sensitive to entrust to a courier. He had concluded that Hitler was "not a single personality but two that inhabit the same body. The one is very soft and sentimental and indecisive. The other is hard, cruel and decisive. The first weeps at the death of a canary; the second cries that there will be no peace in the land until a body hangs from every lamppost!"

In Langer's analysis, Hitler's savage campaign, the entire world war, was an attempt to "compensate for his vulnerability by continually stressing his brutality and ruthlessness . . . for only in this way can he prove that he is not a weakling."

Langer correctly predicted that Hitler's rages would escalate as the Allies won successive battles. He might sacrifice himself on the battlefield when defeat proved inevitable, Langer said, but suicide was "the most plausible outcome."

Eighteen months after Langer delivered his report to Donovan's door, Hitler gave Eva Braun a cyanide capsule, then shot himself in an air raid bunker beneath his chancellery as Red Army troops fought their way into Berlin and American GIs advanced from the west. The Langer report proved that psychiatry could play a role in world events.

Dr. Brussel had seen firsthand the brutal mix of madness and war. He had spent the war's end as a resident psychiatrist aboard the *Queen Mary*, requisitioned for the war effort, as she sailed back and forth across the Atlantic, transporting as many as fifteen thousand combat-worn GIs home to America. On return trips she delivered German and Italian prisoners to Europe for repatriation. In both directions Dr. Brussel ministered to the shell-shocked and war damaged. He never saw battle, but he did know its dark aftermath. On an eastbound voyage a group of American sailors pushed a German overboard and left him to drown. And Dr. Brussel was

once called to a small barracks room where an army lieutenant had put
the muzzle of a Colt .45 pistol in his mouth and pulled the trigger. "There
was no head left on the body," he would recall. "What had been the head
was literally sprayed over the walls and ceiling. Although I'm a physician
and as such am more or less accustomed to the sight of blood, that ghastly
scene tied my stomach in knots. It haunted me for a long time afterward."

On most mornings Dr. Brussel rode the Long Island Rail Road to Penn
Station, then the subway to the Department of Mental Hygiene's offices
across Broadway from City Hall in lower Manhattan. In his briefcase he
carried the .32 Iver Johnson and, without variation, a cottage-cheese sandwich to be eaten for lunch with a glass of skim milk. He also carried *The
New York Times* and *Herald Tribune*. As the train rumbled by Douglaston,
Bayside, and Flushing, he digested the great stories of the day—the Rosen-
berg executions, the McCarthy hearings, the first nuclear bomb tests
in the Nevada desert. His opinionated nature led him to send a series of
dissenting, nitpicking letters to the editor of *The New York Times* on an
expansive array of topics—judicial reform, civil service exams, the hazards of marijuana, the origins of gout, Mideast politics.

Like most New Yorkers, Dr. Brussel followed the story of F.P., the
serial bomber, told with ever bolder, blacker headlines as the explosion
count grew—explosions in theaters, train stations, and the public library.
Dr. Brussel, with his restless intellect, was not content to be an upper-
level administrator and a prolific crossword-puzzle composer. As the
bomber story gained stature in New York newspapers, his puzzle-solving,
diagnostic skills twitched to life. He toyed with a theory that he could
help identify the bomber by applying "common psychiatric principles in
reverse."

Psychiatrists normally evaluate patients and consider how they might
react to the difficulties life throws their way—conflict with a boss or other
authority figures, sexual frustrations, a humiliation at work, the loss of a

parent. As Dr. Brussel read the bomber stories, he began to wonder if he could "reverse the terms of the prophecy." Instead of starting with a known personality and anticipating his behavior, as Langer had, maybe Dr. Brussel could start with the bomber's behavior and deduce what sort of a person he might be. In other words, Dr. Brussel would work backward by letting F.P.'s conduct define his identity—his sexuality, race, appearance, work history, and personality type. And, most important, the inner conflicts that led him to his violent pastime. "It was simply my own way of applying what I had learned about people in the years of studying and wondering," he said, "and my way of taking a step on the road toward unraveling the great mystery of human behavior."

Dr. Brussel called it reverse psychology. Today we call it profiling. Whatever the term, it was still an untested concept in the 1950s. Nobody had yet profiled an offender. Not in real life anyway.

Dr. Brussel's only role models were fictional investigators, most notably C. Auguste Dupin, the reclusive amateur detective from an illustrious but impoverished family invented by Edgar Allan Poe in the 1840s to solve cleverly convoluted murder mysteries in the seamy reaches of eighteenth-century Paris. With Dupin, Poe created a detective genre long before crime stories were consumed like candy. Dupin was the original profiler, a master channeler of the psychotic mind and the forebear of Sherlock Holmes and Hercule Poirot. Dupin, like Holmes, had uncanny analytic powers. Both could divine entire backstories from bits of hair, scratch marks, torn clothing, and other observable details that baffled the police.

Dupin succeeds as a detective because he understands the criminal's viewpoint. In "The Murders in Rue Morgue," Poe wrote that Dupin "throws himself into the spirit of his opponent, identifies himself therewith, and not infrequently sees thus, at a glance, the sole methods by which he may seduce into error or hurry into miscalculation."

To accomplish real-life profiling, Dr. Brussel would have to slip inside the suspect's consciousness, as the fictional Dupin did. Dr. Brussel knew that logic drives every serial offender's actions, however depraved they might seem. Dr. Brussel would have to decode that hidden logic, as he did with the intricate crosswords he labored over. If he understood the offender's logic, he could think his way inside the offender's head. Dr. Brussel could feel the motives and thought patterns.

Dr. Brussel had ample time to toy with these possibilities as he stared at the low hills of Queens sloping to the mild waters of Long Island Sound on his daily commute. Adopting the warped logic of a man such as the bomber might not be enough to catch him. It would take something more—a leap of understanding, an inkling, a presentiment, a hunch. Dr. Brussel, like Freud, considered himself a scientist reliant on logical analysis. He also acknowledged the value of intuition, as he later explained:

> The mind stores enormous amounts of data over the course of years, but not all this data is available to the conscious thinking process. Some of it lies just below the surface. It's knowledge, but you aren't consciously aware of it. Every now and then, however it makes itself felt: it produces a sudden and rather mysterious flash of knowing. A hunch. You don't know where it came from and you aren't sure you can trust it, but it is there in your mind, insistently demanding to be considered. What do you do with it? Throw it out, or use it? This is the choice you must make. In general, I use such intuitive flashes as long as they are consistent with other data I have on hand.

It is unclear how much the bomber's story spurred Dr. Brussel's interest in reverse psychology, but we know that he closely tracked the newspaper coverage. On the morning of March 7, 1953, he would have read about F.P.'s latest strike—an explosion in a locker on the lower level of Grand Central. He would have taken in the description of smoke billowing through the corridors, panicked commuters, and the bomb squad's swarming arrival.

"Like all other New Yorkers I'd been following the Mad Bomber case," he later wrote. "I'd been curious about this strange man. I'd wondered what kind of person he might be. A few tentative theories had suggested themselves to me, but I hadn't considered any of them seriously because I hadn't been required to do so."

Besides, he was busy with his private practice and the demands of his job as deputy commissioner of mental hygiene in a city where half the population often seemed crazy.

"I had real people to deal with," he said, "not ghosts."

CHAPTER FIVE

POPLAR STREET

March 1954

By late afternoon on March 16, 1954, the great marble chamber of Grand Central Terminal was a torrent of wool and gabardine. Broad-shouldered businessmen in gray overcoats and snap-brims, and women with swaying skirts and chignons, collided and converged beneath the azure-painted ceiling. Shafts of sunlight angled from casement windows onto coiling plumes of cigarette smoke.

On this sunny late-winter Tuesday, Grand Central felt like the bustling heart of American prosperity. With European capitals still suffering the lingering detriments of war and beset by corruption and squabbling political factions, New York was ascendant—a city of luster and glittering confidence, a city of gaudy marquees and glass office towers yearning upward, a city where Walter Winchell washed his gossip down with gimlets in leather Stork Club banquettes and Henry Luce ordained statesmen on the cover of *Time*. Half the world's wealth resided in America, and Manhattan presided over most of it.

By 4:30 p.m. Grand Central acquired the upbeat air of a workday's end. A dull roar filled the cavernous hall, a roar of release from the day's burdens and routines. Newsboys raised voices above the hubbub to bark the afternoon headlines: President Eisenhower claimed the right to retaliate without congressional approval if the Soviets attacked London or Paris.

Into the maelstrom slipped a mild figure. He passed unnoticed and un-known through the whorls of commuters on the great marble floor, fleet-ing as a shadow, and walked down a tiled ramp to a men's room off the lower concourse.

The blast came at 5:00 p.m., the manic height of rush hour. It thun-dered like a cannon through the corridors, followed by exhalations of smoke the color of storm clouds. The explosion was forceful enough to shatter a marble partition separating two stalls and fracture a sink and a toilet in a men's room on the terminal's lower level. Three unlucky bystanders—Don Douglas of the Upper West Side, Domenic Zinno of Brooklyn, and Tom Spellett of upstate New York—staggered from the smoke. Police escorted the men to an emergency room, where doctors treated them for shock and contusions.

"It was in the booth next to mine," Douglas said. "I was in the booth to the left, and all of a sudden the partition door all seemed to come to pieces. Pieces were flying all over the place and I didn't know what had happened. I was sort of dazed with ringing in my ears. I was cut on one leg by a fragment that struck me."

The scene still smelled of smoke when the bomb squad double-timed downstairs and began conducting a forensic mop-up inside a cordon of police rope strung up to protect the sanctity of the crime scene. With black suit jackets off and sleeves rolled up, half a dozen detectives photo-graphed and sketched the scene from four angles and knelt to measure the distance from the epicenter of the blast, known as the seat, to the far-thest point of damage. On hands and knees they tagged and bagged shards of exploded pipe and a dozen other bits of evidence found nearby— burn residue, battery fragments lodged in the black-scorched tile wall, strands of copper wire, springs, electrician's tape, and watch parts. Even the smallest shards can tell a story.

Witnesses seated on a waiting room bench described the awful moment—the shuddering jolt of the bomb blast traveling at twenty-six thousand feet per second, the debris thrown across the room, the scraps of who knew what flying around like a tornado. "I felt an explosion and something pushed me in the head," Zinno said. ". . . Just like a force, like a wind, just pressed me down."

What color was the smoke? detectives asked. Was it black (dynamite) or yellow (nitroglycerine) or blue (gunpowder)? Was it loud enough to make their ears ring? Did they see any suspicious figures skulking about?

One man stood coolly apart as the detectives collected evidence. Captain Howard Finney, chief of the crime lab and its subsidiary, the bomb squad, had the hard-eyed look of a career cop. The bomb squad detectives regarded their boss as a tough, clever man, but inscrutable and stern. He never drank. Never joked. Never smiled. When he spoke, which was rare, he did so with a slight Boston accent.

With dark suit and receding steel-gray crew cut, Finney fit the Hollywood image of a New York detective. An intensity of purpose played behind his deadpan gaze. "He has been described as poker-faced," wrote the Associated Press, "but when he gets angry . . . he looks like he's going to explode right out of his well-tailored suit."

Finney was a new breed of cop, a science-minded criminologist with three graduate degrees—he was working on a fourth—and wartime schooling in naval intelligence. In the drab corridors of police headquarters he was known as an advocate for the fast-evolving field of forensics. (He held the same job as Mac Taylor, the fictional *CSI* character played by the actor Gary Sinise.) Finney believed that the scientific analysis of physical evidence could help solve crimes where old-fashioned policing failed. To help prove his point he wrote a technical manual on forensic evidence for New York district attorneys. His convictions were not shared by everyone in the department.

Once the bomb scene was photographed and rigorously combed for evidence, Finney and his men ducked under the police rope and drove back across the Brooklyn Bridge in the dark to their offices on Poplar Street. They climbed three flights of stairs to the crime lab—a suite of whitewashed, fluorescent-lit top-floor rooms where Finney's technicians waged their war on crime with infrared X-ray machines and beakers of chemicals.

The crime lab gave off the same acrid cigarette stench as any other police office of its era, but it was as quiet as a research library. No wise-cracking cops. No cussing perps. Nobody whistled, nobody guffawed. Twenty-two white-coated technicians in rotating round-the-clock shifts leaned over spectrographs, infrared spectrometers, microscales sensitive enough to weigh a single drop of blood, and electron microscopes capable of magnifying an image six-thousand-fold. The instruments consumed so much voltage that the building required special wiring.

Every criminal leaves evidence at a crime scene. The crime lab's job was to find it and interpret its meaning. Technicians compared the structure of hairs found at murder scenes with hairs plucked from suspects' scalps; they matched soil collected from a defendant's shoes with soil found on escape routes; they identified heroin and cocaine by dissolving granules in solvents; they discerned fingerprints left as hidden oil patterns on drinking glasses and doorknobs; they matched the mouths of dead bodies with dental records; they determined when a crime occurred by analyzing blood, semen, saliva, and sweat. When a burned body turned up, they sifted the ashes for bone fragments. When the evidence couldn't get to the lab fast enough, the technicians rushed to the crime scene in a truck, a mobile laboratory, outfitted like a Swiss Army knife with its own power supply, X-ray machine, fingerprinting kit, and darkroom.

Captain Finney and his technicians analyzed more than three hundred pieces of evidence a day—each a miniature mystery—and often testified to their significance in court. They identified bodies, pinpointed the exact time of day a bullet struck its victim, established what type of handgun fired a bullet, matched a shattered car headlight to a make and model, and determined the angle at which blood fell to form a splatter on the floor. Finney kept a storage room filled with objects waiting to be admitted as courtroom evidence—whiskey bottles with fingerprints, broken glass smeared with dried blood, photographs of bite marks. In addition, Finney's crime lab put into practice the first sobriety test for drivers, a balloon device known as the Drunkometer, which determined if a person had more than .15 percent of alcohol in their respiratory system.

Captain Finney built and operated the most sophisticated crime lab of any municipality in the world. It was a showcase for the scientific treatment of evidence and was naturally the object of attention. Within one week in 1952 the lab received visitors from police forces in Iran, Pakistan, India, Israel, England, Tokyo, Ecuador, and Hawaii.

The crime lab had moved to Poplar Street because subways rumbling beneath its former offices on Mulberry Street, in Manhattan, had rattled the more sensitive instruments. The new location, above the borough police academy, also hinted at the crime lab's marginal standing in the Byzantine police hierarchy.

The crime lab was still a relatively new undertaking in 1954. Scientific methods had not entered police work in earnest until the early 1920s, when Berkeley police chief August Vollmer, known as the father of modern policing, hooked burglars and gunmen up to a crude lie detector that read telltale changes in pulse, blood pressure, and breathing during interrogation. He also directed detectives to use blood, fiber, and soil analysis to solve crimes.

Vollmer's example inspired J. Edgar Hoover to start an FBI crime lab, known as the Technical Laboratory, in 1932. It began with a single agent, a World War I veteran named Charles Appel, equipped with a camera and a cast-off microscope set up in an unused break room. Hoover assigned him the space because it was the only one available with a sink. (The ransom note for the Lindbergh kidnapping was among the first pieces of evidence Appel analyzed.)

Forensic science was still struggling to establish itself when Captain Finney assumed control of the NYPD crime lab in 1950. He was an advocate of fast-developing methods such as blood analysis, ballistics, fingerprinting, odontology, and forensic chemistry. But he struggled to win over the hidebound police culture of the nightstick and arm twisting. The police brass on Centre Street had, to a man, come up the ranks as patrolmen on a beat. They had learned to put their faith in the persuasive powers of brawn and intimidation. Street wisdom held that most breaks in a case came from neighborhood informants—bodega clerks, bartenders, stoop sitters—and from leaning on suspects in interrogation rooms.

If the rougher street types were reluctant to divulge what they knew, they could always be persuaded. Lewis Valentine, the police commissioner under Mayor Fiorello La Guardia, tacitly gave cops license to rough up suspicious characters before bringing them in for formal questioning. He bristled at the sight of suspects assembled in the lineup room with hair neatly parted. "That velvet collar should be smeared with blood," he said. "I don't want those hoodlums coming in looking as if they stepped out of a barber's chair. From now on, bring 'em in mussed up."

The rank and file resisted the authority of a specialized central agency such as the crime lab manned by cops with college degrees—and in some cases graduate degrees. What could scientists in white coats possibly teach patrolmen about collaring a fugitive? Who had ever heard of a crime cracked with a microscope? What did chemists know about battery and burglary?

Captain Finney was uncomfortably aware that the crime lab was still on probation. To convince the brass of its effectiveness, he would have to demonstrate its investigative value in a high-profile case—a case such as that of the Mad Bomber.

The problem was that Captain Finney had yet to learn much about F.P. He assumed that the bomber was a man because he slipped unnoticed into men's rooms. (Finney may also have assumed, with his 1950s mind-set, that bomb fabrication could not be a woman's work.) F.P. would have to be a skilled machinist with access to a lathe because he made the bombs by hand, inscribing with great precision the threads for the screw-on caps that enclosed both ends of the pipe. He drilled holes in the pipe for loading gunpowder, then plugged the holes with a three-eighth-inch Allen screws. Captain Finney suspected that F.P. worked a night shift because his letters bore postmarks of daytime hours, and his bombs were generally deposited in the late afternoon with the timer set between 5:00 p.m. and 6:00 p.m. Aside from that, he was a mystery.

In the days after the Grand Central blast a stream of outside experts—fingerprint men, demolition engineers, machinists—came to Poplar Street to examine the fragments of iron pipe and copper wire. The men handled the evidence, turned it over. They stood around, hands thrust in pockets, discussing it with Captain Finney the way perplexed mechanics might worry over a car that stubbornly refuses repair.

After much discussion, Captain Finny and his men came to the troubling conclusion that F.P. had adopted a more advanced timing mechanism. They suspected that he had removed the minute hand from a $5 wristwatch and inserted a screw into the watch crystal. A wire connected the screw, a battery, and a flashlight bulb filled with black gunpowder. The bulb was pressed to the back of the watch. When the hour hand swung around and touched the screw, the electrical connection was complete. The charge from the battery ran through the watch to ignite the powder siphoned into the bulb, which, in turn, combusted the larger store of powder stashed in the pipe.

If Captain Finney could locate the stores that sold the bomb materials, he might turn up a lead. But the watchmaker had distributed more than thirty thousand watches of that type in New York. At Captain Finney's direction, Sergeant Dale and his men began canvassing stores throughout the city. Neighborhood by neighborhood, street by street, they flashed their badges in jewelers', watch repair shops, and department stores—always with the same result. "The dealers acted as if we were crazy when we tried to track the watch down to the individual buyer," Captain Finney said.

The most harassed man in New York that season may have been a timid watch repairman who eked out a humble living by going shop to shop scrounging broken timepieces to fix, polish, and resell. Jewelers hoping to ingratiate themselves with the local cops reported him over and over as a possible suspect. Detectives questioned him eight times, in eight different neighborhoods, though he mostly worked the Yorkville section of the Upper East Side. Finally, so that cops wouldn't waste their time on him anymore, a detective in the Bronx made up a sign for the repairman to wear: I AM NOT THE MAD BOMBER.

Meanwhile, another team of detectives fanned out among plumbing outlets and sporting goods stores to ask about iron pipe and shotgun shells loaded with black powder. At each stop detectives found that F.P. had shrewdly avoided using specialized components traceable to specific suppliers.

By now a touch of desperation had infected Captain Finney's cool methodology. With the pressing certainty of more bombs to come—and the threat of newspaper headlines mocking police failures—he persisted in sending detectives to store after store in the blind hope of a break-through. In each case the men returned to Poplar Street shaking their heads in frustration. "I personally have taken the watch-timing mechanism from one of the bombs this clown has made to seventy-five stores around Times Square," said Detective William Schmitt, who was assigned to catalog the exploded-bomb parts. "Every one stocked that watch."

While Schmitt canvassed watch stores, his colleague Detective Joseph Rothengast visited plumbing-supply outlets with a sample of F.P.'s trademark iron coupling in hand. "Every one stocked the kind of pipe I had," the detective said. "And every one looked at me as if I had holes in my head when I asked if there was any way to trace this particular piece."

In the end, the physical evidence added little to Captain Finney's understanding of F.P., beyond the obvious grudge against Con Ed stated in his letter to the *Herald Tribune*. The growing list of targets—train stations and movie theaters—with no connection to the utility muddled even that bit of evidence.

In desperation, detectives tried to decipher any pattern they could, however far-fetched. A bomb had exploded inside the overhead ventilation box of a telephone booth in the New York Public library on April 24, 1951, a day after the full moon. The next four bombs went off within three days of a full moon. Perhaps the bomber was what police call a mooner, a person with spells of madness induced by lunar cycles. The fire department had found arsonists who lit fires on full moons. As a result, the bomb squad decided to dispatch extra patrolmen to potential targets during the next full moon.

If the physical evidence would not reveal F.P.'s character and motivations, Captain Finney reasoned, maybe they would show up in a paper trail. Police searched thousands of court documents dating back to 1936, four years before the first bombing, for the names of customers who had sued Con Ed. They probed the records of nearly ten thousand mental patients, parsing those who had worked as toolmakers, machinists, or electricians. In veterans hospitals they looked for patients who had handled military ordnance. Finny also asked the US patent office if any inventors had tried to patent a bomb similar to those used by F.P. As the investigation expanded, the detectives collaborated with the postal service, the unions representing engineers and machinists, and vocational schools where bomb parts could be made.

Back in the crime lab, Captain Finney's handwriting expert, Detective Joe McNally, pored over the blocky features of the capital lettering in the note F.P. had sent to Con Ed with the original bomb, as well as the letter he sent to the *Herald Tribune*. "The G was a C with two horizontal lines," Detective McNally said. "The center line on the M comes all the way down to the baseline of the writing. The Y is a V at the top and you've got a vertical on it. The S seems to flat out at the bottom. And then the pictorial effect of it . . . it's sort an arrhythmic type—it's just sort of jumbled, there's no rhythm to it, no regularity to it. If you look at the slant pattern, at one time it's vertical, then forehand, and it jumps back and forth."

The closest thing to a certainty in the investigation was that F.P. harbored a violent grudge against Con Ed. In late December 1954 Finney sent Detective Hugh Sang to conduct a laborious search of personnel files at Con Ed's Irving Place headquarters with the one-in-a-million hope of uncovering a match with F.P.'s oddball handwriting. It was a daunting undertaking. Con Ed, like any public utility, had amassed oceans of complaints. To make matters worse, company records were fragmented and erratic because Con Ed had absorbed two dozen subsidiaries over the years. Many of the resulting records were lost or destroyed.

Nonetheless, John J. Holland, the affable head of company security, heartily agreed to help. He set Sang up in a vacant second-floor office. Every morning Holland delivered boxes of files on former employees who had been fired or caused trouble. Sang plowed through box after box, reviewing job applications, performance reviews, and the angry correspondence of the dismissed and discharged. He kept a particular lookout for employees with the initials F.P. After several weeks Sang concluded that Holland was delivering only innocuous cases, small-time offenders. And only recent ones. "I kept after Holland," Sang said, "and he said, 'I'm having trouble with the legal department.' "

Captain Finny and Sergeant Dale came to Irving Place weekly to apply pressure. Holland greeted them warmly in his office and showered them with good cheer. Surely there must be a deep archive of files dating back to the 1940s and before, Captain Finney said. No, Holland assured him, Con Ed kept no such files, only the recent ones housed at Irving Place.

While Sang searched at Con Ed headquarters, Captain Finney pursued a separate line of possibility: Might F.P. have served in the military? He had planted two bombs before World War II. The first was discovered on November 18, 1940—five months after the World's Fair bombing— inside a wooden toolbox left on a windowsill at a Con Ed compound on West Sixty-Fourth Street. An employee opened the toolbox to find a piece of iron pipe, about the length of his hand, neatly capped on each end and wrapped in a sheet of paper. He unscrolled the paper to find a message printed with pencil in block letters: CON EDISON CROOKS, THIS IS FOR YOU. The lettering was neat with stilted, awkward phrases oddly separated by dashes. Below the message, written in a gray dust identified as gunpowder, was a second warning: THERE IS NO SHORTAGE OF POWDER BOYS.

The message puzzled Finney. If the bomb had exploded, it would have destroyed the note. Nobody would have read it. Had F.P. written the note for his private gratification, or had he intentionally left an inoperative bomb by way of warning? "The detectives who read the note," *Collier's* magazine later wrote, "never dreamed they were appearing in Act I, Scene I, of a fantastic melodrama that was to have the longest run in New York police history."

The dud was forgettable, and it earned no newspaper coverage. Too many other stories that week demanded column inches—evidence of Nazi organizations in the heartland, city officials caught taking bribes, RAF bombers hitting German gun emplacements on the French coast.

Ten months later, on September 24, 1941, a passerby found a pipe in a red sock lying in the middle of Nineteenth Street, four blocks from Con Ed headquarters on Irving Place. Perhaps F.P. had dumped the bomb from his pocket after spotting a policeman, or otherwise losing his nerve. Like its precursor, the bomb was relatively crude, but it proved that F.P. was not a onetimer.

Then F.P. disappeared, at least for a while. Hours after Pearl Harbor he wrote letters to nine prospective targets—Radio City Music Hall, the Roxy Theater, the Astor Hotel, among others—announcing that revenge would be postponed, but not forgotten:

I WILL MAKE NO MORE BOMB UNITS FOR THE DURATION OF THE WAR—MY PATRIOTIC FEELINGS HAVE MADE ME DECIDE THIS.

True to his word, F.P. withdrew for almost ten years. His hiatus ended on March 29, 1951, when a bomb exploded in a cigarette urn outside the Oyster Bar in Grand Central Terminal, blasting sand and metal bolts across a lower concourse. F.P. assembled his third bomb in the same manner as the first two, but it was bigger with an improved fusing mechanism. "This is a well-constructed mechanism," Detective Schmitt said. "It shows considerable advance in technique as compared with earlier bombs." F.P. had clearly used the war years to improve his workmanship.

The bomber's disappearance after Pearl Harbor suggested to Captain Finney that he might have spent the war in uniform, possibly with a bomb demolition squadron where he could have studied the mechanics of US and foreign-made explosives. This would explain why the first bomb crafted after the war had a semimilitary design. Detective Schmitt, who had handled ordnance with the navy, said the bomb resembled the depth charges he deployed in the Pacific: "The firing device was so intricate that I was sure it was part of military ordnance."

Captain Finney asked an army ordnance group at the Picatinny Arsenal in Dover, New Jersey, to determine if the bomb samples resembled grenades used by the Japanese, Russians, French, or Italians. The response was inconclusive. He also asked the Veterans Administration to go through their entire history of discharged servicemen, a depository with tens of thousands of cases, to look for ordnance workers with a history of unbalanced behavior. Staffers could find no veterans who fit that description.

Then, at last, Captain Finney's deductions led to a break in the case. A former GI called in a description of a suspicious acquaintance he served with in an overseas demolition squad. The suspect was a trained machinist and a former Con Ed employee now operating his own repair shop in the South Bronx. This peculiar character, the informant said, was devoted to feeding stray cats at dawn. "He used to be a feet-on-the-ground guy like you and me, but now he's going nuts. He runs a repair shop here in the city, but he spends a lot of his time locked in a back room, like he's building something he doesn't want people to see."

Captain Finney tallied the corroborating traits: an oddball former Con Ed employee; capable of making bombs; operates a workshop equipped with electrical gear and machine tools. After months of flailing among dead-end leads, Finney had a suspect that neatly matched what little they knew about the bomber.

A rotating team of detectives watched the workshop, day and night, from a big black unmarked Plymouth parked nearby. After six weeks of surveillance they grabbed the suspect. Detectives interrogated him in a precinct house on West Forty-Seventh Street while Captain Finney and his men combed the suspect's home and workshop. Try as they might, they could not find a single scrap of incriminating evidence—no flashlight, no wire, no iron pipe. The police had no choice but to release him. "Some people feed cats," the suspect said. "Some collect stamps. We all have our peculiarities. I once knew a guy who liked rhubarb, for God's sakes."

By the winter of 1953, F.P. was hitting his stride. He went to his garage workshop every day with confidence that his bombs were more reliable, and more volatile, than the crude devices that had preceded them. Until now he had carefully planted bombs for dramatic effect, shrewdly confining them to a downstairs corner of Grand Central and other out-of-the-way locations. But after years of frustration, he had concluded that his restraint had allowed the newspapers to ignore him. He would now demand their attention. He would force them to acknowledge his suffering, even if it cost lives. He was for the first time prepared to use bombs as instruments of death.

Movie theaters, he concluded, were the most promising targets because the close-packed audience increased the chance of injury. So far he had hit the Paramount in Times Square and twice bombed the Lowe's Lexington Theatre, the largest movie theater on the East Side. Now, on the late-winter afternoon of March 10, 1953, he was on his way to Radio City Music Hall, the grandest, most glorious theater in the world. As dusk settled on Sixth Avenue, he walked, ticket in hand, through the art deco lobby, with its sparkling chandelier dangling from giddy heights and its mural depicting man's quest for the fountain of youth. He entered the six-thousand-seat auditorium where organists played popular tunes on a pair of Wurlitzers between showings of a Kirk Douglas movie. He took a seat in row L, toward the rear of the orchestra section. After the houselights dimmed, he followed his normal routine: He cut a hole in the upholstery of a neighboring seat with a forty-cent pocketknife. Moving discreetly in the dark, he slid the bomb and the knife deep in the guts of the seat.

Moments later he stood and shuffled his way down the row of seats. He could see that a latecomer had taken his empty seat. He walked to the lobby with a deliberately measured pace, trying to look like a normal moviegoer slipping out to the restroom or concession stand for a bag of popcorn. The exit was almost within reach when the bomb exploded prematurely. The great room flashed with light. A shuddering boom echoed off the scalloped walls. The woman who had taken his seat was pitched into the air, landing a few rows forward. Amazingly, she escaped with only superficial injuries.

F.P. rushed to the lobby with his overcoat swirling. An usher stopped him with a firm grip on his upper arm. Here was the moment F.P. had dreaded for years.

"We're sorry about this, sir," the usher said. "We regret the inconvenience."

So F.P. was not apprehended after all. He shook his arm loose and adopted the air of a displeased customer. He was unharmed, he told the usher, but he still preferred to leave. The usher handed him a free pass and urged him to come back another night, assuring him the disturbance wouldn't recur.

"If I come back," F.P. thought, "it will happen again, all right."

He vanished into the crowds marching along Sixth Avenue. Midtown was alive with converging sirens. F.P. and Finney—prey and predator—missed each other by minutes.

The Radio City mishap wasn't the only close call. F.P. made a habit of waiting until he was in Manhattan to load the bomb with gunpowder and set the timer. That way he would not risk an explosion as he drove. One day he was parked on West Ninety-Sixth Street siphoning gunpowder into a bomb held steady between his feet when a motorcycle cop pulled alongside. The cop glanced at him without suspicion. He was just checking to see if cars were illegally parked. But the encounter nonetheless spooked F.P. He gathered his gear and drove straight home. "I was so frightened I could hardly speak," he would say. From then on he loaded the powder in his garage and wrapped the bomb in rags to cushion it from shock during the drive to the city.

F.P. couldn't shake the sense that the police were shadowing him. A few weeks after his brush with the motorcycle cop, he was riding the downtown IRT express with a bomb in his coat pocket when he noticed a woman dressed entirely in black sitting across from him. She seemed to radiate malignant intentions. In his mind he named her the Black Queen. She was staring at him—staring long and resolutely. He stared back. She held her gaze with cold purpose. His eyes shifted to her handbag, the same type of long-strapped bag carried by policewomen. F.P. stepped from the subway at Eighty-Sixth Street. The Black Queen followed. He climbed a flight of stairs and boarded the downtown local. She did, too. He waited two stops, then exited at Fifty-Ninth Street. So did she. The police had found him, he was sure. He was about to run when the Black Queen turned a corner and walked away.

He was convinced that the police would continue to trap him. He could see signs of their machinations everywhere. Leafing through a newspaper, he noticed wristwatches, the same brand he used as a timing device, advertised for $3.85. He normally paid $5 to $7. It was obviously a ploy, an ambush. He ripped the ad to shreds.

F.P. knew that he was too smart for their tricks. He gloated over his knack for dodging the police, for showing them up. It was easy—almost too easy. He could toy with them—taunt them—with impunity. By now he was convinced that normal rules of law did not apply to him. He floated above such things, like a hero with supernatural powers.

The bombs kept coming, and the injury list grew. Bomb number eighteen exploded in the fifteenth row of Radio City during a sold-out showing of the Bing Crosby film *White Christmas* on November 7, 1954, inflicting deep puncture wounds on the legs and elbows of two middle-aged women. They were taken to Roosevelt Hospital. Two boys received contusions. "There was a big noise," said thirteen-year-old Edward Paolella, who had ridden the subway from Brooklyn with his brother Larry. "My brother started hollering that his back was hurting him, and I dragged him into the aisle and someone came down and asked what had happened and people started evacuating."

Two months later a bomb ripped through a set of lockers in the Long

Island Rail Road section of Pennsylvania Station, blasting a hole in a concrete wall and igniting a fire, which blew choking waves of smoke through the station's lower promenade during the evening commute. A passing volunteer fireman saw smoke billowing from the lockers and wet them down with an emergency fire hose.

Later, as detectives collected the charred remains of the bomb and other detritus, the local precinct cops guided Captain Finney to a man they had pulled out of the crowd who sold enormous souvenir balloons in Times Square. The peddler frequently stored uninflated balloons and other wares in a station locker. He told Captain Finney that he had glimpsed a man in a dark overcoat depositing something in the same locker that the peddler normally used. Thirty minutes later the locker exploded. The man had turned away before the peddler could get a proper look. It was as if Captain Finney were chasing a ghost. F.P. was tantalizingly close, but never within grasp.

On the afternoon of May 2, 1955, the open *Herald Tribune* newsroom, with its twelve-foot ceilings and clutter of desks, was in full deadline clamor as reporters prepared stories on the Eisenhower administration's decision to train Royal Air Force crews for atomic bomb missions and on the Vietnamese army artillery's pounding of rebels on the outskirts of Saigon. The typewriter clatter rose to a crescendo as the evening deadline neared. Cigarette smoke thickened. At 5:34 p.m., a phone rang on an editor's desk. A man on the line refused to identify himself but said that he had planted a bomb at Radio City.

Sixty police, firemen, and bomb squad detectives arrived at Radio City and roped off the entrance beneath the great art deco marquee. They searched the restrooms and concession stands where attendants dispensed popcorn and soda. The men spent almost two hours inspecting the seventy-four rows—all 5,933 red seats—without finding anything suspicious. Sergeant Dale told the manager he could proceed with the 6:18 stage show, featuring the Rockettes, an acrobat, and performing dogs, followed by *The Glass Slipper,* a contemporary movie version of Cinderella starring the pixieish Leslie Caron.

That night, after the Rockettes had stowed their dance shoes in lockers and Caron had secured her prince's heart, the cleaning crew walked the rows, one by one, sweeping paper popcorn containers and candy wrappers. At 3:15 a.m. a broom knocked against a hard object lying on the floor beneath seat 125 on the far right side of the orchestra section. It was a pipe tucked inside a man's sock. For the second time in eleven hours, the bomb squad pulled up to the Sixth Avenue entrance in a fleet of unmarked police cruisers, sirens blaring, followed by the green station wagon and Big Bertha. The protective gear came out. The bomb was carried to Big Bertha and conveyed to an empty lot on Fifty-Third Street, where detectives applied the fluoroscope. It was early morning now, and the low eastern light reflected down the midtown streets. The squad set off for Fort Tilden, a guided-missile base on the western tip of the Rockaway Peninsula in Queens, before rush-hour traffic made transporting the bomb too hazardous.

For most of a day the bomb sat in a concrete bunker tucked among the dunes, the object of study and debate. The detectives agreed this was likely a live bomb that had miscued because of a faulty timing mechanism. But they could not tell for sure without opening it up by hand for a look. This kind of procedure was by far the most delicate the detectives undertook. The bomb was easily powerful enough to butcher a man if it exploded in his hands, discharging shrapnel into his torso and face. No amount of protective padding could save him. Thus the dissection would have to be made with surgical precision under excruciating stress with almost no margin for error. No trembling hands, no mishandling.

Sergeant Dale huddled with his boss, Captain Finney. The safest course, they agreed, would be to skip the inspection and blow up the bomb under controlled conditions. But this could be their chance—their only chance—to examine F.P.'s handicraft intact. So far they had only guessed at the construction based on the exploded bits of forensic evidence. So that afternoon Detective Schmitt, the squad's steeliest veteran, stepped to the bomb with a special tool kit containing no metal instruments. "If we have to," Detective Schmitt told a reporter, "we can get in and cut the wires with a glass knife we carry—glass is a nonconductor of electricity."

Schmitt wore protective padding without gloves so that he would have unencumbered use of his hands. He methodically, deliberately unscrewed one of the caps enclosing the pipe ends, his right hand twisting counter-clockwise slowly so as not to create a spark by scraping metal against metal. When the cap came off, he laid it aside. He could now safely slide the apparatus out. With hands as steady as a watchmaker's he disconnected a wire leading to the battery—thereby deactivating the charge. He could see that the wristwatch had been set to explode the bomb at 6:30 p.m., but it had malfunctioned. Now the other bomb squad detectives could safely gather around for a firsthand look at how F.P. had wired the wrist-watch, flashlight bulb, and battery together in an electrical loop. The fabrication was more impressive than they had imagined—easily capable of killing. Captain Finney knew that when a serial offender gets away with his early crimes, his methods and behavior usually evolve. So it was with F.P. He was good, and getting better.

CHAPTER SIX

UP FROM THE STREETS

August 1954

ON SUNDAY MORNING, AUGUST 1, 1954, NEW YORKERS WOKE TO A MEA-
sure of relief. A weak line of thunderstorms had passed through overnight, bringing a slight respite from a week of stabbing heat that sunbaked
pavement and singed the edges of maple leaves in Central Park. All the
pleasures of a midsummer Sunday lay in store, with the Giants playing
a doubleheader at the Polo Grounds and young couples unfurling towels
on Coney Island.

That afternoon New York police commissioner Francis W. H.
Adams delivered a half-hour speech, aired on television and radio, which
hit heat-weary New Yorkers like a thump to the gut. The city, he said,
was on "the verge of becoming a community of violence and crime," a
city where "sensible" men and women stayed off the streets at night.

The statistics he cited held no great surprise. Murders and other violent crimes had jumped more than 11 percent in the first half of 1954, as
newspapers had loudly warned in a slew of articles describing rape victims
left to perish and elderly citizens stomped for a handful of dollars. The
Mafia staged hits and ran extortion rings with near impunity. More than
a hundred teenage gangs rumbled in bare-fisted back streets. Editorial
pages called for curfews and citizen patrols. New York, the city of pros-

perity and opportunity for all, was shadowed by gunmen, bookies, muggers, and molesters.

The growing disorder was evident to all New Yorkers, but to hear the police commissioner acknowledge it—describe it so graphically—startled his listeners like a face slap. "Before this hot August Sunday is over, one of us in this city will have been murdered," Adams said. "Three women will have been raped. One hundred and forty of our homes and businesses will have been burglarized. . . . Even in the brief half hour in which I will talk to you, seventeen crimes will be committed in the City of New York—more than one every two minutes."

He added, "Conditions grow worse with each passing month and now have reached a point where they must become a matter of the most serious concern for every citizen of this, the greatest, the richest, the proudest, city in the world."

The tinny sound of Adams's voice played from radios perched on barbershop counters in Spanish Harlem and on the flickering televisions of Third Avenue bars. It played in kitchens of Douglaston ranch homes, on Carroll Gardens stoops where families gathered to escape the heat, and in down-beaten tenements standing shoulder to shoulder on Orchard Street.

The most attentive listener of all may have been Adams's boss, Mayor Robert F. Wagner Jr. He tuned in to the broadcast from Gracie Mansion, the 155-year-old mayoral residence overlooking the swift waters of the East River. Wagner had moved into the mansion seven months earlier, accompanied by great expectations. He grew up as the dauphin of New York politics, the son of a formidable US senator and protégé of Tammany boss Carmine DeSapio. In boyhood he sipped lemonade at Shadow Lawn, Woodrow Wilson's summer home, and played fetch with Cesar and Jeff, New York governor Al Smith's Great Danes. He had earned a medal at Loyola, a Jesuit school on Park Avenue, for his recitation of "Spartacus to the Gladiators," a speech inciting Roman slaves to an uprising. At Yale, he led the campus Democratic club, bucking the rightward campus bent by campaigning for Franklin Roosevelt. When Wagner's father and five New York judges rode by train to New Haven for the Harvard-Yale game, he met them at the station with a fistful of tickets and a pair of black cars rented from an undertaker.

There was no question that Wagner would enter politics. No question that he would advance the agenda of progressive reforms his father had championed as a Roosevelt ally—clearing slums for urban renewal, granting collective-bargaining rights to unions, drawing blacks and Hispanics into city government, expanding affordable access to higher education.

Now, seven months into his first term, Wagner's high-minded plans had smacked hard against a harsh reality: the melting pot had become nearly ungovernable. Of the city's 8 million residents, 5 million were minorities. They crammed themselves into patchworks of jostling ethnic quarters with ever-shifting borders—Haitians in Flatbush, Filipinos in Woodside, Irish in Breezy Point, Germans in Yorkville. Neighborhoods had stronger ethnic identities in those days; their residents rarely intermingled. Enclaves eyed one other with suspicion, or, in some cases, open hostility. It was nearly impossible for a mayor to keep the uneasy peace.

West Harlem, for example, struggled to absorb a new wave of blacks fleeing Jim Crow and poverty in the Deep South. Residents looked warily east to Spanish Harlem and west to Manhattanville, a pair of Puerto Rican neighborhoods swelled to bursting with hundreds of thousands of newcomers arriving by the planeload from San Juan. With Puerto Ricans impinging from both sides, and the Irish of Washington Heights pressing from the north, teenage boys of Harlem mustered themselves into real-life Jets and Sharks. They defended their turf against the Puerto Rican Dragons and Irish Jesters by flashing bike chains, car antennas, switchblades, and baseball bats.

Skirmishes broke out across the boroughs as gang members, known as bops, with greased ducktails, white T-shirts, and cuffed blue jeans, advanced and retreated like miniature militias—the Mau Maus, Bishops, and Barons in Brooklyn; the Fordham Baldies and Golden Guineas in the Bronx; the Saints, Sinners, and Chaplains in Queens. They taunted each other with cryptic messages—gang hieroglyphics—written in chalk on subway platforms and school-yard walls. The rule of the street was an eye for an eye. The black gangs fought the Irish, Irish fought the Puerto Ricans, Puerto Ricans fought the Italians, Italians fought the Jews, and the Jews fought blacks. On and on it went, with teenage combatants stabbed, shot, and occasionally killed. Meanwhile, the gangs' older sibling, the mob, fattened up on an underground economy of extortion and heroin distribution.

Wagner's reform policies rested on the liberal conviction that criminals were not inherently bad; they were merely products of bad environments. If Wagner and the redevelopment czar, Robert Moses, could replace slums with wholesome new blocks of public housing, the inhabitants, Wagner theorized, would be less prone to drugs and petty larceny. So bulldozers cleared the neighborhoods, forcing more displaced families to insinuate themselves into unwelcoming surroundings. Which, in turn, produced more conflict and crime. Wagner's progressive agenda grew harder to defend as stabbings and drug deals overtook the streets and borough leaders agitated for stiffer measures. Crime was the one thing that could undo all his ambitions. To be an effective mayor, he had to show that he possessed the strength to handle the havoc engulfing the neighborhoods.

Wagner was a courteous man, and likable enough. He was certainly businesslike, and highly efficient. But he was strangely undemonstrative for a city that prefers its mayors flamboyant. New Yorkers had begun to wonder if he was too soft to manage a tough city. He barely spoke above a whisper in meetings, and he was a bland presence at public events. Bernard Baruch, the financier and statesman, told a mayoral aide, "Your boss is one of the pleasantest disappointments I've had in a long time." Meanwhile, the middle class was slipping away to the suburbs.

As the ongoing heat wave suffocated the city, Wagner concluded that he must prove that he was in command of the job. His first lesson as mayor: if he wanted to be a reformer, he would first have to become an enforcer.

Adams didn't mention F.P. in his radio address, though he hardly needed to. Nothing made the police look more ineffectual than their failure to catch him. The bombs had discharged one after another—seventeen in all since he'd started his campaign.

By the summer of 1954 the bomber coverage had jumped from one-column items tucked among the mattress ads and death notices on page 8 to a front-page fixture. Each lurid headline read like a rebuke to the police. As the story gained momentum, the tabloids started calling F.P. the Mad Bomber of New York, as if he were a folk hero.

The bomber had not committed the grisliest crimes in New York that year. That honor went to John Francis Roche, a plumber's helper who confessed to four murders, plus the rape-slaying of a fourteen-year-old girl he had attacked on her way to school. But F.P.'s bombings induced nightmares like no other. As the coverage accrued, a weight of fear pressed down on the city. The uncertainty of the bombings, the anxiety of the unknown, the thought of a faceless madman walking the streets with dangerous intent, gave rise to a potent form of terror.

"You thought twice before you used a phone booth or went to the movies," one resident said. "You heard lots of Mad Bomber jokes—you'd laugh, but they weren't really funny."

Adams himself may have been part of the problem. A tall, polished reform-minded lawyer, and a valued campaign aide to Mayor Wagner, he was, however, a creature of the boardroom more than the streets. He had no knowledge of lineups or the fraternal customs of the precinct house. In fact, he complained that his police duties interfered with his oil-painting classes. It came as no surprise when Adams returned to private law practice.

In the early summer of 1955, Mayor Wagner sat in his City Hall office looking out through double-height windows onto the Broadway traffic moving south in fits and starts like a hectic, honking parade of coupes, sedans, and Checker cabs. He faced a critical decision: Whom could he find to replace Adams? Who was capable of restoring order to the city, and thereby solidifying Wagner's authority as mayor? Who could turn back the tide of heroin and violence, the muggers and murderers? Who was shrewd enough to catch F.P.?

On August 2, Wagner's choice, a veteran cop named Stephen Kennedy, raised his right hand for the oath of office under the cut-glass chandeliers of City Hall. Within minutes of his swearing in Kennedy addressed the crime surge. The police, he said, would "stand together and give our utmost—our lives if necessary"—to stop the crime.

By appearance Kennedy was no tougher than Adams. With rimless bifocals and thinning iron-gray hair brushed back, he looked more like a poetry editor than commander of the country's largest police force. No trace of his old Brooklyn neighborhood—*Greenpernt*—inflected his speech. He picked his words precisely and pedantically, as a Latin teacher might. "There is in his tone none of the over-meticulousness of the self-consciously cultured man," *The New York Times* wrote in a profile printed six months after his appointment, "though there is a hint of the 'Harvard A.'" A year earlier, when Kennedy had become chief inspector, the top uniformed cop, Mayor Wagner could at first not remember him. "Oh, yes," he said after a long pause. "That's the man who speaks like a college professor."

Kennedy had never been spotted in a nightclub or saloon. There were no poker nights or rounds of beers with the boys. He spent his evenings reading Shakespeare sonnets and listening to Puccini. His favorite operatic character was Baron Scarpia, the villainous police chief in Tosca.

Kennedy claimed to have gone fishing just once in his life. "I didn't catch anything." He spent weekend afternoons in a less manly fashion: clipping hedges and puttering around the rose garden behind his modest two-story home in Bayside, Queens. "My people came from Ireland and they were farmers," he said. "They'd be ashamed of my gardening."

Looks can deceive. Beneath the bookish affectations lay a hard-nosed, up-from-the-streets cop. Of all the tough cops in New York, Kennedy may have been the toughest.

He was the son of an ornamental-marble cutter who came to Brooklyn from county Wexford, Ireland. The elder Kennedy could turn stone blocks into delicate flights of acanthus foliage and graceful caryatids. He had a light hand, but a granite-hard disposition and uncompromising standards. If he judged the marble delivered to a construction site to be of inferior quality, he crossed his arms and refused to pick up his chisel and hammer.

At night Stephen's father returned coated in marble dust to their cold-water flat in Greenpoint—a world away from Manhattan—to read the Bible and Charles Dickens. The neighborhood was patrolled by the Kent Street Savages, a gang best known for pushing a chimney over on a cop as he walked below. Stephen scouted for the Savages in his peripheral vision as he walked down West Street and up McGuinness Boulevard. He "never bothered anybody," he said. But he "never backed up either."

The father passed his unbending sense of discipline along to his four children, particularly Stephen, the oldest. "There were three cops on our post—Casey, Egan, and Maloney—who straightened us out," Kennedy said. "They'd do more than that. They'd tell our parents and then I'd get belted again at home. Nobody asked me, 'What are your needs?' Nobody asked me, 'Are you happy?' It was 'Look, Bud, do this,' and if you didn't do it, you got belted."

Over dinners of potato soup and corned beef the father told his children about county Wexford, an austere land menaced by British constables and belligerent landlords. The injustices of Ireland could never happen here, he told them. The promise of America—the gift of America—was precious. It had to be resolutely guarded.

Stephen grew up an earnest young man, a reader and thinker. As a boy he appeared older than his years. He might have joined the priesthood if his family could have afforded seminary. As it was, they barely scraped by on the grim Brooklyn waterfront. Orders for ornamental marble dropped off as the spare lines of art deco came into fashion in the 1920s.

Nobody wanted fluted frieze panels or carved pilasters anymore. With his family falling into poverty, Kennedy left parochial school to work as a fifteen-year-old longshoreman. He unloaded bananas on the Manhattan docks by day; at night he trained as a 170-pound middleweight boxer, an above-average prospect with ponderous feet but hands like flying cinder blocks. He made some dollars in a few seasons of Saturday-night bouts staged in dingy Brooklyn arenas thick with cigar smoke and curses bawled by angry bettors. Round after round he circled his opponents on the stained canvas—weaving, jabbing, dodging, and scoring points with uppercuts and left hooks. He sparred and shadowboxed alongside the local cops at the Greenpoint YMCA.

Kennedy was a serious young man who sought out a better life. Within a few years he was selling hand-operated adding machines for office use. He was making good money and engaged to Hortense Goldberger, the sister of his best friend from down the block. Abruptly, without much explanation, aside from a vaguely articulated belief in the dignity and necessity of the law and a wish to guard America from the abuses his parents knew in Ireland, Kennedy quit his plum sales job to join the police. Hortense wasn't happy. Nor were his parents. They associated police with the hated young Irishmen who, down on their luck or driven from home, joined the British army. By tradition, the British gave them a shilling bonus for betraying the Irish cause.

Stephen waited as long he could before breaking the news to his parents. "Tsk, tsk, tsk," his mother said, shaking her head. "So you've taken the king's shilling."

Kennedy began his police career, at age twenty-two, by swinging a leather-covered nightstick on the streets of Hell's Kitchen, the midtown backwater where Irish gangs—the Norsemen and Westies—gathered in dark school yards armed with broomsticks and brass knuckles. He wore a badge and holstered a pearl-handled Colt .38 under his blue uniform coat. He was "on the walk," in police parlance.

In the precinct house on West Forty-Seventh Street, veteran cops teased the rookie for carrying copies of *A Midsummer Night's Dream* and *A Tale of Two Cities* under his arm for the long subway ride home. They called him the Professor. Cops didn't care much for intellectuals, but they came to respect Kennedy. Even then he conducted himself with rare rectitude. "He polished his boots a bit brighter than the rest," said an acquaintance from the precinct house, "and walked his beat with an air of mission."

He might be high-minded, but he was tough. He walked alone, commanding respect on the streets of one of New York's diciest neighborhoods. "A policeman's gun is his cross," he said, "and he carries it always."

The young man who, as a priest, would have heard of sins in confession booths now saw them firsthand—in junkies found dead on stoops, in wives who shot abusive husbands in their sleep, in dive-bar fights where drunken friends exchanged knife wounds over nothing.

Kennedy worked his way up the ranks—patrolman, sergeant, homicide detective, lieutenant, inspector. He led special teams rooting out gambling and corruption on the dockyards. He studied at the FBI academy in Washington during World War II, the first New York cop to attend, returning as captain and an aide to Mayor La Guardia. According to J. Edgar Hoover, Kennedy was "New York's finest career officer."

By age thirty-six Kennedy had a demanding job and a wife and child at home, but he still managed to finish high school by attending night classes. He read textbooks on the subway, and he wrote out his homework assignments while eating an apple and a slice of cheese during lunch hour. "When the rest of the boys were out having a drink or a sandwich," an acquaintance said, "he would be having his lunch alone, reading a book." He subsisted on four hours of sleep and a dozen cups of black coffee a day, cultivating what he called his "night study pallor."

Hortense said, "Nobody will ever know what he went through during those years of living on four hours' sleep a day."

He went on to night school at St. John's University, graduating in three years, and to law school at New York University, also at night, because, he said, "I was a law enforcement officer and I thought I should know what the law is." At his law school graduation he chose to wear his blue dress police uniform rather than the customary academic robes.

Kennedy's rise from the streets was long and friendless. He was a cold-shouldering loner who stood apart from a police culture heavy with backslapping influence peddlers and dodgy favors. He earned grudging respect for his unyielding rectitude, but mixed awkwardly with his colleagues. "Steve has come up through the ranks," a police acquaintance said, "but the force never rubbed off on him."

Now forty-nine, Kennedy had grown stocky with a hint of paunch and a boxer's meaty hands stained nicotine yellow. He was thirty pounds over his fight weight. With his dark suit and gray hair parted high on the left side, he looked more like a prosperous stockbroker than a veteran cop.

After his induction as police commissioner at City Hall, Kennedy kissed Hortense good-bye and rode north to the Centre Street police headquarters, where he pushed through a door with his new title lettered in gold leaf on a frosted-glass panel and entered the wood-paneled commissioner's office. He seated himself for the first time in a swivel chair behind the mahogany desk, as hefty as a Studebaker, that Teddy Roosevelt had installed sixty years earlier. Three phones sat on the desk and an American flag perched upright on a stand. A birdcage elevator stood by for private exits. The office befit the world's most powerful police official.

The long journey from his father's threadbare home in county Wexford to the commissioner's office had been achieved through hard-nosed work and an almost inhuman capacity for discipline. Not surprisingly, Kennedy resisted the fashionable view that criminals were products of their environment and therefore not entirely accountable for their actions. In his first days as commissioner, Kennedy promised an immediate and unrelenting fight against the rising tide of crime and violence. "All Kennedy wants," said a sociologist, "is to swing the big stick, arrest more kids, get more cops, bust up gangs."

Kennedy, the old-school beat cop, took possession of the commissioner's office just as a new way of policing came of age. Two years earlier a be-spectacled criminologist from the University of California named Paul

Kirk published the emerging field of forensics' first authoritative text, a comprehensive eight-hundred-page book called *Crime Investigation: Physical Evidence and the Police Laboratory*. Its publication signaled a modern way of thinking about investigations. Kirk wrote it so that detectives without access to specialized training might learn how to conduct the scientific study of physical evidence. Kirk's message was clear: the logic of forensics could decode crimes that defied resolution by conventional police methods.

Kirk, the forensics evangelist, could not have been more different from Kennedy, in appearance and background. While Kennedy was swinging a nightstick in Hell's Kitchen, Kirk was working as a biochemist. He spent the war years isolating fissionable plutonium for the Manhattan Project, the secret research that led to production of the first nuclear weapons during World War II. Afterward he chaired the department of criminalistics at Berkeley.

Word spread that this unassuming man with horn-rimmed glasses and a suitcase full of scientific instruments could work miracles. Police precincts from Sausalito to Sarasota sought his insights on unsolved cases. He received one such call in 1954 from police sergeant Claude Marchand in Hayward, California. Marchand had recently been summoned to the scene of a hit-and-run death on the outskirts of town. The victim was a retired Presbyterian minister. Marchand had found no broken glass or other telling evidence. The only item left on the road was a bouquet of flowers the minister had been carrying home to his sickly wife.

At Kirk's request, the undertaker mailed him the suit the minister had worn on the night of his death. "Kirk called me the next morning," Marchand said, "and told me to look for a 1953 Buick, color Jordan Gray. He told me it would have a large dent in the front of the hood and a smaller dent in the middle of the hood. That he was sure the victim had been hit in the leg and that his body had been thrown upward on top of the car. He told me the driver must have known he hit him."

Kirk had found microscopic paint chips on the suit that matched paint samples supplied by Buick. Tiny tears in the fabric of the suit revealed that the car had clipped the minister behind his knee. If so, the impact would have flung him in the air like a high jumper. He would likely have landed on the hood, his shoulder leaving a dent. With this scenario in mind, Marchand canvassed local auto paint stores, asking if any customers had shown up looking for Jordan Gray touch-up paint. He found his man within days.

Kirk helped introduce forensics to the wider public, the world beyond law enforcement, by almost single-handedly reversing the outcome of the era's most gripping murder trial. In the fall of 1954, the country was transfixed by the case of Dr. Samuel Sheppard, a tall, good-looking osteopathic surgeon and habitual philanderer convicted of beating his pregnant wife, Marilyn, to death in their suburban Cleveland home while their seven-year-old son, Chip, slept undisturbed in the next bedroom. It was the O. J. Simpson trial of its time, complete with lurid headlines and hyperventilating courtroom dispatches by Walter Winchell, Dorothy Kilgallen, and other celebrity columnists. "Dr. Sam Sheppard, who goes on trial tomorrow, is either a murderer or a man in a nightmare," Kilgallen wrote in her pretrial coverage for the *New York Journal-American,* comparing the case to the "classic puzzle of Miss Lizzie Borden." So many reporters showed up that the court had to arrange additional seating. Broadcasters occupied an entire room of their own.

Prosecutors hinted that Sheppard's affair with a twenty-one-year-old medical technician had driven him to crush his wife's skull with thirty-five hard blows. After nearly five days of deliberation, the jury found Sheppard guilty of murder in the second degree. He was sentenced to life in prison. (The case provided the basis for *The Fugitive,* a television program that aired on ABC. It was later adapted as a movie starring Harrison Ford.)

Two weeks after Sheppard's conviction, the defense team hired Kirk to examine the crime scene. "The case is not closed," he said after searching the home. "I have some experiments to make before I can reach any definite conclusions." His nineteen-page report showed that the murderer was left-handed (Sheppard was right-handed). Kirk deduced from tooth fragments found under the body that Marilyn had bitten her attacker. Dr. Sheppard had no bite marks. Kirk also judged Sheppard's account of an intruder plausible, in part because he found a one-inch blood splatter on a closet door that matched neither Marilyn's nor Sheppard's blood types. "He said that Sam's story was consistent with the known facts, and that the technical evidence presented by the prosecution had been worthless," said F. Lee Bailey, the up-and-coming defense attorney who took over the case.

Bailey recognized that he could use the clear, incontestable logic of Kirk's forensic analysis to repudiate a prosecution reliant on innuendo and aspersion. Bailey eventually obtained Sheppard's acquittal by making Kirk the star witness. On the stand Kirk delivered a master class on blood types, and he used diagrams to explain the elaborate lessons drawn from blood splatters. Americans following the case in newspapers, and on the evening news, could only be impressed by the way Kirk applied scientific techniques to crime analysis.

Captain Finney, as head of the New York crime lab, naturally hoped, that Kirk's high-profile example would promote forensic science within the NYPD. But the country's largest police force was also among the slowest to adapt. Detectives didn't need new ideas, Commissioner Kennedy said. Policing simply required a more rigorous application of old methods, the same methods he had learned walking his beat on the Hell's Kitchen streets. "There are relatively few new ideas about fighting crime," he said by way of rebuttal. "The main thing is to make old ideas work."

A week after Kennedy's installment, an upholsterer named John Sena rode the IRT subway from his home in Flushing, Queens, to the Roxy Theatre on the northern edge of the theater district. He arrived at 8:00 a.m., as he always did, and as usual walked the aisles inspecting the theater's 5,869 seats before the Roxy opened its doors for the early showing. In the rear of the orchestra section he found a chair with a slit in its red cloth covering. He removed the chair to his workshop in the Roxy basement, but didn't start work on it until 3:00 p.m., when an audience of two thousand watched the Bette Davis film *Virgin Queen*. As he tilted the chair on his workbench, a blue sock tumbled from the slit. Protruding from the sock was a pipe capped at both ends. "I examined it, and I didn't know what it was at the moment," Sena said, "and then it dawned on me that it was a bomb because I had read about it in the newspaper."

The bomb squad arrived, led by Sergeant Peter Dale, who had lost part of his right hand a year earlier after seizing more than a thousand homemade grenades stockpiled by Cuban revolutionaries in a storefront on West Ninety-Ninth Street. He was disposing of the grenades at a military base by pulling the pins and pitching them, one by one, when a grenade went off prematurely in his right hand. The explosion broke bones in all five fingers and his palm. He endured twelve operations to repair the damage, but he was still on the job. "It was an accident," he said. "If you get hit by a car, it doesn't mean you never cross a street again."

At the Roxy's basement repair shop, Dale reached his arm into the upholstery and pulled out a pocketknife with an imitation stag-horn handle, one of F.P.'s trademarks since he started hitting theaters. The detectives looked at the capped pipe lying on the workshop floor. Nobody spoke. There was no need. All of them knew it might be a live bomb, and it could be timed to explode at any moment.

Balancing urgency with caution, the bomb squad deposited the unexploded bomb in the steel-mesh envelope and carried it up a back stairway to Fiftieth Street, now closed to traffic. Five hundred curious pedestrians watched from behind police barricades as detectives in protective gear loaded the bomb into the back of Big Bertha. The bomb truck then drove with police cars front and back to a gravel pit at Twelfth Avenue and Fifty-Second Street, where they submerged the bomb in oil. They wanted to avoid transporting the bomb in rush-hour traffic so they waited in the gravel pit, smoking cigarettes and talking. At 7:00 p.m. they continued to Fort Tilden, the military base in Queens.

By now the police had conducted more than a thousand interviews and followed up on at least as many dead ends. In desperation, Kennedy reassigned men with no ordnance experience to the bomb squad, and he sent fifty plainclothes detectives to stand watch in movie theaters and train stations.

One after another, the bombs kept coming. A bomb blew up in the sixteenth row of the Paramount Theater during a showing of *Blood Alley,* a John Wayne sea adventure. A fragment sliced like a meat cleaver into the foot of a thirty-four-year-old man who had come to the theater after a day's work as a pharmacist's helper.

In successive months bombs exploded in a subway stop, a phone booth on the main floor of Macy's department store, and behind a sink in a Grand Central washroom (where men paid twenty-five cents to use a private stall). At the latter, police struggled to contain a crowd of rush-hour commuters pressing forward with macabre curiosity. A washroom attendant told police that he had seen a man exit the stall where the bomb went off. "I only saw him from the rear," the attendant said. "He had his back to me and seemed to be working over something at the washbowl. All I could see was that he wore brown trousers and brown shoes, and I remember that he had small feet. . . . Then there was this frightening explosion."

Next came a bomb in a men's room on the Long Island Rail Road level of Penn Station, directly under the main waiting room. At 3:42 p.m. on February 21, 1956, Lloyd Hill, a seventy-four-year-old washroom attendant, stepped into a stall to unclog a toilet. As Hill pushed down with a plunger, the bomb ignited. Slivers of shattered porcelain broke Hill's glasses in half. They sliced open his face and lodged deep in his left foot. He lay on the bathroom floor bleeding freely from his head.

"People were running in every direction, scared," said an onlooker. "So was I. The porter must have been seriously hurt. He was bleeding all over. I could see blood on his face, hands, arms, and legs as police arrive."

An ambulance rushed Hill downtown to St. Vincent's hospital. He stayed for two months while doctors treated him for loss of motor control in his left ankle and toes. He limped with a cane for the rest of his life.

On Poplar Street the forensics team seated at their black lab tables deduced from the exploded fragments that F.P. had waterproofed the bomb with shellac so that he could submerge it in a toilet. The shattered plumbing and porcelain acted as shrapnel, an ingenious bit of low-tech innovation. Sixteen years after his first bomb, F.P. was still refining his technique.

Nineteen fifty-six was a year of gathering dread. Newspaper headlines told the story of seventeen nuclear test detonations on the Bikini and Enewetak Atolls in the Marshall Islands. The University of Alabama suspended Autherine Lucy, its first black student, on the grounds that the campus was no longer safe for her. The first American, airman Richard B. Fitzgibbon Jr., died in the conflict that would soon be called the Vietnam War. (His son would die in the same war nine years later.)

In New York, the bomb squad had by now responded to twenty-seven bombs, and they were no closer to catching F.P. than they had been a decade earlier. Finney and the crime lab technicians were intimately acquainted with every detail of his handiwork—the capped pipe, the black gunpowder, the cheap watch used as a timing mechanism. "I know that gadget so well," a detective said, "that I could put one together in my sleep." But the evidence stubbornly refused to yield much information about the bomber himself. The detectives knew all about the bombs, but nothing about the man.

"His face remains a blank no matter how you visualize it," wrote one reporter. "And this juxtaposition of feelings, knowing so much yet nothing at all, can suddenly give you the sensation, after hours and days of talking with detectives and thumbing through records, that you are walking down the streets crowded with gray and faceless men, looking for a man you wouldn't recognize."

Miraculously, F.P. had not killed anyone—not yet. Though he easily could have. For years he had deposited his bombs in lightly trafficked locations where they might shatter a bathroom or destroy a phone booth, but probably not kill. His strategy changed when the first round of bombs failed to earn him the consolation he felt was his due. In time his newly reinforced bombs would dismember random victims in packed theaters and other crowded public spaces. Captain Finney knew that his luck could run out any day now.

The persistence of the blasts, more than their size, wore on public anxiety. "It is one thing to live in a cloud of fear," wrote *The New York Times,* "but it is another thing altogether when the lightning strikes again and again." The anxiety merged with a greater fear that civic leaders at all levels might not be up to protecting the public in a time when mushroom clouds flickered on black-and-white TV screens.

The mood turned by increments from angst to anger—anger at Mayor Wagner for failing to safeguard the public, anger at Commissioner Kennedy for not adapting, innovating, and improvising.

"If ever there was an argument for scientific police work, for infinite research and an unending hunt for evidence, this is it," wrote the *Journal-American*. "But what was the Police Department doing for 14 years?"

F.P. studied the newspapers like scripture. He followed the details of the bomb coverage, noting with satisfaction that the articles now routinely ran on the front page, though sometimes below the fold. The editors, he thought, were waking up to the gravity of his campaign. But for some reason they could still not see, or refused to see, what should have been obvious all along: he was engaged in a fight of heroic proportions against a wicked alliance persecuting all the little men, men like him, who toiled honestly and with a reasonable expectation of fair treatment. He would have to explain it to them again. On March 1, 1956, he took up his pencil and wrote a second letter to the *Herald Tribune:*

WHILE VICTIMS GET BLASTED—THE YELLOW PRESS MAKES NO MENTION OF THESE GHOULISH ACTS. THESE SAME GHOULS CALL ME A PSYCHOPATH—ANY FURTHER REFERENCE TO ME AS SUCH—OR THE LIKE—WILL BE DEALT WITH—THESE BOMBINGS WILL CONTINUE UNTIL CON EDISON IS BROUGHT TO JUSTICE—MY LIFE IS DEDICATED TO THIS TASK. . . . ALL MY SUFFERING—ALL MY FINANCIAL LOSS—

WILL HAVE TO BE PAID IN FULL——IT MUST ALARM-ANGER AND ANNOY
THE N.Y. YELLOW PRESS & AUTHORITIES TO FIND THAT ANY INDI-
VIDUAL CAN BE JUST AS MEAN——DIRTY AND ROTTEN AS THEY ARE.
I MERELY SEEK JUSTICE.

A huddle of *Herald Tribune* editors stood around a desk in the open newsroom reading the letter together. Here were the bomber's thoughts and
words, in his own hand, as vivid as if he stood beside them. After second
and third readings, and long deliberation, an editor picked up a phone
and called police headquarters, just as they had when the bomber wrote
to them five years earlier.

At 4:20 p.m. on a Friday afternoon the following August, a security
guard, Patsy De Laurentis, working at the RCA Building, known as 30
Rock, in Rockefeller Center, made a call from a public phone booth in
a shopping concourse off the lobby. When he placed the phone back on
its cradle, a length of pipe fell to the floor. It had been affixed with a magnet to the underside of the phone box. Both the pipe and the magnet
were enclosed in a man's red wool sock. De Laurentis picked up the pipe
and turned it over. His first thought was that a mugger might have used
it as a bludgeon, then hidden it there.

"I didn't realize what the object was," he said. "I went over to one of
the plainclothes men at the time to discuss just what it could have been,
and offhand he didn't know either."

De Laurentis carried the pipe to the guards' locker room and passed it
around, at times tossing it like a football. Thomas Dorney, a guard arriving for his 5:00 p.m. shift, asked to keep it. A sturdy stretch of pipe, he
said, would come in handy for plumbing repairs around his three-story
house. "I've used that sort of pipe before to fix a leak," he said.

Dorney stored the pipe in his locker for eight hours. After his shift
ended, at 1:00 a.m., he carried it in his pocket while riding the bus home
to West New York, New Jersey, directly across the Hudson River from
midtown. He laid the pipe on the kitchen table before going to bed at
2:00 a.m.

The bomb exploded at 6:00 a.m. the next morning, while Dorney, his wife, Betty, and their daughter slept upstairs. The hour hand had misfired at 6:00 p.m. the previous evening, an hour after Dorney arrived for his shift. The bomb went off twelve hours later when the hour hand hit six again.

At first Dorney thought a head-on collision in the street outside their home had caused the house to shake. He and Betty rushed downstairs to find the kitchen filled with acrid smoke. As the clouds cleared, they could see that the bomb had gauged a hole in the metal-topped kitchen table and blown a second hole in the ceiling. The blast embedded shrapnel in their walls and refrigerator, and it shattered their windows. "It looks like an atomic bomb hit it," Betty told her husband.

Dorney recalled how he had stopped at a funeral home near his house before going to work to pay his last respects to an old friend, a longshoreman on the city docks. At the funeral home he had picked up a card with a picture of Christ on one side and a prayer on the other. He'd put the card in his pocket. For several hours after work he had carried the card in one coat pocket and the bomb in the other. "I was saved by the grace of God," he told reporters. "I haven't been as religious as I ought to be before, but I'm very religious now."

The bomb in Dorney's home was the twenty-eighth attributed to F.P. By now newspaper articles and, increasingly, national magazines were implying that the vaunted NYPD might not be up to the task of catching the Mad Bomber. "Left to this evidence," wrote the *New York Journal-American,* "police conceivably never might be able to find this madman, for their work would be like the proverbial search for the needle in the haystack."

CHAPTER SEVEN

THE PARAMOUNT

December 1956

A CUTTING SOUTHWEST WIND BLEW DOWN FLATBUSH AVENUE AS MARY Young walked to the Paramount Theater with her two daughters and a pair of grandchildren on the early evening of December 2, 1956. They passed holiday shoppers carrying bags from Abraham & Straus, a nearby department store. Men and women walked, singly and in pairs, in the direction of Junior's restaurant and Garfield's cafeteria. Mint-green trolleys made herky-jerky headway on steel rails running along the cobbled street.

December, the darkest month, had brought predictions of a coming cold snap. The stoops of Brooklyn brownstones awaited the season's first sprinkling of snow. Thanksgiving was done with, and the buoyant Christmas mood had settled on the city. With Christmas came the incidental joys of the season—the pleasingly pungent fir trees lined up for sale on the sidewalks and the bright sights of department store windows.

Mary lived with her adult daughters, Doris Russo and Joyce Young, on Hancock Street, in the nearby Brooklyn neighborhood of Bedford-Stuyvesant. They were unoccupied that Sunday night so they gathered up the grandchildren to see *War and Peace,* a three-hour Technicolor Tolstoy epic designed to swell hearts at holiday time.

The Paramount alone was excitement enough for little Donna and

Russ, the grandchildren. The family passed beneath the elaborate marquee, wrapped around the corner of Flatbush and DeKalb like a sparkling Christmas ornament, and into the theater, with its grand proscenium gaudy with filigree and row after row of seats plushly upholstered in burgundy velvet. They situated themselves toward the rear of the orchestra, on the left side, beneath a dangling art deco chandelier. The organist played the jazzy standard "There's Honey on the Moon Tonight" on the bulky Wurlitzer, as she did most nights. When the lights dimmed, the small talk hushed and an orchestral overture swelled over opening credits. A cavalry in parade dress marched through the streets of St. Petersburg. Hands were kissed. Departing soldiers swigged wine in a last debauch. A mother embraced a young officer home from the front. A colonel shot in a duel collapsed in the snow. Armies clashed.

The story swept through the full range of life, with all its jealousies and tenderness, fury and yearning, in scenes set among panoramic battlefields and drawing rooms draped with brocaded tapestries. With so much pageantry to take in, the family might not have noticed a man rise from a nearby seat and excuse himself, making his way up the dark aisle to the exits.

At 7:50 p.m., just as Prince Andrei returned wounded to his country home from the Battle of Austerlitz, a string of seats erupted with a searing white light that flashed bright on every cranny of the great auditorium and with a concussive boom. "Suddenly I heard a report like a grenade," said Abraham Blumenthal, a thirty-six-year-old postal clerk who was thrown high from his seat. "Then a column of smoke rose in front of me and drifted across the screen." Blumenthal lay on the floor, a blood vessel in his left leg severed by shrapnel.

The theater filled with screams, voiced in unison like a chorus of terror. In an instant the audience rose together and made for the exits. All except for Blumenthal and five other casualties, including Mary Young's daughters. A spray of metal shards had shot over the interceding seats and embedded themselves in their scalps. Men and women pushed by the sisters as they sat almost motionless, too stunned to move. Blood poured in sheets down their faces; it dripped into their laps. "The shock and terror of what happened that evening," Doris said, "will never leave my memory."

A manager appeared at the rear of the theater to announce, preposterously, that a firecracker had gone off. Then he and several ushers helped the injured stagger to the lobby to await ambulances.

Within twenty minutes Captain Finney and the bomb squad marched down the aisle like a regiment, followed by the Brooklyn district attorney. They roped off the orchestra and searched row by row. After locating the point of explosion, they measured the distance to a dozen far-flung shards. Flashbulbs lit up the dim theater as a police photographer captured the scene from every angle. Captain Finney, the silent boss, looked over the crime scene with his implacable gaze.

The next morning nurses wheeled Doris Russo into an operating room at Kings County Hospital, in Brooklyn, where surgeons saved her life by relieving a punctured portion of her skull pressing down on soft brain tissue. Doctors at the same hospital treated her sister, Joyce, for facial lacerations, and Joyce's children, Donna and Russ, for shock.

While the surgeons laid their scalpels to Doris's skull, Captain Finney stood in the crime lab's Poplar Street offices inspecting a schematic of the bomb extrapolated from fragments found at the Paramount. He was without doubt looking at F.P.'s handiwork—an iron pipe with .22 caliber gunpowder triggered by a cheap wristwatch. In his last letter F.P. had made clear his renewed intent to kill. This time he nearly succeeded.

The Paramount bomb was the most powerful yet, and also the first detonated outside midtown Manhattan. To Finney, the Paramount signaled an escalation of the bomber's campaign and a reach for a broader stage on which to register his grievances. It showed, the *Daily News* wrote, a "new audacity, born of apparent desperation."

The Paramount was the thirty-first bombing. More than any other, it had a galvanizing effect and was an inflection point in the long investigation. Even before Finney had concluded his examination of the Paramount evidence, Commissioner Kennedy had resolved to declare all-out war on the bomber, even if it meant reversing some long-standing policies.

Phone calls went out to every precinct. Within an hour 350 borough and division chiefs arrived at headquarters in blue dress uniforms, shields polished and trousers creased, from far corners of the city—Bushwick and Bensonhurst, Corona and Canarsie—and assembled in the lineup room where victims identified suspects. Kennedy stepped to the low stage, where the lineup normally stood, and addressed the men formally, but with the force of a general on the eve of battle. The bomber, he said, constituted "an outrage that cannot be tolerated." He was "our number one most wanted criminal." The investigation, he said, was the "greatest in department history." He ordered the chiefs to instruct all twenty-three thousand cops and detectives, regardless of their posts, "to make every effort to ascertain the identity of the perpetrator." He offered immediate promotion to the officer who made the arrest.

"Alert every member of the force, regardless of assignment, to the necessity of making an apprehension," he said in closing. "The man is not in his right mind." After dismissing his officers, Kennedy sent word for reporters to gather in his office.

The police reporters were a fraternity of wisecracking hustlers who killed time in a three-story brick tenement, known as the police shack, separated from headquarters by a drab one-block street called Centre Market Place—also known as Press Alley. They worked in a series of rooms crappily furnished with manual typewriters on rickety tables, overflowing ashtrays, and chairs of decrepit upholstery. "In those days a nightlong poker game was played in the back room, referred to as the 'den of the forty thieves,'" wrote Arthur Gelb, who would later become managing editor of *The New York Times*. "Reporters there feasted on clams steamed open atop gas heaters, and washed down with the bottles of Madeira."

Desk drawers clinked with jostling whiskey bottles used, as often as not, to entertain talkative cops who showed up for a drink when their shifts ended. The reporters, like the cops, were mostly high school dropouts from blue-collar neighborhoods in Brooklyn or the Bronx. They drank in the same bars as the cops, and they spoke the same street language.

The reporters ostensibly competed for stories. In reality they worked as a team, covering for each other during beer runs or forays to check the Teletype machine in the lobby of police headquarters, which relayed grisly details from precinct cops of liquor-store stickups, tenement collapses, drownings, fires, and stabbings. The violence of the city never ended.

Reporting the truth was less important than forming a consensus so that no resident of the shack risked embarrassment or caught abuse from a city editor. "Nobody wanted to go in with stuff that wasn't right, so we all settled on the same story. Everybody was more than happy to go along with that. It was communal journalism. And if you were too drunk to talk, somebody else would get on the phone and dictate to your rewrite man," said Nicholas Pileggi, an Associated Press reporter who later wrote *Wiseguy: Life in a Mafia Family,* which was made into the movie *Goodfellas.* The police shack reporters protected each other, and they protected their sources within the department. If a cop stabbed his girlfriend or brawled after too many beers, the reporters might agree not to cover the story at all.

The residents of the shack killed time sleeping, drinking, phoning bets to bookies, and playing cards while waiting for the shortwave police radios installed in their rooms to crackle to life with news of roasts (fire victims), wet divers (bridge jumpers), and other disorder. They might also be jolted into action by the police communications bureau, or CB as they called it, phoning on a direct line from across the street. The CB phone rang in the first-floor hallway, just outside a room occupied by Guy Passant of *The New York Times,* nicknamed Put-Put because he was in perpetual motion. "Passant would yell out, 'CB says three-alarm fire' or 'armed robbery,'" said Pileggi.

When police hauled a handcuffed murderer, madam, gambling boss, or con man from a police cruiser for booking, the reporters met them in Press Alley like a pack of jackals, shouting lurid questions in a full range of nasal New York accents and pressing close with flash cameras. They lifted from their rakish beat stories of betrayal and vice, dissipation and vengeance.

The unofficial dean of the police shack was a dandified night-shift reporter for the *Daily News,* Patrick Doyle, who covered twenty thousand homicides in his career, a milestone that earned him a place in the 1985 edition of *The Guinness Book of World Records.* Doyle was a master at placing his stories on the front page. He perfectly understood what qualities most chilled and entertained tabloid readers: deaths involving the socially prominent, either as victim or perpetrator; acts of violence against children or the elderly; and shockingly brutal killings with a lingering mystery. Within the police shack these traits were known as the Doyle Criteria. If a story had one or more, it stood a good chance of earning a front-page byline.

Doyle was nicknamed the Inspector for his sly way of gathering information by impersonating a detective. He would duck under the police rope at crime scenes in a three-piece suit with pleated pants and suspenders, fedora and trench coat, the same outfit worn by most detectives. An NYPD clip secured his tie. He identified himself to patrolmen as "Doyle from downtown," which was technically true. If the patrolmen assumed he was a high-ranking detective, then that was their problem. Doyle would then question them about the circumstances of the accident or murder. Who fired the pistol? Was he in custody? Did the police find the knife? Or a suicide note? Did the suspect confess? He even told cops to keep reporters away from the scene, thereby assuring himself an exclusive. He reported on as many as four or five murders a night, dictating his raw notes to rewrite men from one of the five phones at his desk on the second floor of the police shack. Next to the phones was a bulbous police radio and an ashtray filled with cigar ashes. When his shifted ended at 1:00 a.m., he headed to his private table in a back room of P.J. Clarke's, a Third Avenue saloon, where his picture still hangs. On the way uptown he would listen to the police scanner in his car, as he always did. He found joy in his work, though it took its toll. He often spent the next afternoon, before his shift began, gardening behind his home in suburban New Jersey. "I like to see things grow," he said. "I've seen so many things dying."

By long-standing practice, the police doggedly withheld all information about the bombing investigation from police shack reporters, even from Doyle. On the record they dismissed F.P. as a crackpot or prankster; in private they made their apprehension known. Kennedy and his aides believed that publicity would only incite panic and encourage the bomber. If deprived of attention, he might grow discouraged and taper off, though so far that had not happened. Kennedy also knew that whenever a serial criminal such as F.P. receives publicity, copycats follow—the last thing the police needed.

Reporters loitering on the steps outside the Centre Street headquarters might question a captain or a lieutenant exiting the building, only to get the official brush-off: the department has nothing to say about the manhunt right now.

So when word reached the police shack that Kennedy wished to brief reporters on the bomber, they scrambled across Press Alley and up a flight of stairs to the dark-paneled commissioner's office. They gathered around his mahogany desk like linemen in a huddle.

Kennedy's eyes hardened and his jaw thrust out as he spoke. He began by admitting that even after thirty-one bombings the police had no solid leads or significant insights. Then, in a reversal of the long-standing policy of silence that had cloaked the investigation for sixteen years, he agreed to show letters and other evidence to the reporters. For the first time, the police would share what they knew in hopes that some observant citizen might provide a breakthrough. An engaged citizenry might be the difference maker.

"At first we requested that no publicity be given to [the bomber's] acts, but this did not deter him," Kennedy said in a prepared statement that he read aloud to the reporters. "Now we are working on the theory that publicity will enable us to learn something from somebody and thus bring about his arrest. . . . I appeal to members of the public to come forward and give to the police whatever information they may have concerning this man. The identity of informants will be kept a closely guarded secret."

Naturally reporters welcomed Kennedy's new openness—a posture we now call transparency—but reassembled back in the police shack, they mocked the policy reversal with hooting hilarity as a sign of desperation.

After years of stonewalling reporters, the commissioner was now asking the press to find the bomber for him!

In the following days the police began sharing with reporters reams of evidence—starting with a chronology and notes on bombings dating back to 1940. "After 16 years of being secretive about the bomber we are no farther along than we were when we started," a police official told reporters. "Every hopeful lead has vanished, and the bomber is still as much a mystery as ever. We are hoping now that somebody, somewhere, may recognize the bomber's writing, or lettering. Perhaps they will be awakened by a familiar phrase that he uses unconsciously and which may have crept into the excerpts we have released."

The false alarms began immediately after police disclosed the first batch of investigative details, as Kennedy feared they would. Six hours after Kennedy met with reporters, an American Airlines plane bound from Rochester to Idlewild Airport (later renamed John F. Kennedy Airport) made an emergency landing in Syracuse after Port Authority police received a call saying a bomb had been placed on board.

At 10:45 the next morning a police dispatcher picked up the phone to field the first of thirteen anonymous calls that day warning of bombs placed throughout the city—at theaters, a freighter, an army base, among other sites. Three of the threats were directed at Brooklyn high schools, presumably by students arranging for a day off. Sergeant Dale led the bomb squad to all thirteen locations, including the Fox Theatre on Flatbush Avenue in Brooklyn, where detectives searched four thousand seats before giving the all clear for a late-evening show of *Rumble on the Docks*.

The hoaxes did not stop Kennedy from sharing more investigative material. On December 10 his press office distributed to reporters of the police shack a sheet containing fragments of F.P.'s unusual handwriting selected from twenty-two letters to the *Herald Tribune*, theaters, hotels, and Con Ed with a request for citizens to notify a precinct house if they recognized the lettering. The snippets, cut out and pasted on a single sheet of paper, read like a nonsense poem:

. . . CALL ME A . . . COMPLIMENTS . . . DEPENDING ON ENERGY . . .
I NOTIFIED . . . MAKES NO MENTION . . . MANHATTAN HOTELS . . .
MY SUFFERINGS . . .

The police department's failures left an opening for the tabloids to hustle up their own dubious investigations. Within hours the *Daily News* had shown the writing samples to a "graphologist-psychiatrist." The expert, identified only as "Europe's foremost expert on identification through handwriting," reported that the author of the block letters was stooped and haggard, a man in desperate need of love—or at least recognition. The letters, he said, revealed a "deterioration of the bomber, mentally and physically, and an increasing aggressiveness in his disordered desire to make his presence felt."

The expert added, "He must speak out again and again, before it is too late."

Meanwhile, the false alarms kept coming. On December 16 the bomb squad convoy pulled onto the Brooklyn-Queens Expressway and drove at reckless speed to a post office on the main street of Flushing, Queens. A postman sorting packages at 3:55 p.m. noticed a rhythmic clicking coming from inside a heavy rectangular package. He removed it to the parking lot while his supervisor phoned the police. The bomb squad evacuated five families from an adjacent apartment building and submerged the box in a tank of oil. Sergeant Dale knelt down and pressed the fluoroscope to the side of the box. A murky black-and-white image came into focus. Inside the box he could see a battery-driven toy locomotive spinning its wheels.

The manhunt had reached an absurd new low. Captain Finney and his men were chasing frauds and false alarms while F.P. took his daily walk and returned to his garage to tinker and refine.

CHAPTER EIGHT

"IT WILL BE BUTTONED"

December 1956

CAPTAIN FINNEY WAS NOTORIOUSLY TIGHT-LIPPED—AT TIMES, HE BARELY spoke—but by mid-December of 1956 he began to express doubts to trusted colleagues. Commissioner Kennedy's outreach to newspapers, and by extension the public, was unlikely to turn up any useful leads, Finney said. Publicizing the bomber's penmanship was a long shot—no more likely to strike lightning than the wanted flyers pinned to post office walls.

If the police were to catch F.P., Finney believed, they would have to find inventive new lines of pursuit. Otherwise they faced the ugly prospect of body bags hauled from theaters and train stations. It was only a matter of time—months, or maybe weeks—before F.P. would kill, possibly kill scores at a time.

As head of the crime lab, Captain Finney had so far confined himself to the scientific treatment of physical evidence. Now, in the wake of the Paramount bombing, he wondered if it was possible to interpret the evidence in ways that nobody had yet considered. Could the letters and scorched bomb fragments help investigators grasp not just what the bomber did, but why he did it? Could they shed light on what strange motivations arose from F.P.'s life circumstances?

If Captain Finney was to make a leap into new ways of thinking about the evidence, he would have to do so quickly. Sixteen years after his debut, F.P. was delivering more powerful bombs and shrewdly depositing them where dense crowds congregated—a strategy that would present grave dangers during the holiday season ahead.

While Commissioner Kennedy looked outward to the public for answers, Captain Finney sought to look inward, to the bomber's emotional life. Finney quietly, discreetly, began to make inquiries: Who could help him understand F.P.'s mind and motivations?

Of all Finney's police colleagues, none was more sympathetic to the experimental path than Captain John J. Cronin, the shy and brilliant head of New York's missing persons bureau. Cronin had spent his entire thirty-year police career trying to solve puzzling and bizarre disappearances. The difficulty of his job had driven him to accept the unconventional. For example, he hosted a local television show, *The Bureau of Missing Persons,* which aired photographs of the lost and unaccounted for. He invited viewers to phone in clues. He also advocated the use of extrasensory perception in investigative work and petitioned police brass to staff a psychic in every precinct.

In the atmosphere of heightened urgency that beset the Poplar Street offices that December, Cronin offered Captain Finney a long-shot proposal. Six years earlier Cronin had spoken at a convention of police chiefs in Elmira, New York, alongside Dr. James Brussel, whom Cronin described as a sharp-witted psychiatrist with uncommon insight into the workings of the criminal mind. Dr. Brussel's long tenure as assistant commissioner of the State Department of Mental Hygiene, and his frequent turns as an expert witness, had earned him a number of friendships within the police department. All would describe Dr. Brussel as a psychiatrist with a nuanced, up-close understanding of how mental illness could sway a person to particular types of unlawful behavior. "That the human mind works at all—that anything so fantastically complex could even begin to operate as a unit—is itself rather remarkable," Dr. Brussel would write. "That most of us manage to keep this intricate and enormously variable mechanism under some sort of control most of the time, living with one another in tolerable harmony, is more remarkable still."

Dr. Brussel had given a memorable talk from the dais that day in Elmira, attributing the rise in teenage gangs to a culture of violence inculcated by wartime training. The talk was riveting and startlingly original. Cronin had made a point of staying in touch with Dr. Brussel over the years. Might a psychiatrist such as Dr. Brussel be useful in the bomber case? Cronin asked Finney. Cronin had no idea that Dr. Brussel was closely following the case from the privacy of his home in Queens. Nor could Cronin know that Dr. Brussel had already worked out a hypothetical plan for profiling F.P. by employing his theory of reverse psychology.

In 1956 there was no such thing as criminal profiling; nobody could recall an instance when the police had consulted a psychiatrist. It was a collaboration fabricated in detective novels, but never found in real life. Still, Captain Finney was intrigued by the possibility. A physical description of the bomber was unobtainable, he reasoned, but maybe Dr. Brussel could use the evidence to draw a profile of the bomber's inner self—an emotional portrait—that would illuminate his background and disorder. It was a radical notion for 1956.

At Captain Finney's urging, Cronin called Dr. Brussel to ask if he would be willing to discuss the case. Dr. Brussel at first demurred, despite his long fascination with the bomber. He began by citing his workload. The New York Department of Mental Hygiene had 120,000 patients, and the caseload grew by 3,000 a year. Patient files were stacked high on his desk. In addition, he shouldered a full schedule of lectures and meetings and the demands of private practice.

Dr. Brussel had other reasons to hesitate. The police had never before asked a psychiatrist to draft an emotional portrait of a fugitive. He hesitated to test his theories in such a high-profile case. "I felt that my profession was being judged, as well as myself," he would write. "And curiously, I was one of my own accusers in this bizarre trial of wits. Did I really know enough about criminals to say anything sensible? . . . I'd seen hundreds of offenders in my career, but had I learned enough from them and about them?"

What if his analysis failed to break the case or, worse, sent the police in the wrong direction? "I don't know what you expect me to do," Dr. Brussel told Cronin. "If experts haven't cracked this case in more than ten years of trying, what could I hope to contribute?"

"Maybe you'll come up with something," Cronin answered. "Captain Finney needs a break. The commissioner is pressing him for results. Give it a whirl, Doctor. Sometimes the difference between failure and success is a new thought."

In the end Dr. Brussel couldn't resist the chance to participate in a prominent investigation. The man who put his name forth in outpourings of journal articles, crossword puzzles, and letters to the editor was not about to turn away when the police invited him to work on the city's greatest manhunt.

Captain Finney, accompanied by two bomb squad detectives, arrived at Dr. Brussel's office on the twelfth floor of the Department of Mental Hygiene, on Chambers Street, with a satchel full of photos documenting the bomb wreckage, copies of the bomber's letters, and other evidence from his sixteen-year campaign.

Captain Finney took a seat facing Dr. Brussel's desk. "We'd appreciate any ideas you might have on this case, Doctor. Our case is one of straw-grasping. We're stumped. Here's a bundle of letters and photographs. Solve it."

Dr. Brussel would describe Captain Finney as a "tough, clever man . . . a man of many accomplishments and few words." Dr. Brussel knew that he wasn't going to impress Captain Finney with psychiatric babble. "Nor was I going to satisfy him with hedged statements: 'Maybe—but on the other hand—' No, not this man. I knew he would want direct answers or none at all."

Dr. Brussel could tell Captain Finney sincerely wished to explore how psychiatric insights might advance the investigation, but his sidekicks smirked and rolled their eyes. "I'd seen that look before," Dr. Brussel later wrote, "most often in the Army, on the faces of hard, old-line, field-grade officers who were sure this newfangled psychiatry business was all nonsense—and worse, was a sign of softening in the Army. The way you handled men was you told them what to do, and if they didn't do it you clapped them in the stockade. You didn't waste everybody's time talking to a bad soldier and asking why he was bad. What did the Army need headshrinkers for? And here was that same attitude in my New York office."

Dr. Brussel recognized that no matter what he said, no matter how insightful he might prove to be, these detectives, and many like them, would reject psychiatry as a legitimate tool for solving crimes. He was right. Years later one of the detectives who was in Dr. Brussel's office that day still insisted that he had no use for the "scientific types" who knew nothing about the street-level realities of crime fighting.

However skeptical they might be, the detectives watched in silence for two hours as Dr. Brussel pored over the evidence. "They showed one thing very plainly," Dr. Brussel would write. "At large somewhere in New York City was a man who was quite definitely mad."

Dr. Brussel's mind sifted in increments through patterns and proclivities, drawing on psychiatric theory and probabilities.

"People sometimes ask what proportion of my psychiatric deductions is science and what proportion is imagination," he later wrote. "I don't really know the answer—not in precise terms. I can only say that I always start such a deduction with a solid basis of science, but somewhere along the way intuition and imagination begin to take over. When you think about an unknown criminal long enough, when you've assembled all the known facts about him and poked at them and stirred them about in your mind, you begin to see the man. You see him more and more plainly. You picture his face, hear his voice."

After a long ruminative pause standing by a window overlooking City Hall, Brussel turned to his visitors and offered a description so specific—a profile almost photographic in its detail—that F.P. might have been seated beside them in Dr. Brussel's twelfth-floor office. However fantastic Dr. Brussel's diagnosis may have been, it was rendered believable by his charisma and loud, confident voice.

The bomber, Dr. Brussel began, was a textbook paranoid schizophrenic, a condition he later defined in print as "a chronic disorder of insidious development, characterized by persistent, unalterable, systemized, logically constructed delusions." People suffering from this disorder, he explained, often have a cool and distant demeanor. They may hear demonic voices calling them to action or see things that are not real. They may believe other people are controlling them or plotting against them. They are typically reclusive, antisocial, and consumed with hatred for their imagined enemies. For all their derangement, they're capable of acting quite normal—until, inevitably, some aspect of their delusions enters into their conversation. "The paranoiac is the world's champion grudge-holder," Dr. Brussel would explain. "We all get mad at other people and organizations sometimes, but with most of us the anger evaporates eventually. The paranoiac's anger doesn't. Once he gets the idea that somebody has wronged him or is out to hurt him, the idea stays in his mind. This was obviously true of the Mad Bomber."

The condition, Dr. Brussel told Finney, worsened over time, progressively clouding normal logic. Most paranoids don't become fully symptomatic until after age thirty. If the bomber was about that age when he planted his first bomb, in 1940, he would now be at least in his midforties, probably older. His guess about the bomber's age "could have been wrong," Brussel acknowledged, "but, I thought, the laws of probability were on my side."

The laws of probability, or what Dr. Brussel called "inferential deductions," played into most of his conclusions. "They are not infallible," he said, "but neither are they mere guesses." Like Sherlock Holmes, he was playing the odds.

Now Dr. Brussel paused, "trying to screw up the courage to articulate my next deduction." The bomber, he continued, is "symmetrically built . . . neither fat nor skinny." From across the desk Finney shot him a skeptical look. "How did you arrive at that?"

Dr. Brussel cited a German psychiatrist, Ernst Kretschmer, who correlated body type with pathologies. In a study of ten thousand patients, he found that a majority of paranoids had "athletic" bodies—medium to tall with a well-proportioned frame. The probability was seventeen in twenty that the bomber fell into that category.

Dr. Brussel continued: Like most paranoids, F.P. felt the need to convey his superiority. He did so with a self-righteous insistence on order. A fastidiousness verging on prissiness showed in the letters he'd hand-printed in nearly perfect block letters free of smudges or erasures. F.P., Dr. Brussel said, "was almost certainly a very neat, proper man. As an employee, whether of Con Ed or any other company, he had probably been exemplary. He had turned out the highest-quality work. He had shown up precisely on time for work each morning, neatly dressed and clean shaven. He had never been involved in brawls, drunkenness, or any other messy episodes. He had lived a model life—until the alleged injustice, whatever it was, had occurred."

The same care surely applied to his grooming. "He's probably very neat, tidy, clean shaven," Brussel predicted. "He goes out of his way to seem perfectly proper. . . . He wears no ornament, no jewelry, no flashy ties or clothes. He is quiet, polite, methodical, prompt."

Captain Finney nodded. The man who had eluded him for years was coming into focus.

The bomber, Dr. Brussel continued, was afflicted by a sense of persecution caused in the formative stages of his gender development, roughly age three to six. In his young life he'd confronted the shameful knowledge of a forbidden sexual desire—most likely an erotic fixation on his mother. He protected himself from the shame and horror with a twisted bit of oedipal logic: *I desire my mother. But that's horribly unacceptable. She's married to my father. I'm now competing with him for her affection. I'm jealous of him. He's jealous of me. He hates me. He persecutes me.*

The original cause of the hate never surfaced in the young F.P.'s consciousness, and it gradually faded. All that remained, like a residue, was the sense of persecution and the searing desire for revenge.

According to Freudian theory, the Oedipus complex normally resolves itself. Most boys come to recognize that their grievance is misconceived, and they reconcile the sexual impulses that originally shamed them. But in a diseased mind such as F.P.'s, the paranoia spreads like a contagion. Any two entities with something in common would, no matter how illogically, meld into one in his mind. His sense of persecution could therefore disburse from his father to a boss, to a company, to politicians, and to any organization that could plausibly symbolize authority.

To Dr. Brussel, the paranoid's inclination to assign guilt by association explained an inconsistency that had stumped the police. In his letters the bomber had singled out Con Ed, but he planted only the first of his bombs on Con Ed property. He would see people or organizations with the remotest connection to Con Ed as conspirators, no matter how illogical that might be. He might blame Con Ed for some unstated offense, Dr. Brussel said, "but he twists it around so that wherever a wire runs, gas or steam flows, from or to Con. Edison Co., is now a bomb target."

F.P. seemed convinced, as a paranoid would, that a range of companies and agencies had conspired with Con Ed. By way of evidence his letters mentioned "Con Edison and the others" and "all the liars and cheats." This, Dr. Brussel said, helped to explain why F.P. had bombed theaters and train stations. He was at war with a world colluding against him.

Once F.P. decided that somebody, or some organization, had wronged him, nothing would dissuade him. He would operate with absolute conviction; he could not even imagine being wrong. A paranoid cherry-picks corroborating details from the world around him. "He marshals all kinds of compelling evidence to support his central premise," Dr. Brussel said. "His delusion is rooted in reality in such a way that it baffles efforts to dispel it." Hence the arrogant, self-righteous tone of F.P.'s letters.

For the bomber, the drive for vengeance, the need to correct what's amiss in the world, had likely assumed a religious ardor. He had, Dr. Brussel explained, formed a covenant with God to carry out a private mission of revenge, which would only make it harder to catch him. "This pact is a secret between him and God," Dr. Brussel said. "He would never let a hint drop. Why should he ever let you catch him doing something wrong?"

Divine standing could lead the bomber to commit ever more drastic acts, Brussel warned, if the earlier blasts had not yet accomplished his goals. Like a vengeful God who inflicts blight and earthquakes, the bomber would feel that he possessed the righteous power to punish those who failed to accept the validity of his claims.

With godliness came omnipotence, and with omnipotence came contempt for lesser beings. The bomber's confidence in his superiority, his arrogance, would make it hard for him to hold a job. So he was likely to be, if not impoverished, then at least penurious. But even in poverty he would find a way to keep up a smart impression in his grooming and wardrobe. "He would always have to give the appearance of being perfect," Dr. Brussel said.

The bomber, Dr. Brussel continued, almost surely operated as a lone wolf. Self-contained and self-sufficient, he found gratification from the solitary contemplation of his elaborate schemes. Paranoids "have confidence only in themselves," Dr. Brussel explained. "They are overwhelmingly egocentric. They distrust everyone. An accomplice would be a potential bungler or double-crosser."

Dr. Brussel knew that the three detectives in his office had waged a long, frustrating manhunt. Paranoid schizophrenics, he explained, were the hardest of deranged criminals to catch because their mind splits between two realms: Even as they lose themselves in warped delusions, they continue to follow logical trains of thought and lead outwardly normal lives. They watch the world around them with a wary, distrustful eye.

"For a long while, as the three police officers sat and waited in silence, I studied the Mad Bomber's letters," Dr. Brussel would recall. "I lost all sense of time. I tried to immerse myself in the man's mind."

F.P.'s reliance on clunky, old-fashioned phrases, such as "treachery" and "dastardly deeds," erratically spaced with phrases set off by dashes, suggested a foreign background. It was hard to imagine an American referring to Con Ed as "the Con Edison Company," as F.P. did. "There was a certain stilted tone in the letters, a total lack of slang or American colloquialisms," Dr. Brussel would recall. "Somehow the letters sounded to me as though they'd been written in a foreign language and then translated into English."

The police had long suspected F.P. was German, or of German extraction, because of his vaguely Teutonic lettering, particularly his *G*'s, which ended their circular form with a pair of horizontal slashes, like an equal sign. Dr. Brussel thought of the many bombings by anarchists and other radicals in Eastern Europe and said, "He's a Slav."

The three detectives shot Dr. Brussel a startled look. "Mind giving the reasoning behind that?" Captain Finney asked.

"Historically, bombs have been favored in Middle Europe," Dr. Brussel answered. "So have knives." Of course, those weapons are used throughout the world. "But when one man uses both, that suggests he could be a Slav."

Captain Finney looked skeptical.

"It's only a suggestion," Dr. Brussel said. "I'm just playing the odds."

Dr. Brussel wasn't finished. If the bomber was a Slav, that also suggested his likely religion: Roman Catholic. It could also be a clue to his location. Dr. Brussel flicked through the postmarks, noting that most of the letters were mailed in Westchester, the county immediately north of the city. Dr. Brussel guessed that the bomber was disguising his whereabouts by posting his letters halfway between New York and one of the industrial towns in Connecticut where Slavic immigrants had settled.

Now Brussel focused on the handwriting. The penmanship was nearly flawless, as Dr. Brussel would expect from a fastidious paranoiac. F.P. had formed almost perfectly rectilinear letters—with one exception. The *W*'s looked like double *U*'s, in a literal sense, with no overlapping diagonal arms. The sides were curved instead of straight. They also had peculiar rounded bottoms. "The misshapen *W* might not have caught my eye in most people's hand-printing, but in the bomber's it stood out. Consider the paranoiac: a man of obsessive neatness, a man who will not tolerate a flaw in what the world sees of him. If there is any little untidiness about this man, anything even slightly out of place, it catches a psychiatrist's attention immediately."

The *W* "was like a slouching soldier among twenty-five others standing at attention, a drunk at a temperance society meeting," Dr. Brussel continued. "To me, it stood out that starkly. . . . Language is a mirror of the mind. That odd curved *W* had to reflect something about the Mad Bomber, it seemed to me. . . . Something subconscious had compelled the bomber to write this one particular letter in a distinctive way—something inside him so strong that it dodged or bulldozed past his conscience."

Might the *W*'s resemble breasts, or maybe a scrotum? Dr. Brussel wondered. If so, had F.P. also unconsciously fashioned bombs shaped like penises? "Something about sex seemed to be troubling the bomber," Dr. Brussel thought. "But what?" He deliberated for long moments, his eyes scanning the evidence.

For a moment Dr. Brussel thought he might put the question directly to Captain Finney. Dr. Brussel was working in mysterious territory, and he felt the need for help. But when he saw the faces of Finney's two sidekicks, Dr. Brussel looked down again. "To talk about these things now, before my own mind was made up, would only court additional disbelief," he would recall. "The ideas I was forming were going to sound far-fetched. To present them in half-baked form would only make them seem more so. I decided to wait until I had made the ideas clearer to myself."

He told Finney, "Sorry I'm taking so long."

"Take all the time you want," Finney said. "We didn't come here expecting pat answers."

Dr. Brussel had already established that an Oedipus complex had caused F.P. to develop into a full-blown paranoid. His oedipal hatred for his father had spread in adulthood to a broad range of authority figures. "The bomber obviously distrusted and despised male authority: the police, his former employees at Con Ed," Dr. Brussel would write. "To the bomber, any form of male authority could represent his father."

Dr. Brussel now looked back through the evidence for signs of sexual disturbance. His eyes rested on photos of theater seats the bomber had slit open to secrete his penis-shaped explosives in a dark place. "Something about the bomber's method of planting bombs in movie houses had bothered me since I'd read the first newspaper account years before," Dr. Brussel would say. "There was something strange, something not fully explained by the available facts." The slashing was an uncharacteristically violent act. Everything in the evidence suggested a careful man, a man who would avoid unnecessary risks and minimize signs of his presence. Why did he go to the trouble of slitting open seats and stuffing his bombs in the upholstery?

"Could the seat symbolize the pelvic region of the human body?" Dr. Brussel wondered. "In plunging the knife upward into it, had the bomber been symbolically penetrating the woman? Or castrating a man? Or both? . . . In this act he gave expression to a submerged wish to penetrate his mother or castrate his father, therefore rendering the father powerless—or to do both. . . . It fit the picture of a man with an over- whelming, unreasonable hatred of men in authority—a man who, for at least sixteen years, had clung to the belief that they were trying to de- prive him of something that was rightfully his. Of what? In his letters he called it justice, but this was only symbolic. His unconscious knew what it really was: the love of his mother."

Dr. Brussel hesitated to explain these graphic psychiatric details to the detectives. They seemed too far-fetched. Instead he gave them a shorthand version, saying the bomber was probably unmarried and unattached—the classic loner. He was unfailingly courteous, but without close friends. "He wants nothing to do with men—and, since his mother is his love, he is probably little interested in women either."

He was, Dr. Brussel added, "quite possibly a virgin. . . . I'll bet he's never even kissed a girl." Slavs valued family ties, so he probably lived with "some older female relative who reminded him of his mother."

A long silence followed as the detectives absorbed what Dr. Brussel had said. It was a lot to take in, and it may have sounded preposterous to those uninitiated in the strange ways of Freudian reasoning. At least they weren't arguing with him, Dr. Brussel thought.

"What is his illness?" Captain Finney asked, referring to the chronic ailment that F.P. had hinted at in his letters. "I am not well, and for this I will make the Con Edison sorry," he had written to the *Herald Tribune*. He had also warned that "all of my physical, mental and financial sufferings will be paid for in full." But what exactly was he suffering from? "There are hundreds of chronic conditions, and if we wanted to, we could go through a medical textbook and come up with a list a yard long," Dr. Brussel told Finney. "But let's stick to the usual. Let's place our bets on chronic conditions that are statistically the commonest." Dr. Brussel ruled out cancer because it would likely have killed F.P. by now. He eliminated tuberculosis as well because the antibiotic streptomycin had proven effective, provided F.P. sought out medical help and took his prescription. "Had I thought about it a little more carefully, I'd have realized that the paranoiac typically doesn't seek or heed medical advice," Dr. Brussel would later write. "He needs no advice from anybody, about anything. . . . The bomber was God, punishing an unjust world that had made him suffer and had failed to recognize his superiority. What could any doctor do for God? But no, I was too cocky to stop and think of these things. So I diagnosed the bomber as a heart case."

By now the shadows of the December dusk had obscured the city outside Brussel's office window. After four hours with Dr. Brussel, the ghost in the streets had assumed humanly form in Captain Finney's mind—a fastidious middle-aged loner of Slavic descent with a history of run-ins with neighbors and colleagues. He lived in a northern suburb, probably in Connecticut, with an elderly female relative, and secretly nurtured a grudge against Con Ed and other powerful institutions.

Finny and his men put on their coats and packed the evidence.

"What are you going to do with what I've given you?" Dr. Brussel asked as the detectives prepared to leave. "You can't simply tell policemen to look for a middle-aged Slav from Connecticut." Dr. Brussel didn't wait for an answer. "I think you ought to publicize the description I've given you. Spread it in the newspapers, on radio and television."

F.P. craved attention, Dr. Brussel continued. In their outward appearance paranoids tend to be quiet, mild-mannered people. They are reserved, and a little diffident. "When he went into a store, he probably had to wait a while before anybody would serve him," Dr. Brussel said. "People would push ahead of him in line. The butcher would give him the last-choice cut of meat. All this must bitterly frustrate him. He was the bomber but this didn't help him in his daily life."

Like most paranoids, F.P. was dying to compensate for his ineffectual nature by impressing people with his superhuman acts. His letters never failed to boast that his bombs were growing stronger, and the police could do nothing about them. "He knows how clever he is," Dr. Brussel said, "but he wasn't sure whether everybody else knew." He had to be frustrated by the lack of public notice. Given the intensity of his feelings, he might be unable to resist the chance to respond to a published profile, if only to correct any inaccuracies.

"You might prod the bomber out of hiding," Dr. Brussel said. "He'll say to himself, 'Here's some psychiatrist who thinks he's clever, thinks he can outfox me—me the bomber!'"

Dr. Brussel added, "I think he wants to be found out now. I think there's a chance he'll come forward by himself if we handle him right."

And if Dr. Brussel's description was at all accurate, he said, it might provoke some acquaintance into providing useful information. The informant could be anybody—"a mail carrier, a local merchant, a fellow employee."

"A million and one crackpots," added one of the detectives, referring to the well-established tendency for copycat crimes and hoaxers to follow publicity for a crime.

"They'll drive us crazy," Captain Finney agreed. "But I guess it has to be done. I agree with you, Doctor. This ought to be put in the papers, and I'll see if I can get the commissioner to go along."

The two men shook hands, then the three detectives moved to the door. In the parting moment Dr. Brussel closed his eyes. An image of the bomber came to him with cinematic clarity. He wore outdated clothes since his contempt for others would prevent him from holding steady jobs. His attire was old-fashioned, but clean and meticulous. It would be prim, perhaps with an enveloping, protective aspect.

"Captain, one more thing. When you catch him," Dr. Brussel said, "and I have no doubt you will, he'll be wearing a double-breasted suit."

Dr. Brussel added, "And it will be buttoned."

CHAPTER NINE

"KEEP OUT OF THIS"

December 1956

IT RAINED HARD AND LONG IN THE DAYS LEADING UP TO CHRISTMAS. A cold, dispiriting downpour swept the midtown sidewalks, drenching decorations and soaking holiday shoppers looking for last-minute gifts. Red and green lights shone on the wet pavement.

It was still bucketing on Christmas Eve when David Cruz, a nineteen-year-old clerk in the main branch of the public library, on Fifth Avenue, spent the morning shelving books. The library was particularly busy that day, with students off from school finishing papers and research projects before the holiday began in earnest. They filled the broad oak reading-room tables with books about medieval history and parliamentary procedure, French poetry and statistical theory.

While Cruz ferried carts of books among the closed stacks, an electrical engineer named Ezra Cohen strolled down Fifth Avenue with a friend. The two men ducked into the main library, climbing the steps between the marble lions and the Corinthian columns to escape the persistent rain. They admired the Christmas tree and wreaths decorating the lobby, then browsed among the open-faced science books in a technology display set up along a corridor. Cohen was leaning over the exhibition glass to read book titles when a shabbily dressed man nudged him and urged him to read the description of a chemical compound that exploded when exposed to air.

"It is similar to that used in the atomic bomb," the man told Cohen and his friend.

"We knew that this was false," Cohen later reported, "and knew then that the man was not an authority on the subject, although he tried to pass himself off as one. I looked at him closely as the thought flashed through my mind that maybe he was the one responsible for the bomb explosion in the Brooklyn Paramount Theatre. So I offered him this leading question: 'Maybe that's the stuff the Mad Bomber is using?'—and watched his face for some reaction. There was none. He appeared quite calm."

"Oh, no," the man replied, "he's using a watch mechanism."

"I asked him how he knew this," Cohen said, "and again observed him intently."

"I read about it in the papers."

"Why does that man plant those bombs?" Cohen asked.

"He must be a lunatic."

Cohen and his friend nodded at each other, signaling that it was time to make their escape. They walked north along the corridor and down a flight of stairs to the Forty-Second Street exit. "He fell in alongside of us and pressed for further conversation," Cohen said. "He started to talk about another type of bomb which he said his father told him the Irish had used on the English. I tried to move along, but he insisted on talking, disregarding my attempt to get to the street and away from him. When he persisted in talking, I tried to humor him and explained we were in a hurry to get somewhere. We stepped rapidly away from him toward Fifth Ave., but didn't see where he went."

Meanwhile, Cruz was busy reshelving books on organic chemistry and social anthropology in the science department upstairs. He waited all morning for a chance to call his girlfriend; he wanted to shore up plans for a date that evening in the Hunts Point section of the Bronx where they lived. He was finally granted a lunch break at 1:30 p.m. and descended the marble stairway to a varnished wood phone booth on the second floor. It stood directly above a first-floor booth where F.P. had detonated a bomb five years earlier.

As Cruz opened the accordion door, a dime slipped from his fingers. While leaning down to retrieve it, he noticed a bulky maroon sock attached with an ordinary black square magnet to a metal ringer box on the underside of the phone. He pulled off the sock and absentmindedly fiddled with its contents, an iron pipe, while dialing his girlfriend. "I think I just found a bomb," he told her. He laughed, and she laughed with him.

After hanging up, he examined the pipe more carefully. The pervasive newspaper descriptions sprang to mind—red sock, pipe, bomber. He wasn't laughing any longer. He ran upstairs and sprinted down a marble hall, holding the pipe at arm's length, to the science reading room where he held the bomb out for his boss to see. But his boss was too busy answering readers' questions to give Cruz more than a cursory glance. Now Cruz's face twisted itself in panic. He carried the pipe to a storage room at the end of the hall where he showed it to three other clerks. "That looks like the bomber's work," one said. "I saw the police circular describing it."

Unsure what to do, Cruz tossed the bomb out a door-size casement window. It landed in an ivy bush in Bryant Park, at the rear of the library, near a row of tables where, in more favorable weather, old men passed afternoons playing chess. While Cruz tried to calm himself, a clerk, Mario Soriano, notified a security guard, who ran to a police call box at Forty-First Street and Sixth Avenue.

Within minutes, sixty uniformed police poured into the empty park like an invading army. A row of two-toned police cruisers pulled up to Forty-Second Street, followed by Big Bertha and the green station wagon. The car doors swung open. Captain Finney and the bomb squad marched into the park. Captain Finny stood impassively while rivulets of rain dripped from his brimmed hat and darkened his trench coat. A puddle formed at his feet. Inside the library Sergeant Dale and the bomb squad detectives cleared hundreds of patrons from the grand reading room at the back of the building. Crime lab technicians photographed the phone booth and dusted for fingerprints.

Captain Finney looked more embattled than ever. With the nonstop demands of the previous week he had barely made it back to his modest two-story home in the Ditmas Park section of Brooklyn. His wife, Rita, passed the hours alone by designing and sewing a line of dresses.

The bomber had now struck thirty-two times, each incident a tense drama unto itself. Each with its own stomach-souring anxiety. And Captain Finney had little to show for it. If anything, the police were losing ground. "We're completely stymied," Deputy Police Commissioner Walter Arm told the press later that day. "We're no closer to capturing him than we were when he started leaving his bombs sixteen years ago."

An accepted fact of police work is that violent crimes against strangers are the hardest to solve. Even by that standard F.P. had come to seem un-catchable. Captain Finney had waited patiently for F.P. to make a mistake. He was beginning to think F.P. might never take a false step. "You can call him mad, a crackpot, and a psychopath," a police official said, "but for my money he's a pretty cute individual. He hasn't exposed himself so far, and I believe it's too late for him to start now."

Commissioner Kennedy had reversed his policy of confidentiality in hopes of a breakthrough. So far, sharing information with the press had only turned up the heat on Captain Finney. Newspapers responded to the release of handwriting samples, timelines, and other investigative details with a carnival of lurid speculation and pseudoscience. Editors hired an inventory of experts only too eager to second-guess the police. The *Journal-American* published an illustrated spread explaining how to make pipe bombs. Its afternoon rival, *The World-Telegram and Sun,* printed an artist's rendering of the bomber's face based somehow on the inferences of a handwriting expert.

Worst of all, the publicity induced another flood of false alarms—or what the police called "scare bombs." In addition to the frustrating pur-suit of F.P., the bomb squad was now obliged to respond to every hoax, no matter how far-fetched. "We treat every one as if it were the real thing," Sergeant Dale said. They dutifully chased down twelve false alarms on December 4 alone in a perpetual pell-mell state of emergency stretching from midmorning to almost midnight. The crisis assumed the quality of farce. Some of the cranks had even gone to the trouble of planting a reproduction of the bomb, complete with capped ends. The police log of false alarms for the day looked like this:

10:42 a.m.: Prospect Heights High School, Brooklyn

10:44 a.m.: New Utrecht High School, Brooklyn

10:50 a.m.: Samuel J. Tilden High School, Brooklyn

11:05 a.m.: Brooklyn Army Terminal

11: 39 a.m.: IRT subway station, 34th and 7th Ave

11:40 a.m.: Office building, 853 Broadway

12:18 p.m.: West Side Airlines Terminal, Ninth Ave and 42nd Street

1:00 p.m.: Paramount Theater, Times Square

1:30 p.m.: Office building, 630 Broadway

9:00 p.m.: Freighter Cheyenne Trader, Brooklyn Terminal, Greene Street

9:05 p.m.: Fox Theatre, Brooklyn

11:10 p.m.: Mark Hellinger Theatre, West 51st Street

Three of the prank calls almost certainly came from high school students trying to arrange a day off. It's harder to say what motivated the rest. According to psychologists consulted by *The New York Times,* the fraudulent callers sought a momentary sense of power, or revenge, in their otherwise impotent lives. They wanted to be noticed, to be talked about. "They made something happen," *The Times* wrote, "something that would be read in the newspapers and seen on television." One caller, after he was caught, said he simply wanted to "raise hell" for the police.

Whatever their incentives, the cranks and kooks had shifted focus away from the investigation. Some within the police department murmured that Commissioner Kennedy's publicity effort had only made matters worse, but he defended it as a way of reassuring the citizenry. "The public can cope with the known," he said. "It is fear of the unknown that causes apprehension."

The library bomb clearly wasn't another December hoax. Captain Finney knew it was real as soon as he saw the pipe lying among the ivy. The police had shared reams of evidence with the press since Commissioner Kennedy ended the policy of investigative secrecy three weeks earlier. But they were careful to withhold detailed photos of F.P.'s bombs for fear that the copycats would mimic its appearance. Fake bombs with accurate appearance would only make it harder to recognize the real version. It made no difference to Captain Finney. He could spot the bomber's handiwork the way a curator recognizes a Matisse. He could tell the bomb in the bushes was the bomber's heftiest device yet, an explosive capable of dismemberment and death.

Finney stood in the rain while carols blared incongruously from a tinny speaker outside Stern's department store on the corner of Fifth Avenue. A heaving throng of five thousand last-minute Christmas shoppers massed behind blue police barricades quickly erected on the north side of Forty-Second Street. Hundreds more watched from office windows as a detective dressed in a steel helmet, bulletproof gloves, and body plating crouched behind a shield of bulletproof glass. He scuttled on his knees like an armored crab and touched the bomb with a stethoscope. He listened for the tick, tick, tick. Nothing. Maybe the thirty-foot fall from the casement window broke the timing mechanism. Or maybe the mechanism was intact, quietly clicking down the moments to discharge. Moving deliberately, the detective placed the bomb in the steel-mesh envelope. Two policemen hoisted it on a pole and slowly—very slowly—walked a few steps down to the street and three hundred feet to Big Bertha, parked behind the library on Forty-Second Street. Then the truck sped, heavily escorted fore and aft, to the gravel yard on the West Side riverfront.

By then it was late afternoon, and a darkening sky hung over the westside docks. The bomb squad waited until the rush-hour traffic subsided, then transported the bomb to a military facility in Queens. If the bomb didn't explode within seventy-two hours, they would blast it themselves. "Under no circumstances do I want any member of this department to try to take the thing apart," said Chief of Detectives James B. Leggett. "Why take a chance on someone being killed or injured." Captain Finny and his men had no idea that the bomb squad's busiest days lay just ahead.

Ezra Cohen, the engineer who had stopped by to see the holiday decorations in the library lobby, was by now back in his Brooklyn apartment where he heard a radio news report about the bomb. He called the police to disclose his encounter with the strange man who seemed to take an inordinate interest in the explosive compound. In a two-hour interview he gave detectives a detailed description of the man—middle-aged, shabby clothes, about six foot tall. Patrolmen fanned out to search midtown, but the attributes fit nearly half the people on the street. Whoever he was, the suspect was gone.

The next day's newspapers introduced a lurid note to Christmas morning: "The Mad Bomber yesterday sent his Christmas greeting to eight million whom he so bitterly hates," wrote the *Daily News*.

The front-page *New York Times* account, headlined "Bomb in Fifth Ave. Library Spurs Hunt for Psychotic," laid bare the department's long, frustrated investigation, with all its fumbles and false leads. "The bomb squad, the Police Bureau of Technical Service, fingerprint men, handwriting experts, demolition engineers, all have worked on the case with fierce concentration—and gotten nowhere."

The last section of the article, titled "Psychiatrist Conceives Image," revealed for the first time that police had enlisted Dr. Brussel "in the hope that the psychiatrist might work up from the material a kind of portrait of the bomb-planter." The article said that Dr. Brussel had "conceived this image" of the suspect:

Single man, between 40 and 50 years old, introvert. unsocial . . . cunning. neat with tools . . . contemptuous of other people. resentful of criticism of his work but probably conceals resentment . . . might flare up violently at work when criticized . . . feels superior to critics. resentment keeps growing.

Dr. Brussel was gratified to see that the police had followed his advice and released the profile to the press. "The news story didn't contain all my predictions," he said, "but it crystallized the major ones. The profile told enough to embarrass me severely if I turned out to be grossly wrong."

A few nights later the phone rang in Dr. Brussel's Queens home. Because he treated so many violent criminals, Dr. Brussel had an unlisted number, but anybody could reach him by calling Creedmoor. The hospital switchboard forwarded calls to Dr. Brussel's home, taking care to patch in the police if the caller sounded suspicious. Dr. Brussel suspected that was the case when his phone rang at 1:00 a.m. as he entered the cottage after a late night out.

"Is this Dr. Brussel, the psychiatrist?"

"Yes, this is Dr. Brussel."

"This is F.P. speaking. Keep out of this or you'll be sorry."

"I started to say something," Dr. Brussel would recall, "hoping to keep him talking long enough for the police and phone company to trace the call. But F.P. was too clever to fall for a trick like that. Without even waiting to hear my reaction to his threat he hung up."

On a late-December day, F.P. climbed the steps leading up from the Columbus Circle subway stop and stood momentarily at the spot where the long diagonal run of Broadway crosses Eighth Avenue. The two converge in a grand rotary encircling a marble statue of Christopher Columbus, his gaze affixed downtown. On the west side of the rotary stood the newly opened Coliseum, a low, windowless four-story exposition hall adjoining a twenty-six-story office block.

In the lobby F.P. bought a $1.50 ticket for the auto show, the Coliseum's inaugural event, and rode an escalator to the second-floor exhibition hall. The show was New York's most heavily attended annual attraction. It was more crowded than usual this year, having opened in a brand-new modernist venue. A surging crowd swept F.P. along, an inconspicuous figure admiring the shiny tail fins and whitewall tires. As he walked among the spoke-wheeled Gaylord sedans and graciously rounded Sunbeams, he could feel the pleasing weight of the two-foot bomb stashed in the pocket of his overcoat. He had planned to hide it somewhere on the showroom floor—in the undercarriage of a shiny new Buick, perhaps, or behind one of the many expansive cardboard displays. But he was in no hurry. There was so much to see—girls in bathing suits reclining on long-nosed Jaguars with gaping grilles, a large-finned Packard spinning slowly on its own rotating stage, a three-wheeled bubble car made by Messerschmitt.

F.P. could barely navigate the aisles, as rows of people encircled attractions. The show was so thronged that he began to wish that he had brought more firepower. For years he had deliberately placed his bombs where they would provoke terror, but cause minimal injury. He was done with that now. No more solicitude. He wanted to kill. As he negotiated the pressing crowd, he began to picture in his mind the bloodshed and horror a bigger bomb would inflict. He could hear all the smug, smiling people around him screaming and stampeding for the escalator. He decided to come back another day with a cluster of more powerful bombs in his pocket.

CHAPTER TEN

THE PUBLISHER

December 1956

Seymour Berkson may have been the only New Yorker to recoil at the sight of Dr. Brussel's bomber profile published on the front page of *The New York Times* on Christmas Day. The paper lay across the kitchen table of his Fifth Avenue apartment like an unwanted holiday gift.

Five years earlier Berkson had succeeded William Randolph Hearst Jr., son of the press baron, as publisher of the brassy *New York Journal-American,* flagship of the Hearst empire and New York's most read afternoon newspaper. At age fifty, Berkson was among the youngest ever to hold the position of publisher on a big-city paper. Hearst, father and son, had positioned the *Journal-American* in a middle ground between the decorous uptown broadsheets (*The Times* and *Herald Tribune*) and the obstreperous tabloid pack. It was respectable, but not too respectable.

The *Journal-American* upheld the notorious Hearst bent for hot-blooded headlines ("Mob Makes Morbid Show of Death" and "Giants Lucky When Mays Muff Puts Leo in Daze"). Its output was uneven, but it was capable of tenacious reporting, particularly on the grimy city beats discounted by *The Times* and *Herald Tribune* that fixed their gaze more intently on Washington and foreign capitals. "Let it latch onto an exposé, and Hearst's *Journal-American* will rip in like a mongoose attacking a cobra," *Newsweek* wrote. "The *Journal* jabs again and again until its story falls limp and exhausted."

The *Journal-American*'s ragtag team had an underdog's ardor for beating its high-minded uptown rivals. "No one had more fun covering the heartache and happy times of the city," Hearst Jr., would write in his memoir. "We were a wild and often sentimental bunch who loved New York because it was our town. We wrote about it with affection, anger and despair. . . . New York was then the most exciting city in the world. We were good. At times, magnificent."

The *Journal-American* was like a dissolute boxer capable of rising from the mat and landing a knockout punch. It rightly prided itself on smart feature articles and a murderers' row of big-name columnists, drawn by the generous Hearst payroll, including the ardently anticommunist Westbrook Pegler and a society correspondent who wrote under the picturesque pseudonym Cholly Knickerbocker. The paper also benefited from Hearst's International News Service, which fed stories from major European cities. While manager of the news service, Berkson had coined the unofficial company motto: "Get it first, but get it right."

Berkson was the modern journalist in every way, but he had a nostalgic streak. On his desk he kept a clanging typewriter of wartime vintage, known as a mill, which produced only capital letters. "This may be dated," he said, "but I have always used a noisy mill. Never could get used to a noiseless. I like to pound away at the keys, and when I pound, I like the mill to answer me back."

Berkson was an unlikely publisher for a louche operation like the *Journal-American*. He was serious-minded, with dark eyes and neatly parted black hair doused with bay rum. He wore double-breasted suits ordered from a Rockefeller Center clothier and patterned neckties by the Italian company Countess Mara. "He had fine features," his son, Bill, recalled, and was "considered handsome and charming by most people who knew him. He had a ready smile and laughed heartily, but not loud."

Berkson was a steadfast company man, but not one of the shrill anticommunists or dubious tabloid types that Hearst favored. "If he cared about anything, it was journalism," Bill said, "and that it should be done correctly."

When Bill was in danger of failing chemistry at Lawrenceville, a New Jersey boarding school, his father demanded an explanation. Science didn't much matter to him, Bill said. He wanted to be a writer. "If you're going to be a writer," Berkson answered, "you need to know everything." (Bill went on to become a distinguished poet and art critic.)

As a Hearst correspondent based in Paris and Rome, Berkson had distinguished himself with a series of exclusives on the maneuverings of European leaders headed to war. His key sources included Signora Margherita Sarfatti, Prime Minister Benito Mussolini's confidante and mistress. A collection of Berkson's articles about Il Duce's rise and ruinous collapse was published as a book. He wrote a second book about the dissolution of royal families. "We think he is one of the few European correspondents we have known who looks like a European correspondent, except that he does not carry a cane," Damon Runyon wrote in a 1938 column. "He is slim and dapper and quite active and smokes cigarettes out of a long metal case and wears his hat with a rakish slant."

In 1934, as Rome bureau chief, Berkson received an urgent cable from his boss, William Randolph Hearst. The Whitney Museum in New York was curating works by Edward Hopper, Georgia O'Keeffe, and other contemporary American artists for exhibition at the Venice Biennale. Hearst had offered to pay for shipping and installation if the Whitney agreed to include a jarringly old-fashioned portrait of his mistress, the actress Marion Davies. The Whitney refused. Hearst was accustomed to getting his way. He instructed Berkson to work surreptitiously with Count Giuseppe Volpi di Misurata, the Italian industrialist and president of the Biennale, to hang the painting in the vestibule of the American exhibition so that Hearst and Davies would see it as they entered. Hearst hinted that in return for Count Volpi's cooperation, Hearst's newspapers would give Mussolini favorable coverage.

Eleanor Lambert, the Whitney's press manager, arrived in Venice with orders to remove the portrait. Hearst instructed Berkson to make sure it stayed. Lambert was a petite blonde with steely resolve. She threatened to withdraw the entire American collection if the portrait was not immediately taken down. What's more, she promised to leak the whole embarrassing story of the mistress and her portrait to the Associated Press. (Hearst was still married to Millicent Hearst.)

In the end Lambert and Berkson struck a compromise: the portrait would stay, but an accompanying panel would state that it was not part of the exhibition. With the standoff settled, Berkson invited his adversary to dinner. He was married to Jane Eads, a barnstorming Chicago reporter who, among other things, broke the story of King Edward VIII's romance with Wallis Simpson, the American divorcée for whom he would abdicate the throne. Lambert was likewise married, to an architect, though long separated. Berkson and Lambert nonetheless fell hard for each other. They married in New York two years later.

By the 1950s they were living in a thirteen-room Fifth Avenue apartment. She had become a prominent fashion publicist and originator of Fashion Week and the International Best-Dressed list. He was publisher of the *Journal-American*. Their parties mixed witty and hard-bitten newspaper types such as Bugs Baer and Bob Considine with Valentina, Bill Blass, and other fashion designers. Movie stars such as Judy Garland and Mary Martin also showed up. "There was a lot of laughter in the house," their son, Bill, recalled.

A generation earlier Berkson might have been the kind of progressive publisher, such as Horace Greeley or Adolph Ochs, who influenced policy and promoted social betterment. But by the mid-1950s newspapers had begun surrendering advertising to television. Walter Cronkite was ascendant, newsprint in retrograde. The long Darwinian winnowing would soon begin.

As a matter of survival publishers now appealed to what the philosopher William James called the public's "aboriginal capacity for murderous excitement." Berkson had come over from the International News Service to lead the fight for murderous excitement in the mudslinging low ground of newspaper warfare. It was a fight tinged with desperation.

William Randolph Hearst had died of a brain hemorrhage at his Beverly Hills home on an August morning in 1951 with five sons at his bedside. Also in attendance was Richard Berlin, a bean-counting company president whose primary ambition was the containment of profligate spending. Rigid and parsimonious, he was a corrective to the famous Hearst extravagance that led to the Hearst Castle in San Simeon and a long string of media acquisitions. Berlin succeeded Hearst as chief executive officer. His mandate was to right a foundering company. After taking stock of Hearst's eighteen newspapers, plus its radio and television stations, magazines, paper mills, lumber plants, mines, and cattle ranches, Berlin warned Berkson that newspapers were now the company's weak link. The cost of newsprint was up, advertising down. He would consider closing newspapers, including the flagship *Journal-American,* if things didn't pick up. The romance of newsprint left Berlin unmoved.

A publisher fighting for his newsroom's survival could ask for no greater gift than a serial bomber such as F.P. The story sold newspapers, and it kept going and going. The *Journal-American* had followed the bomber story with glee and gusto for more than a decade. Earlier that month, when Commissioner Kennedy began opening the investigative files to the press, Berkson had dedicated a team of reporters to the bomber story. He expected them to break news and develop stories ahead of Patrick Doyle and other residents of the police shack. But unexpectedly the *Journal-American* was in danger of falling behind. Bad enough that the bomber had twice written letters to the *Herald Tribune.* Now, on Christmas morning, Berkson woke to find *The New York Times* story about the psychiatrist, Dr. Brussel, and the profile that he had come up with for the police. The *Journal-American* had a lot of catching up to do.

Berkson mulled his next move over Christmas brunch with his wife, Eleanor, and their son, Bill. He faced humiliation if the *Journal-American* trailed the uptown broadsheets on the red-hot bomber story. He needed to respond with something creative, a gambit that would distinguish the *Journal-American* from its seven newsstand rivals.

Deliberating over work matters on Christmas morning was entirely in keeping with Berkson's reputation as a boss with a high-voltage capacity for work. "Seymour was one of the most dynamic creatures I've ever met in the news business, an exasperating lint-picker, demanding, deflating, and the hardest-working man in the shop," said Bob Considine, a war correspondent and columnist.

So it surprised no one when, with brunch dishes cleared, Berkson placed a Christmas-morning phone call to the Brooklyn home of Paul Schoenstein, an assistant managing editor who oversaw the reporters assigned to the bomber story. Schoenstein was a dapper figure with short gray hair combed straight back. He sat stone-faced at his desk from 6:30 a.m. to 4:00 p.m., dressed in a pressed white Brooks Brothers shirt with neatly folded sleeves and a bow tie arranged just so, dispensing disturbingly dark jokes and shouting savage put-downs across the newsroom in a distinctive baritone while editing endless accounts of strangulations, stickups, and graft with a cigarette in his left hand and a black grease pencil in his right. He dropped the pencil occasionally to slam pages unfit for print onto a large spike sitting on his desk. He spent so many hours with a phone pressed to his ear "that I sometimes answer 'Hello' in face-to-face conversations," he said. The only place he could relax, he said, was in the mezzanine of Radio City Music Hall. "And there, I confess, I usually fall asleep," he said.

Schoenstein wasn't too busy to cast hooded eyes on the Smith and Vassar girls, cashmere interns, who slummed it in the newsroom en route to marriages or more respectable jobs at *Time, Parade,* or other midtown magazines. He had at least one affair among their ranks.

Whatever Schoenstein's foibles, his colleagues respected his steadying hand on a newsroom made unruly by the rowdy and wayward. He'd won a Pulitzer Prize twelve years earlier by mobilizing the staff to locate a supply of penicillin, still a relatively scarce drug, at a Squibb factory in New Jersey. He then arranged for doses to be rushed in a police-escorted car to a Brooklyn hospital in time to save the life of a two-year-old Queens girl afflicted with a rare blood disease. "He beat death by three hours," *Time* magazine wrote, "and *The Times* by a good deal more."

Over the phone Berkson told Schoenstein that *The Times* might have broken the news of Dr. Brussel's profile, but the manhunt would surely yield more scoops. In newsroom parlance, the bomber story had legs. Gazing out over the winter-dead branches of Central Park, an idea came to Berkson: maybe the *Journal-American* could contact F.P. by publishing an open letter, possibly cajole him into revealing the exact nature of his grievance. Better yet, maybe the paper could play the role of negotiator, luring the bomber out of the shadows with the promise of legal and medical help.

Schoenstein liked the idea. He had a knack for upstaging competitors by ginning up stories from his own wits and imagination. During the war Schoenstein had directed overseas photographers to send portraits of wounded soldiers, sailors, and marines to their families as a Mother's Day gift from the newspaper. His reporters infiltrated the German American Bund, a Nazi group, so successfully that the FBI came to Schoenstein for leads. And he published an exposé of Rockland State, a psychiatric hospital known for its cruel conditions, after convincing doctors to admit a reporter as a patient. "No city editor dare sit back and gloat," he once wrote. "He knows that he is in a constant race with the opposition to get the news first—and he must be alert to use all his ingenuity to scoop the competition. No one can know blacker despondency than a city editor when, walking unsuspectingly to a newsstand, he picks up the opposition newspaper and his heart skips a beat—there is a sensational story on Page One, and he doesn't have it."

Schoenstein warned Berkson that his plan could backfire. If F.P. interpreted the open letter as a trap, he might ratchet up his campaign, in which case the police—or worse, the readers—would likely blame the *Journal-American*. Still, the potential upside clearly outweighed the risks. A letter to the mystery bomber, with the electrifying possibility of a correspondence, would set the *Journal-American* apart from the pursuing pack and outdo the hated uptown broadsheets. Schoenstein urged Berkson to put the plan in motion.

"As a stab in the dark, we decided to write him an open letter in the hope that it would pique his interest and tempt him to bring his grievance into the open," Berkson later said. He would describe the plan as "a rather innocent and almost absurdly simple thing."

After speaking with Schoenstein, Berkson embarked on his daily commute from the silken heights of Fifth Avenue to the *Journal-American*'s sooty sandstone building across from the Fulton Fish Market, just south of the Brooklyn Bridge, where the sidewalks stank of seaweed and tomcats gnawed on codfish gristle. The sixth-floor newsroom hummed like a high-gear factory, despite the holiday, when Berkson arrived in the early afternoon. Rewrite men hunkered behind a row of black metal desks, their shoulders crooked to the phones, taking dictation from reporters at City Hall or the police shack. Given the breakneck urgency to update the news for five afternoon editions, reporters had no time to return to the newsroom and compose articles. The reporters were glorified legmen, some barely literate. "There was a no-nonsense spit-on-the-floor and do-the-story attitude," said Mickey Carroll, a business reporter. "The people who reported the stories didn't write the stories. There wasn't time for that. You put out a new edition every hour."

Chain-smoking editors yanked pages from Underwood typewriters and bellowed for copyboys to lower texts to the composing room in a dumbwaiter. The room rang with the *clacka-clacka-DING, clacka-clacka-DING* of typewriter carriages at full tilt. Smoke choked the air. Dead butts filled brass ashtrays. Casement windows admitted a sickening stench from the warren of slimy fish stalls on the far side of South Street piled high with scallops, cod, snapper, and oysters. "I felt like throwing up," Marilyn Bender, a reporter, said of the summer days when warmth required that the windows be thrown wide-open. The windows stayed open all winter, if only a crack, as relief from the choke of cigarette smoke. In the morning, editors wiped down desks and typewriters covered with a dusting of soot from incinerators and smokestacks on the East River. They called it "the black plague."

When the last of five afternoon editions went to print at 4:00 p.m. the rewrite men and pressmen, their hands smeared with grease, marched off to Moochie's Saloon, a waterfront dive with rickety stools and a slanted floor at the corner of Market Slip and South Street, where the staff gossiped, conspired, clowned, and griped while throwing back hard-boiled eggs and glasses of whiskey with beer chasers. The worst off might stagger back to the newsroom and fall asleep on giant rolls of newsprint stored in the composing room.

At Moochie's the rewrite men mingled with Marvin the Torch, a notorious arsonist, and Johnny the Radio, a neighborhood gossip. Bookies, gangsters, and fishmongers crammed in beside the pockmarked bar drinking from dirty glasses and eating meatballs with bent knives and forks. "I never had the nerve to try the meatballs," said William Randolph Hearst Jr., who, in his tenure as publisher, routinely slummed it. "They looked like badly scuffed mini-baseballs hit out of the park by murderers' row."

The place had a penetrating odor that the patrons facetiously attributed to the eggs. In actuality the smell came from the tidal waters rising and receding in the basement. The stench was more than compensated for by the generosity of Moochie, a widowed barkeep who lived above the saloon. He bought the rewrite men drinks, cashed their checks, and covered for them when wives or editors called. He paid for at least one reporter's funeral.

The rewrite men had not yet decamped to Moochie's when Berkson arrived on Christmas afternoon. Schoenstein was composing the letter to F.P. on a typewriter with help from Eddie Mahar, a two-hundred-pound city editor with a shock of white hair and an ample nicotine-stained mustache who berated reporters at every turn in a voice consistently dialed up to a full-throated bellow. "His natural volume was a yell," said Mike Pearl, a reporter.

They faced a tricky piece of writing. The letter had to sound a sympathetic note, but not so consoling as to arouse F.P.'s suspicion. In the final draft the editors gave the bomber "guarantees" against "illegal action," promised him a "fair trial," and offered to publish his grievances. The letter, accompanied by an account of the "All-Out Search for Mad Bomber," ran big and bold across all eight front-page columns:

AN OPEN LETTER
To The Mad Bomber
(Prepared in Co-operation with the Police Dept.)
Give yourself up.
For your own welfare and for that of the community, the time has
    come for you to reveal your identity.
The N.Y. Journal-American guarantees that you will be protected
    from any illegal action and that you will get a fair trial.
This newspaper is also willing to help you in two other ways.
It will publish all the essential parts of your story as you may choose
    to make it public.
It will give you the full chance to air whatever grievances you may
    have as the motive of your acts.
We urge you to accept this offer now not only for your own sake but for
    the sake of the community.
Time is running out on your prospects of remaining unapprehended.
You can telephone the City Editor of this newspaper at COrtland
    7-1212, or you can go to any police station or even the policeman
    on the street and tell him who you are.
In all cases you will be given the benefits of our American system of
    justice.
Give yourself up now.

The letter met with laughs in the city's seven other newsrooms. "Typical Hearst stunt," editors said. "Don't hold your breath waiting for a response. The *Journal-American* must be desperate."

On the wall of Berkson's newsroom office hung a taxidermic sailfish caught on an Acapulco vacation. "Keep your eyes open and your mouth shut," he liked to tell reporters. "That sailfish did neither."

Berkson regarded the open letter to F.P. as another kind of fishing expedition: it was a lure cast into the deep, mysterious waters of New York. Over the following days the newsroom waited for the bomber to take the bait. Clerks checked every envelope and package for F.P.'s blocky handwriting. Every jangling phone brought a clutch of anticipation.

The last days of December deteriorated into the worst of times for Captain Finney and the bomb squad boys. The false alarms had mercifully dwindled as the holidays neared. Then the Christmas Eve bomb found at the library and the publicity surrounding Dr. Brussel's profile whipped up a new round of press coverage, which provoked an epidemic of prank calls—more than a hundred in the final week of the year—as if callers were intent on ending 1956 on a splurge. Police precinct switchboards flooded with tip-offs, each of which required investigation, no matter how implausible. "Every time we find a real bomb, every whack in New York writes or calls in about imaginary ones," one detective said. "This city has plenty of whacks with a screwball sense of humor."

One policeman checked for bombs at the same theater so many times that he saw almost the entire movie in short increments. He needed one more well-timed bomb scare, he told a reporter, to learn how the story ended.

Commissioner Kennedy installed plainclothes cops, many of them women, in public places with the remote hope of catching F.P. in the act. The plants sat in orchestra sections of theaters watching the top-run movies of the season—*Giant* with James Dean, *Oklahoma!* with Shirley Jones, *Julie* with Doris Day—over and over while scanning for patrons making suspicious maneuvers in the dark. They loitered for hours in train station waiting rooms peering over magazines and sports sections at the comings and goings of middle-aged men.

Detectives worked in shifts, day and night, trying to follow up every tip, no matter how flimsy, without recklessly smearing the suspects' reputations. "We can't just barge into these places and let everybody know that we are checking over such-and-such person as a bomber suspect," one detective said. "Even after the person is cleared his employer will remember that he was under investigation in a case like this and it will count against him."

It was as if F.P. had released a viral madness and suspicion into society. An informant wrote the police urging them to "check brown-eyed people, they're no good. I love humanity, except where brown-eyed." A man spent $50 in long-distance fees to call police headquarters from Anchorage, Alaska. He talked for an hour, demanding that he be flown to New York to help solve the crime. A short time later a white-bearded man appeared unannounced in the *Journal-American* newsroom and declared that he would contact F.P. telepathically in exchange for $56,000. "Not only that," the newspaper reported, "but he'd keep the Mad Bomber under a 'telepathic spell' and would lead him down to Police Headquarters by sort of rolling in his brain waves as one would a fish line."

After weeks of deliberation, a commuter in Darien, Connecticut, reported that his next-door neighbor—a man he considered a friend—conducted mysterious weekly trips to New York, always carrying a blue canvas suitcase. The commuter had seen the neighbor furtively ferrying the suitcase to and from the trunk of his car, always when his wife was out. The man matched most of Dr. Brussel's criteria: he was a middle-aged former Con Ed employee, an electrical engineer, who favored double-breasted suits. Earlier in his life he had been diagnosed as a paranoiac and had spent time in a psychiatric hospital. He was married, which did not square with Dr. Brussel's description. "But since his wife was some ten years older than he," wrote Dr. Brussel, who was following the case, "it was conceivable that he had married her in order to find a mother—and this could be thought of fitting the image."

Two state troopers confronted the man as he pulled into a parking spot at the Darien train station. They asked him to unlock his trunk and produce the suitcase. Inside the suitcase troopers found a provocative pair of high-heeled boots. He confessed that he hired prostitutes in the city as a respite from an unhappy marriage. He asked the women to indulge him by wearing the boots.

Captain Finney invited Dr. Brussel into the inquiry whenever a tip originated from a doctor or a medical facility. "Not a few times I sat in the rear of an unmarked police car as it cut in and out of traffic," Dr. Brussel wrote. "Every time we started out, Inspector Finney and I hoped anew that we had caught up with the elusive bomber." As the car navigated the close-packed streets, Dr. Brussel and Finney rode in the back discussing the possibilities. They were like opposites seated side by side. One wiry, the other stout. One manically talkative, the other almost mute.

Captain Finney rode with Dr. Brussel to an uptown hospital after administrators alerted police that they had repeatedly treated a patient of Czechoslovakian descent for heart failure, the exact ethnicity and ailment Dr. Brussel had specified in his profile. The patient was also a former Con Ed employee and a bachelor. He fit "to a T," Dr. Brussel wrote. He leafed through the patient's medical history in the hospital records room while Finney waited in the car. The file was thick with corroborating details. "As I read, I could feel my heart pound," Dr. Brussel wrote. "Perfect!" Before leaving to discuss his findings with Finney, Dr. Brussel paused to check the suspect's hospital admissions against the bombing dates. "That ended it," he wrote. "On two bombing dates the patient had been in the hospital—once in an oxygen tent."

A short time later a colleague at the New York Psychiatric Institute called Dr. Brussel to say that a rageful patient in his care, a Westchester resident, believed that Con Ed was responsible for his heart palpitations, shortness of breath, and chest pain. X-rays and lab tests uncovered no heart problems. The patient was delusional. However, the doctor said he could not reveal the patient's name without violating the confidentiality agreement. "I want to do my duty as a citizen," the doctor said, "but I refuse to lose my license or go to prison for the state or you."

As a state psychiatric official, Dr. Brussel had the right to examine patient records during routine inspections. "Why couldn't I stumble over

his file?" Dr. Brussel asked the doctor. "You give me the name, but nobody need ever know." The doctor agreed.

"Once more, I made a flying trip uptown in a police car," Dr. Brussel
wrote. "I obtained the record. Again, the patient and my description fit
like a hand in a custom-made glove. More, this man's vituperative feeling against Con Ed was sheer fire-and-brimstone. Then came the disappointment: on one of the bombing dates he, too, had been confined in
the institute.

"While we were following down such leads as this and trying to swal-
low our disappointment each time, we still kept hoping that the publicity
campaign would make the bomber do something to reveal himself."

Captain Finney wasn't counting on any such misstep. At his urging,
Commissioner Kennedy added sixteen detectives to the bomb squad,
bringing the roster to thirty-four men. The beefed-up squad responded
to fifty warnings on Friday, December 28, alone, the single busiest day
in bomb squad history. The *Daily News* called it "a prankster's holiday."
At one point the calls came in at a rate of one a minute. In the late afternoon Finney ordered the squad to investigate only those reports where a
device was found—which in each case turned out to be an air filter or short
pipe left in imitation of F.P.'s handiwork. Even so, there were enough reports to create a dizzying daylong whirlwind of emergency as the bomb
squad's fleet of police cruisers, trailed by Big Bertha and the green station
wagon, careened from one corner of the city to the next, roping off train
stations and evacuating theaters.

"The way we work, ninety percent of our calls are false alarms," Detective Schmitt said, "but any one of them might be something planted
by our friend, or someone else. Sure, the chances are it's a package or dirty
shirts dropped by some guy, or it's a practical joke by some weak-witted
kid, or it's a phony planted by a nut. But how do you know? . . . Ninety-
nine times out of a hundred, the innocent-looking object is just what it
looks—innocent. It's that one in a hundred that sprays a quarter pound
of rusty steel into you."

In the course of one endless, unrelenting day, a porter in Madison

Square Garden found a white sock containing a length of pipe stashed in a lower-level men's room during a college basketball triple-header attended by ten thousand. The bomb squad dismantled it to find a firecracker. Another dud was found at the Commodore Theatre on Second Avenue. The squad spent more than an hour searching the lobby of the Waldorf Astoria Hotel—every cranny of the lounges, restaurant, and bar—without finding anything. On and on it went, with all manner of counterfeit bombs turning up at Grand Central, the Port Authority bus station, a Brooklyn department store, a church, hospital, office buildings, subway stations. "It's a screwball's delight," Sergeant Dale said of the hoaxers. "Honestly, for the life of me, I can't understand what they get out of it."

Not all calls were hoaxes. Some came from well-intentioned New Yorkers who had read Dr. Brussel's profile and found in it confirmation of their worst suspicions about the people around them. They called to report a neurotically tidy acquaintance or a coworker with a Slavic accent. Any man indifferent to women got suspicious looks. Workers with a history of job disputes, middle-aged men living with aunts, neighbors with tool shops, acquaintances who kvetched over utility bills, any who mumbled to themselves—they all could be culpable. It began to seem that everyone was suspect, everyone was shady.

"It's amazing how suspicious people can be of each other," a police official said, "and how vicious."

Wives began to wonder what their husbands were doing in the basement on Saturday afternoons. Neighbors eyed neighbors, friends sized up friends. "A man called here today with a complaint about a neighbor who has been a respected figure in the community for more than thirty years, a lawyer without a blemish," a detective said. "He's sure the lawyer is the bomber because he has a workshop in his basement and has been acting strangely. They never think that maybe *they're* acting strangely."

A Queens woman called a local police precinct to announce with certainty that her husband was F.P.: "He's plain crazy. Take my word for it, and don't bother checking. Just arrest him and put him away. It'll be good riddance for everyone."

Amid the chaos of December 28, a bystander called to report that a strange-looking man was "snooping" around telephone booths and bathroom stalls in Grand Central. Policemen stationed nearby picked up a lugubrious sixty-three-year-old named George Cernac, a track-maintenance worker carrying two paper shopping bags containing a new pair of red wool socks, the exact type F.P. used to conceal bombs. He spoke with a Slavic accent, one of the characteristics Dr. Brussel listed. An application for US citizenship found in his bags indicated that he was born in Yugoslavia. His belongings also included a key to a locker at the Rye train station, in Westchester, which heightened suspicion, since that was the area F.P. had mailed his letters from. Cernac was, the *Journal-American* wrote, "a startling new avenue of investigation."

The cops marched him to a police precinct on East Thirty-Sixth Street and locked him in an interrogation cell. They had begun to question Cernac when he started to perspire and swoon. His eyes acquired a vacant aspect, then he toppled to the floor. He died of a coronary thrombosis before an emergency-room doctor could be summoned from Bellevue Hospital. His identity remained elusive. Cernac had given the police a home address in Bethlehem, Pennsylvania, but nobody at that address claimed to know him. He might have been a legitimate suspect, but detectives didn't have anything to go on. Cernac's life was a blank.

As the bomber story spread to front pages of newspapers across the country, the bomb scares rippled outward. A stick of dynamite with a timing device was found in Kansas City's Union Station, and crank calls propelled police on wild-goose chases in Hartford, Dallas, Wichita, Chicago, Kansas City, and Philadelphia. The hoaxes occurred as far away as London, where a phone call warned of a bomb at the Chelsea Arts Ball, a costume party held at the Royal Albert Hall.

On the afternoon of December 28 the bomb squad sprinted, sirens howling, to the Times Square Theater on West Forty-Second Street, where, seven minutes before the end of the feature, the assistant manager had discovered a piped contraption on the floor near the stage. Without alerting the audience of 350, he folded his jacket around the pipe and carried it out a fire exit to an alley and covered it with a metal drum. Detectives found it be a harmless imitation of F.P.'s handiwork, a pipe stuffed with paper.

Instead of chasing F.P., the police were now chasing the hoaxers. "Their task was endlessly complicated," wrote the *Journal-American,* "by the pranksters, psychos, busybodies and false-alarmists who crop up with most major crimes."

The police arrested a pair of Brooklyn girls and held them on $2,500 bail for calling in a fake bomb threat. Eight Long Island boys were taken into custody for coercing a classmate into phoning in a scare so they could skip school. "Our policy is to arrest these people and bring them to justice," Commissioner Kennedy said. "We regard them as nuisances. . . . We believe that some making these calls are sick people who are more to be pitied than censured, but despite this they will be dealt with firmly, because they are in many ways hampering the search for the bomber." District attorneys and judges joined with the police in making an example of these cases and others like them. No specific law forbade false alarms, so prosecutors charged the hoaxers with malicious mischief or disorderly conduct, both misdemeanors.

If the hoaxes had an upside it was that the swarming police presence in public places throughout the city seemed to have cowed the real bomber into hiding. At least that was the hope at police headquarters. Though Dr. Brussel warned Captain Finney that the opposite was likely true: the hoaxes would only spur the bomber to greater acts of violence. "I didn't believe the man could turn down any challenge to his self-conceived superiority," Dr. Brussel wrote. "As I imagined him, he would feel compelled to show off his cleverness by throwing some kind of taunt at the aroused, wary city."

It wouldn't take long for F.P. to prove Dr. Brussel correct. At 7:25 p.m. on December 28, at the end of the bomb squad's busiest day, Grace Maylott, a switchboard operator at the Paramount in Times Square, fielded a call from a deep-voiced man who said that he had hidden a bomb in the theater. "Now listen carefully," the man said in an accent Maylott described as guttural, possibly German. "At 7:55 there will be a bomb exploding in your theater."

Maylott stalled for time in hopes that the call might be traced: "I'm sorry, I can't hear what you're saying."

The man repeated his warning.

"Why do you do these things?" she asked.

"Never mind." The man hung up.

If the man was F.P., then George Cernac, whose body now lay unclaimed in a city morgue, could be struck from the list of suspects.

Fourteen policemen and detectives from a West Forty-Seventh Street precinct entered the theater and fanned out like a squadron of ushers. Somewhere in those dark rows a bomb might be tick-tick-ticking inches from an unsuspecting young couple on a date or a lonely widow seeking a few hours of distraction in an absorbing story. With twenty minutes to go before the time of detonation specified by the caller, the police searched row by row with flashlights looking for seats with torn upholstery or other telling irregularities.

It may seem odd that the police did not evacuate the theater, recalling these events now as we do from a culture of utmost caution. In this case, and others like it, the police were reluctant to alert the audience for fear of causing a panic. For better or worse, their operating policy was to avoid disrupting a crowd unless necessary. And given the volume of prank calls, Sergeant Dale and his men were half-convinced the call was another hoax—though they could never know for sure.

The appointed time, 7:55 p.m., came and went. Up on the screen Alfred Hitchcock's latest suspense drama unspooled, a case of mistaken identity called *The Wrong Man*. A bass player in the Stork Club's house band was wrongly accused of robberies. He struggled to clear himself from a preponderance of evidence. He finally managed to exonerate himself and reunite with his wife, only to find her clinically depressed. Credits rolled and the audience of twenty-five hundred filed up the aisles and dispersed into the blinking glare of Times Square.

With the houselights turned up, the police conducted a more thorough search. They found their bomb at 2:40 a.m. buried deep within a leather-upholstered seat in the fifteenth row. After a day made frantic by fifty hoaxes, here at last was the real thing. It was the second bomb found in the Paramount within a year, and nearly identical to the Christmas Eve bomb thrown into the ivy bush outside the library four days earlier.

The bomb squad removed the device in the usual manner. Detectives lumbering in protective suits carried it in the steel mesh envelope to Big Bertha, which still contained the bomb collected from the public library. Big Bertha sped from Times Square to Fort Tilden in Queens.

The only way to dispose of unexploded bombs such as the ones found at the Paramount and the public library was to detonate them in a controlled manner. The two bombs were laid together in a three-foot-deep trench, shaped like a shallow grave, dug from sandy ground on a lonely stretch of beach, and packed with sandbags. Detective William Schmitt of the bomb squad and Lieutenant Clifton Pruett, commander of an army ordnance unit, leaned across the bombs in order to attach plastic explosives and connect the wires used to ignite them. They wore no protective garb; it would have done little good if the bombs had gone off beneath them. Besides, they needed full mobility to set the charge and get away fast. The bomb squad designed the blast for a particular effect. "The purpose is to split the bomb so as to conserve as much of the debris as we can, to study it, and for use as evidence in court," Captain Finney said.

The detectives unspooled a wire 125 feet over a low dune and through a stand of shrub pine to a bunker known as the Hell Box, where Captain Finney huddled with a few bomb squad detectives. Press photographers stood on its roof. Sergeant Dale shouted, "Fire in the hole!"—a traditional warning of imminent explosion originated by miners. He twisted a handle, which sent a charge of current through the wire to the plastic explosives. For a moment the men could hear only the shush of waves and the faint soughing of the ocean breeze through pine branches. Then came three muffled reports, like rifle salutes in a distant field. The blast kicked a sandbag five feet in the air. Down from the bunker, their black lace-ups sinking in the sand, came Finney and his men to collect the exploded remains of the metal pipe, the cheap wristwatches, and granules of gunpowder for study in the crime lab. "It looks as if both were real bombs," Finney said after reviewing the evidence in his Poplar Street office later that day. "We found fragments of a watch and particles of plumbing in the debris that indicate the bombs were the same type left by the bomber in the past."

With that he closed the file and leaned back in his desk chair. "The question now is, Where do we go from here? The bomber now has the know-how and technique. Is he going to try for something bigger?"

That afternoon Alfred Hitchcock settled his considerable bulk into a chair in his suite at the Sherry-Netherland Hotel overlooking the Plaza and the southeast corner of Central Park. He was in New York to promote his latest, *The Wrong Man,* the movie showing at the Paramount when police retrieved the bomb from a theater seat. It was the story of a man's long fight for vindication, which seemed to be the story F.P. was trying to tell about himself. For that reason, and because the director had a genius for capturing criminal psychology, a *Journal-American* reporter asked Hitchcock what he thought of the bomber case. "The Mad Bomber is a man with a diabolical sense of humor," Hitchcock replied, as if F.P. were a character of Hitchcock's own creation. "And he is not a stupid man. You could hardly say that a man who has avoided being caught for sixteen years is stupid. Whatever it is that has made this man an enemy of society, one can only see a man who is enjoying this thing. He apparently is as much concerned with taunting the police to try and catch him as he is in blowing people up."

Hitchcock also expressed sympathy for the beleaguered detectives: "All of us are schooled by TV to expect police miracles. We see crime labs and microscopes and such—a continuous indoctrination on police skills. Hard to live up to."

A series of phone calls interrupted the interview. Every time he picked up the phone, Hitchcock asked, "Are *you* the Mad Bomber?"

The prank calls slackened slightly that day, December 29, down to twenty-four, one of which presented an enormous challenge. At 11:40 a.m.

a commuter found a note in a Grand Central telephone booth warning that a bomb would explode in the Empire State Building at 11:02. The note neglected to specify morning or night. The bomb squad, along with a pack of enlisted patrolmen, rode the elevator to the 102nd floor and laboriously worked their way downward, floor by floor, searching restrooms, offices, and corridors. They abandoned the search at 1:45, having swept the world's tallest building without finding anything.

While the bomb squad was working their way down the floors, the city Board of Estimate, a council of elected officials that controlled the city budget, authorized a $25,000 reward for information leading to the bomber's conviction. The Patrolmen's Benevolent Association pledged another $1,000. It was the first time since the 1940 World's Fair bombing that the city had posted a reward. Over in the police shack the reporters laughed. The reward, they said, only made the police look more desperate.

Commissioner Kennedy chose this moment to address the press. It may be a measure of Dr. Brussel's influence that Kennedy couched his remarks in psychiatric terms, as if in deference to the field's new effect on law enforcement. "He is a killer type," Kennedy said of the bomber. "Not a mastermind but a mental defective who is under the delusion that he is a superman. He uses the bombs for a psychic kick. He needs help."

Kennedy also authorized the release to the press of a photograph of the small pocketknife found with the bomb at the Paramount Theater with an accompanying description: single two-inch blade, imitation-pearl handle, made by the Remington Arms Co., and distributed before 1950 by the Pal Razor Co. It was the fourth knife found, each by a different manufacturer. Kennedy appealed to retailers to report any information they might have about suspicious customers.

Ushers and theater custodians phoned in dozens of reports of torn or abraded seats, and the bomb squad responded accordingly. "I can't tell you how many nights I spent in theaters, opening and fluoroscoping the seats, whenever there was a rip in the upholstery," said James Falihee, a bomb squad detective.

For years the bomber's campaign had been a source of titillation for newspaper readers. Now, as 1956 came to a close, titillation turned to terror. Curiosity gave way to a sense of siege and a sinking conviction that the mighty NYPD, the largest police force in the world, might not be capable of protecting the public.

A weight of doubt and fear pressed down on the city. Headlines spoke of nuclear bomb tests and interrogations by the House Un-American Activities Committee. The more immediate fear—the visceral fear—centered on the wraith loose in the streets. Mayor Wagner's midcentury city of collective will and ambitious public undertakings succumbed to suspicion, anxiety, and, for the first time, raw fear.

"There was a lot of fear, especially in the subways," recalled Arthur Gelb of *The New York Times*. "People thought twice before taking the subway. Many people took buses because they felt the subways were where he would attack." The press began comparing the bomber to Jack the Ripper, the serial killer who, like F.P., wrote anguished, disjointed letters. It went unstated, but understood, that Scotland Yard never caught Jack.

Hours after the detonation at Fort Tilden, the *Journal-American* newsroom jumped with deadline juice. Its metabolism coursed after a day invigorated by bomber news—the fifty false alarms, the live bomb removed from the Paramount, and the arrest of a suspect who died in police custody. Editors shouted for copy. Chain-smoking rewrite men clacked away on massive manual typewriters perched on rolling stands. Copyboys ferried text to the composing room. In all the deadline bustle nobody much noticed when, at 8:10 p.m., a copyboy dropped a special delivery letter postmarked Mount Vernon, New York, on the desk of a night city editor named Richard Piperno.

Two days had passed since Berkson printed the front-page letter inviting the bomber to come forward. Since then the newsroom had held its collective breath. The mood was made more anxious by news that WNEW, the radio arm of the *Daily News,* had begun broadcasting its own cryptic appeals to the bomber at the conclusion of its hourly news summaries.

Then, out of the blue, the letter landed on Piperno's desk like the answer to a prayer. It bore F.P.'s block lettering in heavy pencil. The letter was written on a stamp-embossed, unfolded air-mail envelope, just like the two he'd sent to the *Herald Tribune*. For once, all motion stopped in the newsroom.

An hour later Commissioner Kennedy stepped into the sixth-floor newsroom and looked around like an envoy from a hostile country. As always, he wore a dark gray suit, set off by the navy-blue uniforms of the officers who trailed him like pilot fish. Police and publisher were by long habit adversaries, an authority figure and a professional questioner of authority. But circumstances now cast Kennedy and Berkson as collaborators. Seated beneath the sailfish, the two men reviewed the letter, which was incongruously written on Christmas stationery decorated with snowmen. It began with a rebuke:

TO THE JOURNAL-AMERICAN—I READ YOUR PAPER OF DEC. 26—WHERE WERE YOU PEOPLE WHEN I WAS ASKING FOR HELP? PLACING MYSELF INTO CUSTODY WOULD BE STUPID—DO NOT INSULT MY INTELLIGENCE BRING THE CON. EDISON TO JUSTICE—START WORKING ON LEHMAN-POLETTI-ANDREWS . . . THESE GENTS KNOW ALL.

The letter bore out Dr. Brussel's prediction that publishing F.P.'s profile would help lure him from the shadows. A paranoid schizophrenic could not resist the chance to correct the record and gloat over the terror he had rained down upon the hated world around him. His tone perfectly matched the personality sketched by Dr. Brussel—haughty, superior, proudly defiant. The letter suggested a psyche unbowed by remorse or tortured by doubt.

Among other things, the letter would allow the police to narrow the search window. The three men cited—former governor Herbert H. Lehman, former lieutenant governor Charles Poletti, and former state industrial commissioner Elmer Andrews—had all left office by 1942, suggesting that the bomber's grievance originated as a worker's compensation issue with Con Ed before that date.

Then F.P. proposed what he called a truce. He pledged that he would not plant any more bombs until mid-January if the *Journal-American* promised not to publish his letter until January 10:

THE METHOD OF BOMBING WILL THEN BE DIFFERENT. BEFORE I AM FINISHED THE CON EDISON CO. WILL WISH THAT THAT THEY HAD BROUGHT TO ME IN THEIR TEETH WHAT THEY CHEATED ME OUT OF. MY DAYS ON EARTH ARE NUMBERED—MOST OF MY ADULT LIFE HAS BEEN SPENT IN BED—MY ONE CONSOLATION IS—THAT I CAN STRIKE BACK—EVEN FROM MY GRAVE—FOR THE DASTARDLY ACTS AGAINST ME.

To prove that he would not be breaking his word if the police uncovered bombs during the truce, F.P. provided the locations of nine undiscovered bombs, including one in an Empire State Building phone booth that has not been found to this day. He wrote out the list as follows:

1 Broadway Paramount—center aisle (seat)
2 Penn Station—wash room
3 Times Square subway—phone booth
4 Subway train—vestibule
5 Empire State bldg.—phone booth
6 Macy Dept. store—phone booth
7 Public Library—phone booth—"found"
8 Radio City—phone booth—blew four days later "Jersey"
9 Brooklyn Paramount—under seat

In closing, he demanded that newspapers stop calling him the Mad Bomber: CALLING ME NAMES—IS JUST FRUSTRATED STUPIDITY IN ACTION.

Kennedy and Berkson read and reread the letter side by side in Berkson's office. Kennedy judged it "unquestionably genuine." Naturally Berkson was burning to declare his scoop in a banner headline blazing across the late editions. The bomber had already written angry, scornful letters to the *Herald Tribune,* but to write F.P. a letter and get a response—to engage in an actual dialogue with the serial bomber—was a triumph, a newspaperman's dream. The story would catapult the *Journal-American* to the front of the pack and hold off the tightfisted Hearst CEO, Richard Berlin, whose threats hung over the newsroom like a death sentence.

Better not, Kennedy said. The *Journal-American* would jeopardize the investigation if it published the letter before the crime lab had time to examine it and detectives could decipher its contents. Besides, F.P. would surely never write the newspaper again if it ignored his request to withhold the letter until January 10. The two men stared each other down. Berkson, by virtue of pluck and initiative, had landed a whopping exclusive, and Kennedy was telling him he couldn't print it. Berkson was not accustomed to being told what to do. In fact, he didn't need Kennedy's permission. He was free to publish whatever he wanted. But he had maneuvered himself into an accord with the police, and with F.P. He was beholden to both, and they to him. He was reluctant to blow the fragile trust for a single headline. In the end he agreed to withhold the letter from publication. "We were in the awkward position of being honorbound not to print a line about it until January tenth," Berkson said.

Meanwhile the teeming life of the newsroom persisted. Deadlines came and went. Editors with their neckties hanging loose worried over headlines for strikes and scandals, gambling raids and celebrity divorces. Reporters clattered away on their typewriters, pausing to light cigarettes or sneak sips from ninety-cent cardboard containers of beer delivered from Moochie's.

For Captain Finney, the year's end brought a brief respite. The pace of hoax calls slackened unaccountably in the final two days of 1956. For fourteen hours on December 30—from midnight to 2:05 p.m.—the city went without a scare, only to spike as New Year's approached. On the afternoon of December 30, a frigid winter Sunday in the thick of the holidays, hoaxers called in three bomb scares within twenty-one minutes. A dud was found in a grandstand phone booth at Yankee Stadium where 56,836 watched the New York Giants rout the Chicago Bears in a championship football game. Only a handful of fans noticed the bomb squad's presence, and the game continued without interruption.

Meanwhile three Continental Airline flights en route to Denver were ordered to land after a caller reported a bomb aboard. They were searched in the air, and once again on the ground. Nothing was found.

A few minutes after 3:00 p.m. a transit cop found a length of galvanized iron pipe inside a phone booth in a passageway leading from Grand Central to a subway shuttle connecting the terminal with Times Square. The bomb squad took no chances. Sergeant Dale and his men shut down the shuttle for more than two hours, rerouting thousands of passengers during the onset of rush hour. They dismantled the device to reveal only a handful of harmless graphite.

Cowering in an adjacent phone booth the police found a smiling, semicoherent little man, a thirty-seven-year-old clerk in a Bronx fruit store named Morris Ruben. He had $9.70 in dimes weighing down his pockets, along with thousands of private phone numbers, including home numbers for Mayor Wagner and Commissioner Kennedy. He admitted to phoning in a number of bomb warnings. "I always help the police," he said. "I helped them in another bomb case." He was arrested and sent to Bellevue Hospital for observation.

The phones kept ringing at police precincts over the following day. A pebble-filled flashlight tucked within a gray-and-red-striped sock was discovered in a phone booth in the Fordham Road subway station, and similar fakes turned up at the Roxy Theater, the Egyptian consulate, and a Coast Guard office. The scare calls came from as far away as Zurich, Switzerland.

On December 30, the afternoon newspapers reported that FBI agents were spotted standing among the New York detectives at the bomb scare scenes, adding to speculation that the feds might take over the case from the besieged NYPD detectives. An FBI spokesman dismissed the conjecture, saying the bureau was unlikely to enter the investigation unless a bomb was found in an airport, a train, or some other interstate location where the agency had jurisdiction. Nonetheless, Kennedy's people sounded defensive about the federal presence on their turf. "We solicit the aid and cooperation of all law enforcement agencies as well as the public and the press in this investigation," an NYPD spokesman said. "This is not a matter of seeking glory, but of stopping the actions of a man who is a menace to the city."

Through it all Berkson tried to delicately play the bomber. He quietly, gently coaxed him to continue the correspondence with a series of semisecret messages. For three days in the first week of January the *Journal-American* published the same unmarked overture hidden among dozens of notices of union meetings and lost cats in the announcements section. It was signed "C.D." for city desk:

> We received your letter. We appreciate truce. What were you deprived of? We want to hear your views and help you. We will keep our word. Contact us same way as previously.

The message was like Morse code transmitted to a faraway ship. It was sent out into the world in hopes of finding its intended audience. Thousands of readers might see the communiqué. Berkson could only hope that the bomber was among them. On those anxious days he sat beneath the sailfish, his oxford shirt crisply folded twice below the elbow, hoping for a response.

CHAPTER ELEVEN

THE TRUCE

January 1957

ALL EYES RESTED UNEASILY ON THE NYPD AS THE MANHUNT STRETCHED into mid-January of 1957. More than a month had passed since Commissioner Kennedy opened the investigation files to the press. The resulting publicity had led the bomb squad to spend weeks chasing down copycat calls while the real bomber planned his next moves with impunity. The police looked more hapless by the day.

From behind his imposing mahogany desk on the second floor of the Centre Street headquarters, Commissioner Kennedy commanded a police force like no other—23,000 patrolmen, 5 helicopters, and a cavalry of 259 horses. This street army was trained to uphold the civic order. But the bully force of nightstick and revolver had proven useless in the face of madness and terror. After sixteen years and boxes of carefully cataloged physical evidence—pocketknives, powder samples, letters—the bomber was still faceless. "For all we know," said a detective, "the person we're looking for is a blonde who lives on Park Avenue."

Mayor Wagner's New York, the city that embodied America's better self, the highest hopes of a progressive-minded postwar society, a city of public education and fresh starts for immigrants and refugees, was reduced to gnawing anxiety. Neighbor looked on neighbor with mistrust.

Meanwhile, F.P., in his long defiance of authority, had come to seem like an almost-sympathetic figure—an underdog who defied the exalted NYPD. It was hard not to root for him, at least a little, as one might root for Butch Cassidy. By design or not, he played the role of antihero, the kind of subversive figure that caught Hollywood's notice, particularly in the conformist 1950s. "All those bomb-scare headlines obviously have impressed the powers at Twentieth Century Fox," wrote *The New York Times* in its announcement that the studio would rush a feature film called *The Mad Bomber of New York City* into production. Within a week *The New Yorker* answered with an unsigned article by a staff writer who wanted to return a pepper shaker to Lord & Taylor but stayed in his office for fear that guards would mistake his package for a bomb. "By now, we suppose, every New Yorker worth his salt has his own bomb, or bomb-hoax, story, and Fox is welcome to ours, if it can just come up with a suitable ending."

Fortunately for Commissioner Kennedy, no bombs would explode in the coming days. In his letter to the *Journal-American,* the bomber had granted a truce, a bomb-free hiatus, to end on some unspecified mid-January date. However welcome it might be, the truce came with a cost: it brought added pressure to catch F.P. before the truce expired. His letter had warned, ominously, that when he resumed, "the method of bombing will then be different." Different could only mean bigger, and deadlier. Now was the time for an all-out push to capture F.P.

Kennedy's first move was to disregard an important aspect of Dr. Brussel's advice. The psychiatrist had warned that the bomber lived well north of New York City, most likely in Connecticut, where Slavic enclaves had formed around mills and manufacturing. By early January detectives had concluded that the bomber lived not in Connecticut, but in Westchester County—more specifically White Plains, the county seat, where F.P. had postmarked six of his letters. They based their assumption on a small but significant difference in dialect. In canvassing plumbing supply stores the police had found that New York plumbers called a short stretch of galvanized connecting pipe *line pipe coupling*. In Westchester, just fifteen miles north of Manhattan, the same item was known as *well-coupling*. The bomber had used *well-coupling* in his letters.

The police believed—or hoped, anyway—that the discrepancy in terminology had led them to the bomber's hometown, or at least his county. So on January 3, bomb squad detective Michael Lynch gathered seventy-five police officials from thirty-nine Westchester police departments at the columned, foursquare Westchester County Office Building in White Plains to announce that the search was shifting to their precincts. In the following days an occupying army of New York cops fanned out among Mount Vernon, Rye, and other Westchester towns to check the handwriting of 357,000 driver's license applications; 26,000 court files; 150,000 jury lists; 20,000 pistol permits; 15,000 supreme court cases; and 9,000 judgments in the Westchester County Clerk's Office. In addition, the police cunningly obtained handwriting samples from all Con Ed employees living in Westchester by asking them to fill out bogus civil defense forms.

Thirty veteran detectives enrolled in a refresher course at the police academy were abruptly pulled out of a lecture and ordered to Westchester to help with the search. Their reassignment led to speculation within the police shack that an arrest was imminent. The *World-Telegram and Sun* wrote that "a new lead had triggered the outburst of police action. High police sources attempted to quash the rumor, but the unprecedented manner in which the detectives were corralled for the hunt seemed to indicate some sudden and urgent development."

Patrick Doyle, Put-Put Passant, and the other residents of the police shack waited for the break. They stationed themselves on the street so as to grill police brass exiting headquarters, and they worked their sources in the police ranks. But the break never came. Instead, a discreet paper chase commenced in sparsely furnished courthouse cubicles and municipal back rooms throughout the county. Huddles of men in shirtsleeves sat among disposable coffee cups, half-eaten sandwiches, and overfilled ashtrays. They leafed through hundreds of thousands of appeal notices, affidavits, foreclosure forms, arraignments, and bail postings. Card by card, sheet by sheet, they checked the forms against samples of the bomber's handwriting with its *R*'s made in a continuous cursive with a little loop in the center, Y's that looked like a V with a serif flourish, G's ending in double horizontal bars. "That German G," one detective said, "you couldn't miss that anywhere." It was tedious, exacting, eye-glazing work. The hunt proceeded like a marathon game of bingo, with men singing out when they found a match.

Within three days investigators turned up several hundred possible matches. They delivered samples of each suspect's handwriting to the crime lab, where Joe McNally and other handwriting experts whittled the suspect pool to forty-two. They opened files on each man, and a small infantry of detectives, working in shifts, trailed all forty-two, day and night. Unmarked police cruisers with supplies of deli coffee and dough-nuts perched on dashboards conducted all-night vigils outside the suspects' homes in Scarsdale and New Rochelle, Pound Ridge and Tarrytown. Plainclothesmen surveilled from a discrete distance as suspects walked to Mount Kisco diners and Bronxville groceries. One by one alibis or ex-culpatory information disqualified suspects from the list until, finally, none were left to follow.

Still the search continued. College students who had placed orders with chemistry suppliers for explosive powders used in laboratory experi-ments were questioned, and cleared. Because F.P. had written that his "days on earth are numbered" and most of his "adult life has been spent in bed," the police asked Westchester hospitals and clinics to watch out for men who matched Dr. Brussel's profile.

On the evening of January 10, the police learned of a sixty-seven-year-old widower, Andrew Kleewen, who had died from bronchial pneumo-nia at Fordham Hospital in the Bronx three days earlier. Kleewen roughly matched Dr. Brussel's criteria: He was a retired Latvian machinist with a gravelly accent and high-flown grudges who had lived alone in the Bronx near the Westchester border since the death of his wife five months ear-lier. Detectives knew from a job application that he was six feet tall and two hundred pounds—roughly the size Dr. Brussel had anticipated. Klee-wen's pneumonia would explain the bomber's contention in his last letter that his "days on earth are numbered."

NYPD patrolmen examine debris after a bomb shattered lockers in Grand Central Terminal on May 6, 1953. The blast thundered through the corridor at 4:45 p.m., just as crowds of commuters were making their way home. (John Rooney/AP)

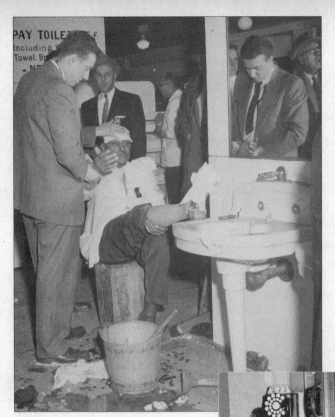

Doctors treated Lloyd Hill, washroom attendant, after a bomb exploded in a Penn Station toilet on February 21, 1956. He limped with a cane for the rest of his life. (*World Telegraph & Sun* Collection Library of Congress)

On December 30, 1956, a detective removed a fake bomb from a telephone booth in a subway station adjacent to Grand Central Terminal, one of dozens of false alarms complicating the manhunt. (Edward Hausner/*The New York Times*/Redux)

ABOVE: On December 27, 1956, bomb squad detectives carried an unexploded bomb from Grand Central Terminal and loaded it into Big Bertha, a flatbed truck rigged with a protective canopy of woven steel cable left over from the construction of the Brooklyn Bridge. (Neal Boenzi/*The New York Times*/Redux)

LEFT: Seymour Berkson, publisher of the *New York Journal-American*, with his wife, the fashion publicist Eleanor Lambert, and their son, Bill. Berkson's correspondence with the mystery bomber helped lure him from the shadows. (Bill Berkson)

After examining the evidence, psychiatrist James A. Brussel predicted that the bomber was a Slavic middle-aged man with a history of workplace disputes. He would be unmarried, and living with an older female relative. Lastly, Brussel guessed that the bomber would be wearing a double-breasted suit when arrested. Brussel is widely credited with conducting the first case of criminal profiling. (*New York Daily News* via Getty Images)

Police Commissioner Stephen P. Kennedy, known as New York's toughest cop, briefed police shack reporters on the manhunt. After years of keeping investigative details secret, he reversed himself. He began sharing what the police knew, in hopes that the public might provide a breakthrough. (Meyer Liebowitz/*The New York Times*/Redux)

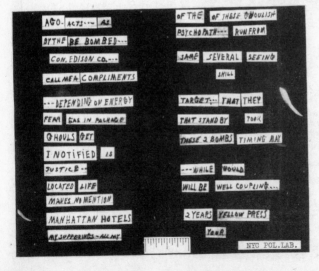

In desperation, the NYPD crime lab pasted snippets of the bomber's letters on a sheet of paper and distributed copies to newspapers with a plea for readers to notify a precinct house if they recognized the odd block letters. (New York City Municipal Archives)

After years of setbacks, dead ends, and frustration, bomb squad detectives arrested George Metesky at his home in the middle of the night. (Left to right: Detectives Richard Rowan, Edward Lehane, James Martin, and Michael Lynch.) (Al Ravenna/*World Telegram & Sun* Collection/Library of Congress)

George Metesky lived with two unmarried sisters on the first floor of this house in the rundown Brooklyn neighborhood of Waterbury, Connecticut. Neighbors called it "the crazy house." (Ed Ford/*World Telegram & Sun* Collection/Library of Congress)

Detectives found pipe sections, copper wire, batteries, and other bomb components hidden behind a laundry sink in Metesky's home. (Al Revenna/*World-Telegram & Sun* Collection/ Library of Congress)

Watchful neighbors had noticed that Metesky spent long stretches alone in the corrugated tin garage behind his house, and that he always locked the door on his way out. The windows were frosted to prevent snooping. (Ed Ford/*World–Telegram & Sun* Collection/ Library of Congress)

Metesky, flanked by Mike Lynch of the NYPD bomb squad (left) and Waterbury Police Captain Ernest Pakul (right) at the Waterbury police headquarters during his booking on January 22, 1957. The next day's newspapers would report that the Mad Bomber, who terrorized New York for years, looked like a church deacon or small-town clerk. (Phil Stanziola/*World-Telegram & Sun Collection*/Library of Congress)

Metesky behind bars in the Waterbury police station. During interrogation he became eagerly forthcoming, sharing information about himself like a keen job applicant. (Al Revenna/*World-Telegram & Sun* Collection/Library of Congress)

Reporters and press photographers stood five deep as detectives led Metesky from a police cruiser at New York headquarters. "The face might have been that of a successful political candidate or a winner of a Nobel Prize," Dr. James Brussel would write. (*The New York Times*/Redux)

Metesky's defense lawyer, James D.C. Murray, was known as the champion of lost causes. He was a gentle, grandfatherly figure who had represented a procession of public enemies — rapists, kidnappers, mobsters, crooked cops, and more than one hundred accused murderers. (*World-Telegram & Sun* Collection/Library of Congress)

A judge committed Metesky to Matteawan State Hospital, an upstate asylum for the criminally insane, where he spent sixteen years without a jury trial. (New York State

When police entered the dead man's three-room walk-up apartment in a drab postwar brick building near Van Cortlandt Park, they found ample evidence of a disordered mind. A mad clutter of newspaper clippings littered the floors and kitchen countertops. Two entire bureaus spilled hospital receipts and other detritus. The heaps contained copies of unhinged letters complaining of elaborate, fantastical injustices mailed to Secretary of State John Foster Dulles, Mayor Wagner, and other public figures.

When police found a stash of Con Ed bills dating back twenty-five years, they called Captain Finney. It looked for a moment as if his man had finally been found. Kleewen's handwriting had some of the same European characteristics as F.P.'s, but the resemblance was not strong enough to satisfy Joe McNally, the handwriting expert. McNally's doubts, and the absence of any pipes or bomb-making gear, obliged Captain Finney to strike Kleewen from the suspect list.

In his letter to the *Journal-American,* F.P. had indicated that Lehman, Poletti, and Andrews knew about his grievance, but the three former state officials could not recall anything that would distinguish his case from the thousands of other disputes that had crossed their desks. When pressed, Andrews, the former state industrial commissioner, remembered that in the late 1930s he had fired a security guard in the New York office of the Workmen's Compensation Board for being drunk and discourteous. When Andrews refused the guard's appeal for reinstatement, he became "a little deranged," Andrews said.

"I'll get even for this," the man shouted on his way out. "You'll never forget this."

The guard was a suspect for other reasons as well: He was of German descent and had previously worked for Con Ed. The utility had fired him for repeatedly showing up drunk.

Andrews told detectives he recalled that the guard lived in Haverstraw, a town in Rockland County, just across the Hudson River from Westchester. Two decades had elapsed since the incident, but Captain Kennedy dispatched a team of twenty-five policemen to find the guard. They knocked on doors and checked registries. In the end they could find no trace of him.

On January 14, the coldest stretch of weather in two years swept into New York City. The thermometer hit 3.1 degrees that morning, a record for the date. Patches of ice covered the cobbled stretch of Poplar Street. From his third-story window in the crime lab Captain Finney could see icicles hanging from the scaffolding on the undercarriage of the Brooklyn Bridge. It was the grimmest of winters. Captain Finney still had no viable suspect, and time was running out. "For all we know, we may have had him in for questioning," a police official said. "Any man clever enough to have eluded detection for sixteen years is certainly clever enough not to give himself away."

F.P. had granted a moratorium—in his words, a truce—that would last until mid-January, or as long as he chose to honor it. Kennedy and Berkson, unlikely allies, were uncomfortably aware that any affront might disrupt the fragile peace and return F.P. to action. Cultivating F.P.'s trust presented a particular problem for Berkson, who planned, after an awkward delay, to publish F.P.'s letter to the *Journal-American*. If the bomber saw the newspaper as exploiting their correspondence, he might decide to end their agreement.

As the January days ticked by, Berkson paced the newsroom, fretting that another newspaper might catch wind of the correspondence before he could publish F.P.'s letter. His fear was realized when Richard Starnes, managing editor of the *World-Telegram and Sun,* the *Journal-American*'s afternoon rival and long-standing adversary, spotted Berkson's message to F.P. half-hidden among the dark columns of personal ads. Starnes shrewdly recognized a scoop. Working the phone, he found an obliging police source who confirmed that the *Journal-American* was waiting to publish a letter sent by the bomber. On the afternoon of January 7, the headline "Mad Bomber's Letter Hints Brief Truce" ran on the front page of the *World-Telegram and Sun.* The accompanying article dropped the bombshell: an unnamed "New York newspaper" was corresponding with F.P. The article said that police believed the letter to be genuine, and it quoted the *Journal-American*'s secret message in full. "The paper that received [the letter]," the police source said, "is still trying to make contact with the bomber again."

Berkson found himself in the infuriating position of standing by while his primary rival snatched the most precious scoop of his career. To make matters worse, a pack of other newspapers jumped on the story. The *Journal-American* had to scramble to keep up with the coverage of its own letter.

As if that weren't frustration enough, the fragile trust Berkson had forged with F.P. was all but shattered by an article written in his own newsroom that quoted a police official describing the bomber as "a psychopathic enemy of society." Whether editors printed the article with Berkson's approval is not known. Berkson was the publisher, not the editor. He therefore stood at a slight remove from the story lineups and copy flow. The article may have made its way into print without his knowledge. Whatever the case, F.P. took it as a form of betrayal. He responded with outrage in a letter that landed in the newsroom four days later:

> . . . YOU INSIST UPON POISONING THE MINDS OF PEOPLE AGAINST ME—YOU PUT ME IN THE WORST POSITION—DELIBERATELY—THEN YOU ASK THAT I CONFIDE IN YOU—I HAVE BEEN BETRAYED ONCE AGAIN—I DO NOT TRUST YOU—YOU HAVE THE CHOICE OF PLACING THE MAIN CONTENTS OF THE LETTER I SENT YOU BEFORE THE PUBLIC—OR YOU HAD BETTER HAVE A VERY GOOD REASON FOR NOT DOING SO . . . YOUR TIME IS RUNNING OUT—ARE YOU GOING TO TELL THE TRUTH OR WILL YOU BETRAY THE PEOPLE—I WILL BUY A PAPER ON THURSDAY—THE RESPONSIBILITY IS YOURS.

The *Journal-American* article, and the bomber's angry response, raised fears that he would resume bombing immediately. On the evening of January 9, Commissioner Kennedy made his second emergency visit to the *Journal-American* office. Once again he huddled with Berkson beneath the sailfish. By midnight they had reached an agreement: since the *World-Telegram and Sun* had broken the news of F.P.'s letter, Berkson would now publish it with the exception of passages that Kennedy redacted. The next day's *Journal-American* contained a photograph of the bomber's original letter beneath the headline "The Mad Bomber Writes!"

The *Journal-American* newsroom had received a steady stream of letters claiming to be from F.P. To throw forgers off, Berkson shrewdly asked his art department to alter the bomber's letter in its published form so that pencil lines looked like ink and readers could not tell that the letter was written on an unfolded air-mail envelope. Disguising these traits made it easier for the watchful mail-room clerks to weed out the counterfeits.

Berkson published F.P.'s original letter to the *Journal-American* above the fold, accompanied by a second open letter back to him written by Berkson himself and edited by Commissioner Kennedy, inviting F.P. to elaborate on his grievances. Every scrap of information they could get the bomber to divulge would help the police narrow the search window:

> Please make yourself clear enough for us to understand. We cannot help you air your grievances unless you help us ascertain what they are. . . . We realize, too, that time is running out on our chances to be in touch with each other. You will get best results by answering quickly.

More than 757,000 readers bought that day's edition of the *Journal-American,* including F.P. If he was antagonized by the headline referring to him as the Mad Bomber, he didn't show it. Two days later F.P. dropped his response into a White Plains mailbox:

> I WAS INJURED ON THE JOB AT A CONSOLIDATED EDISON PLANT––AS
> A RESULT I AM ADJUDGED––TOTALLY––PERMANENTLY DISABLED––I

DID NOT RECEIVE ANY AID—OF ANY KIND FROM COMPANY—THAT I DID NOT PAY FOR MYSELF—WHILE FIGHTING FOR MY LIFE.

He went on to provide details of his compensation claims:

I INSISTED ON "HEARINGS"—MY CASE WAS MARKED "CLOSED" 4 TIMES—THE CON. EDISON KEPT INSISTING THAT I PLACE MY CLAIM BEFORE WORKMAN'S COMPENSATION—THAT THEY CON ED WOULD NOT BLOCK ANY EFFORT ON MY PART TO GET COMPENSATION—THEY BLOCKED MY EVERY EFFORT—THEY EVEN TRIED WITH PERJURERS

Then the letter swelled with anger:

I TYPED TENS OF THOUSANDS OF WORDS (ABOUT 800,000)—NOBODY CARED—I GOT A SAMPLE OF WHAT YOU CALL "OUR AMERICAN SYS-TEM OF JUSTICE". . . YOU PEOPLE ASK ME TO SURRENDER MYSELF—WELL SIR—WHO IS REALLY GUILTY—YOU OR I?

He closed on a conciliatory note, extending the truce another few weeks. "A lot depends on what can be done by March 1st by you people," he warned.

Dr. Brussel had predicted that anonymity would eventually frustrate the bomber: "He had conceived himself as God and over the years he had grown more and more frustrated by the need to conceal himself. He wanted to dominate the world, wanted it to know who he was."

The bomber's letters seemed to be proving Dr. Brussel right. F.P. clearly yearned for people to admire his cleverness and moral superiority. He could not resist sharing bits of his background and biography. His second letter, for example, mentioned that Con Ed had invited him to file an appeal with the Workmen's Compensation Board. In each letter he re-vealed a little more about himself. In doing so he brought the manhunt a little closer to his door.

But did F.P. reveal enough to be caught? Detectives didn't know for sure that F.P. had worked for Con Ed. He might have worked for a sub-contractor, or one of the subsidiaries that Con Ed had acquired. If that was the case, the Con Ed files would be of no use. With that possibility in mind, a search began in the almost impossibly vast files of the Immigration and Naturalization Service for citizenship papers and alien registration records matching F.P.'s handwriting.

Berkson published a slightly abbreviated version of F.P.'s second letter on January 15, along with a third letter back asking F.P. for more particulars about the compensation case, ostensibly so that a new, more equitable hearing might be arranged:

> We want to help you, but can only do so if the partial portrait of injustice you have begun to paint is brought into sharper focus. Once it is, we promise to tell your full story to the world. If you have been cheated, as you point out, we will procure the best counsel to aid you. . . . If you can give us further details and dates we are assured by competent legal authority that your case can indeed be reopened with a fair and just hearing of all the evidence you have. We know you will keep your word. We will keep ours.

F.P. had written the second letter, like the first, on a No. 8 envelope that unfolded to double as stationery. It was postmarked White Plains with a special delivery stamp. The day after the second letter arrived, Paul Schoenstein sent a reporter named Douglas Hearle to the White Plains post office. Hearle found a clerk named Donald Caputi who said he'd sold an envelope of that kind, along with a special delivery stamp, to a middle-aged man on the day F.P. mailed the letter. The customer was a "big, smiling man with a jolly air," Caputi said. "He was wearing a gray fedora and a dark topcoat. He had a round face and he was in his fifties."

The customer's age and features matched Dr. Brussel's profile.

Schoenstein alerted the police, and they rushed Caputi to Centre Street police headquarters, where he spent hours looking through photographs of criminals in a room known as the rogues' gallery. He leafed through hundreds of photos of middle-aged arsonists, anarchists, and murderers without finding a match. A police artist then sketched a plump-cheeked postal customer with a brimmed hat and eyeglasses based on Caputi's description. "We never did quite make it," Caputi said. "But we came very close, and at least police knew approximately what the man looked like."

Even with the police sketch, Commissioner Kennedy concluded that his detectives might never catch the bomber—unless he wanted to be caught, as Dr. Brussel had suggested. "As matters stand," a police official said, "he has a much better chance of finding us than we have of finding him." With that in mind, the *Journal-American*'s letter ended with an invitation to "present your case in person."

The helping hand Berkson extended to the bomber was not false, at least not entirely. Like a hostage negotiator, Berkson was both manipulator and confidant. He intended to make good on his promise of "the most scientific medical care" and "top legal counsel" while continuing to draw bits of revealing information from F.P.

With the help of police contacts, Berkson secured a pledge from Isador R. Lubin, the New York industrial commissioner, that he would grant a review of F.P.'s case. "If an injustice has been done to this person by the Department of Labor," Lubin wrote in a letter published on the front page of the *Journal-American* on January 15. "I will do everything in my power to see it rectified." Lubin ordered state workers to begin combing through the roughly two hundred thousand compensation cases a year dating all the way back to 1914, a search of herculean proportions. A race of sorts was now under way between Con Ed and the state to see who could find a match first.

The January 15 edition of the *Journal-American* also contained a letter from Con Ed president Harland Forbes addressed to Berkson saying that "examination of our records yields no clue to the identity of

'F.P.'" Forbes stated that he would welcome more information, including the date of the injury. "We wish to assure 'F.P.,'" Forbes wrote, "that we will make a thorough and impartial reappraisal if we have some facts to work on."

By now the correspondence between the *Journal-American* and F.P. gripped the newspaper's readers like a real-life noir novel, complete with a thrillingly uncertain ending. Danger at proximity incited panic. But danger at a distance was entertainment. New Yorkers lived in suspense, waiting to see how F.P. would respond to the *Journal-American*'s latest letter. The topic was constantly discussed at bodega counters and on rattling subways. From Red Hook to Riverdale, the city held its collective breath, awaiting the outcome.

It felt to everyone as if a resolution was at hand. A letter containing F.P.'s handwriting, or a fair approximation, arrived at the *Journal-American* to say that he would give himself up at the far end of the Coney Island boardwalk at 2:30 p.m. on January 18. A reporter and a photographer waited with a band of police all afternoon in a freezing rain. Six inches of snow had fallen a day earlier, and the biting ocean wind blew it in swirls down the boardwalk. Nobody showed. The police dismissed the overture as another in the long series of hoaxes.

The next day, a Saturday, a third letter from the bomber, this one authentic, arrived at the *Journal-American* city desk with a crucial bit of missing information: F.P.'s injury, he said, occurred on September 5, 1931.

I HAD TO LIE COLD ON THE CONCRETE. LATER PNEUMONIA. THREE MONTHS LATER T.B. . . . I DO NOT GO OUT EVERY DAY, AND IN THE COURSE OF A WEEK I AVERAGE AT LEAST 16 HOURS A DAY IN BED.

He ended his letter by saying that he might take Berkson's suggestion:

THINK THAT A FACE TO FACE MEETING COULD BE FIGURED OUT AS THERE ARE SO MANY THINGS THAT COULD THEN BE FREELY DISCUSSED.

F.P. had lived a concealed life for sixteen years. Editors and rewrite men at their black metal desks now went about their daily tasks with the electrifying awareness that the bomber could walk out of the shadows and into the *Journal-American*'s smoky newsroom at any moment to clasp hands with his correspondents. The schizophrenic was all but at their door.

CHAPTER TWELVE

THE DEAD FILES

January 1957

IN THE EARLY MORNING OF JANUARY 20, A UNIFORMED POLICE OFFICER drove Commissioner Kennedy in a city-owned Cadillac from his modest Bayside home, with its scruffy rose garden and downstairs rental flat, to Seymour Berkson's Fifth Avenue address. Kennedy stepped from the elevator on the eleventh floor and entered another world—an apartment with formal French furniture, a pair of maids' rooms, a Salvador Dalí watercolor, and a wood bust of Berkson's wife, Eleanor Lambert, carved by the sculptor Isamu Noguchi.

Berkson sat down with Kennedy in a book-lined library overlooking the Central Park reservoir, where the two men, boxer and reporter by background, planned the manhunt's endgame. The biographical details conveyed in F.P.'s letters had brought the first hope that the two men might identify the bomber, but he could easily slip away if they made a clumsy move.

Dr. Brussel had predicted that F.P. would ache to share his story of martyrdom and vengeance with the world. Berkson and Kennedy played to that inclination as they composed a letter urging him to give himself up. "We feel as you do that we have established a bond of mutual trust," they wrote. "It is on that basis we urge you now to come forward to avail yourself of the opportunity for justice offered you. . . . You can decide where, how and when to meet us. . . . Please write us in the same manner as previously, outlining the procedure you would like to follow for the face-to-face meeting."

The letter would never be published.

The police had by now reluctantly concluded that Westchester was a dead end. While Berkson and Kennedy played their trust games with F.P., and each other, the massive behind-the-scenes paper chase shifted to the Con Ed offices in New York. F.P.'s successive letters had contained critical details of his personal history—his injury as a Con Ed employee, his frustrated fight for workman's compensation, his infirmity with pneumonia and tuberculosis. Investigators narrowed their search accordingly.

By mid-January they confined themselves to the rows of beige filing cabinets at a Con Ed warehouse at 157 Hester Street, in lower Manhattan, containing the "dead files," compensation cases of former employees now closed for good. A few years earlier Con Ed had claimed no knowledge of this archive. The police picked their way through all sixty thousand files looking for employees with the initials F.P., and for characteristics that matched Dr. Brussel's description.

The dead files contained paperwork dating back to 1940. A thirty-four man police detail finished searching by the morning of January 18. That afternoon Lieutenant Herbert Schenkler, the detective leading the paper hunt, called Con Ed and asked to see the older employee files, from 1930s. Con Ed insisted that files dated prior to 1940 no longer existed.

In reality, Con Ed was hiding them, possibly because they contained embarrassing information about injury and illness caused by air quality at the company's plants. The company had removed one thousand files marked "troublesome" to a set of filing cabinets housed on the second floor of their Irving Place headquarters, where they could examine them without police meddling. Four Con Ed clerks and a supervisor had begun a secret review of the files on January 15, the day the *Journal-American* published the bomber's second letter. They had about two hundred files to go when the police began asking for the files on the afternoon of Friday, January 18.

At 4:20 p.m., forty minutes before the workweek's end, a Con Ed clerk named Alice Kelly saw the keywords "injustice" and "permanent disability" scrawled in red ink at the top of a file. The paperwork inside looked unremarkable at first; it contained the same application forms and claim letters found in hundreds of other files. Scanning the contents, she noted that the company had hired a George Metesky as a generator wiper in 1929 at the Hell Gate power plant in the Bronx at a salary of $37.50 a week. A boiler explosion had injured him on September 5, 1931. He was dropped from payroll a year later and submitted a compensation claim in 1934.

The file contained six of Metesky's letters, none of which sounded sinister or violent until Con Ed rejected his appeal in 1936. At that point his tone turned menacing. In one letter he threatened to "take justice into my own hands" for Con Ed's "dastardly deeds." Kelly recognized the stilted, belligerent phrases.

"As I pulled this typewritten letter, I knew I had something," she later said. "I saw some words that I had seen in the *Journal-American*. These words indicated that the writer intended to do something about injustices."

She read the letters through a second time. "I think we have it," she shouted to three nearby clerks. They gathered around her to read the rest of the file over her shoulders.

Kelly turned the letter over to her supervisor, Herbert Schrank, a compensation manager, saying, "This is it."

Shrank read it through and agreed, "Yes. This is it." He then read parts of the file over the phone to Lieutenant Schenkler. Unaccountably, Schenkler did not fetch the file that afternoon. Instead he and a team of detectives debated whether Metesky warranted investigation. He matched Dr. Brussel's profile in several respects, but after years of embarrassing false steps, the detectives were wary of chasing down another false lead. They decided to gather more information.

According to the file, Metesky lived in Waterbury, an industrial city of one hundred thousand in western Connecticut. The next morning Captain Finney called the Connecticut Motor Vehicle Bureau to request a photocopy of any license or car registration found in Metesky's name.

The clerk could find none. Three hours later the detectives sent a Teletype message to the Waterbury Police Department asking for a "discreet check" on George Metesky of 17 Fourth Street. In police circles a Teletype implied a medium-level priority; if the NYPD was convinced that Metesky was F.P., they would have phoned.

The request came to Captain Ernest Pakul, a chief of detectives with generous lips and a broad face that squeezed itself into a squint as if he were biting a lemon. He could find no Metesky listed at that address, though there was a George Milauskas. Pakul suspected it was the same man. Lithuanians living in Waterbury's poorest neighborhoods often Americanized their names without bothering to change the official record. He sent Detective Paul Salvatore to snoop around under the pretext of investigating a hit-and-run.

Manufacturing had provided Waterbury with a modest measure of industrial prosperity. From hulking redbrick factories bound by the slopes of the Naugatuck Valley came brass screws, washers, buttons, buckles, cocktail shakers, and a popular $1 pocket watch. The city sold itself as "the brass capital of the world."

Detective Salvatore could find no sign of prosperity at 17 Fourth Street, a sagging three-story home near the top of a short, steep hill. The house was like a vagrant trying to look presentable, with sloping floors and ragged triple-decker porches propped up by squat white columns. The patch of lawn consisted of neatly mown weeds. The mailbox beside the house had both names—Milauskas and Metesky—thereby confirming Pakul's hunch. It was later suggested that a teacher afflicted with a stutter had provisionally changed George's name to Metesky when she stumbled over Milauskas. He permanently adopted the new version because it sounded more American.

The house was in Brooklyn, a downtrodden neighborhood cut off from the rest of Waterbury by the murky Naugatuck River. It was named after the New York borough; like its namesake, it lay across a bridge from the center of town. There, on the wrong side of the Naugatuck, the promise of middle-class America lay tantalizingly close but forever beyond reach. Generations of immigrants had toiled without advancement. Grime smeared warehouse windows. Factory smoke hung in the air. Trash tumbled across unshaded yards. Buckled sidewalks gave way to pitted paths. Laundry flapped on lines strung across lots where weeds grew high and fences wanted mending. Unemployed workers smoked on street corners. Brooklyn was a long way from the Connecticut of well-heeled commuters and country roads lined with picturesque stone walls.

Detective Salvatore walked among treeless streets and rickety buildings asking passersby about George Metesky. Neighbors described him as an invalid and a loner who resided in the weather-beaten house with his spinster sisters. In Brooklyn it was known as "the crazy house." Residents considered the family cold and peculiar.

At 4:37 that afternoon Pakul teletyped the NYPD to report that a chronically ill unmarried man lived at that address with his two sisters. Acquaintances described him as "strange" and "aloof" with a history of run-ins. Finney could see that the description exactly matched Dr. Brussel's profile.

At 9:00 a.m. on Monday, January 21, Detective Bertram Scott, a ten-year police veteran and former marine, finally picked up the Metesky compensation file that Alice Kelly had found three days earlier. On the ten-minute return trip to Centre Street headquarters, he read through the material with growing certainty.

"This sounds an awful lot like our man," he told Deputy Chief Captain Edward Bynes.

Within the hour they had found the clincher: Con Ed's Metesky file listed his date of injury as September 5, 1931, the same date cited by F.P. in his third letter to the *Journal-American*. He must have known that the date was a crucial bit of evidence, but he chose to disclose it anyway. He was, Dr. Brussel wrote, "like a supremely confident boxer who, jeering at a weaker opponent, momentarily drops his guard and offers his chin, daring the opponent to try for the kill."

CHAPTER THIRTEEN

FAIR PLAY

January 1957

AT 3:00 P.M. ON JANUARY 21, SIX HOURS AFTER DETECTIVE BERTRAM Scott obtained the George Metesky file from Con Ed, three bomb squad detectives left Poplar Street in an unmarked police cruiser for the eighty-mile trip to Waterbury, where they would lay the groundwork for an arrest. They were led by a tall, lean-faced detective, Mike Lynch, who had departed so hastily that he still wore a plaid shirt from home under his obligatory gray suit. A gray fedora with a black band was pushed back on his head.

Captain Pakul waited for them in the Waterbury police station, a sparse suite of rooms in the back of a Georgian city hall. While the detectives drove north, Pakul continued his probe. He began by asking a relative who lived across the street from Metesky to describe his neighbor. The answer was "eccentric" and "queer."

The neighbor explained that Metesky and his unmarried older sisters, Anna and Mae, occupied the ground floor of the crudely painted three-story home. Boarders rented the two floors above them, though none stayed long. The sisters shut off the tenants' water if they squandered too much on laundering or mopping floors. Televisions had to be turned off by 10:00 p.m. When a tenant's mother died, the Meteskys denied the bereaved the use of the house's front staircase. The coffin had to be carried out the back way, the same as the trash. The sisters banned kids from play-ing in the yard, and they met tenants with a scowl while compulsively sweeping the porch and dusting the picket fence George had built in front of the house. "I'd knock on the front door and hand them the check," a tenant said. "They'd take it and slam the door on my face."

Mrs. DiChiara, who lived next door, once had houseguests with a baby. Every day she would wash the diapers and hang them on an out-door laundry line. "The day the baby and her mother left, the diapers disappeared from the line," she said. "One of the sisters, noticing this, said to me over the fence, 'You must have dug a hole and buried the baby.' She wasn't joking, either."

When a black woman named Alice McDaniel moved nearby, the Meteskys threatened her family. "He and his two sisters came up on my porch and shouted at us through the door that they hated us because we were colored and because we had children," she said. "He was especially mean and vicious. He wanted us to move, or else."

The house Metesky and his sisters occupied was built in 1924 by their father, George Milauskas, a Lithuanian immigrant who worked as a night watchman in a Waterbury lumberyard. Stolid and broad shoul-dered, he was a hard worker with steadfast principles and the fortitude to back them up.

"Gangs used to break into the lumberyard," an acquaintance said, and the father "would go right after them, eight or ten at a time. He was all guts. He'd chase them, too."

His wife, Anna Mary Buraitis, never learned to speak English, and she adapted only grudgingly to American life. She doted on George, her youngest. When she died, her two daughters, Anna and Mae, pampered their baby brother as their mother had. They never got married, never raised families of their own. Instead, they plodded along at menial jobs in a buckle factory and brass mill. At home they mended and remended the same outdated dresses, sacrificing so that they could indulge their brother, who lay at home racked with coughs.

The Metesky family's grim bearing had become neighborhood lore.

The more daring local children, with some parental encouragement, snuck close enough to peer in the windows, hoping to glimpse satanic masses and other sinister doings. One winter day two girls inched their way up to the house. Anna burst from the front door brandishing what the girls later described as a wand. The Waterbury Lithuanians were only a generation removed from the Gypsy superstitions of home. Their darkest suspicions were confirmed when one of the girls contracted the mumps the next day. A week later her friend slipped on an icy patch and broke her thumb.

Metesky sent reams of letters to neighboring parents complaining of nosy children. One fall afternoon two ten-year-olds were playing football when their ball bounced away. It skittered down Fourth Street and rolled along the packed-dirt Metesky driveway, coming to a rest near the corrugated-tin garage behind the home. Neither boy wanted to fetch it, given the family's reputation. "You get it," Jimmy said. "You threw it."

"Yeah, but you were supposed to catch it," Nick answered. "You get it."

The boys crept down the driveway together. They were almost within reach of the ball when George Metesky stepped between them and the ball.

The impassive face he normally offered acquaintances was contorted with rage. "What are you boys doing? Spying? Spying, are you?"

The neighbors noticed that Metesky spent hours alone in his garage nearly every day. They could hear the *clank clank* of metal tools, and they noted that he always locked the doors on his way out. He had equipped the garage with six small smoked-glass windows, so nobody could see in. What, they wondered, could he possibly be up to? "I hear him out in that garage of his, pounding, pounding away, like he was hitting some kind of metal with a hammer," a neighbor said. "Only he never seems to actually make anything out there. He never brings anything out."

Notes on Captain Pakul's reconnaissance were waiting for the three New York detectives when they pulled into the Waterbury police station at 5:30

p.m. and went to work. They matched samples of Metesky's handwriting drawn from the local motor vehicle bureau with his Con Ed file, and they checked to see if he had a criminal record in Connecticut. (He did not.)

At 8:00 p.m. Captain Pakul took the detectives to the home of Miles Kelly, a former Metesky tenant who had clashed with George in 1942 while both men worked for a local company that manufactured hydraulic hoists for the wartime navy. Kelly called Metesky "an unstable person" with a history of disputes. Metesky had written their boss a series of overwrought letters containing far-fetched claims about Kelly.

Then, in the thick of World War II, the Waterbury draft board rejected Metesky because a chest X-ray revealed a history of lung disease. Metesky blamed his rejection on Kelly, who worked part-time at the draft board. Metesky wrote President Roosevelt and other high federal officials, demanding that Kelly be sent to frontline combat. The detectives heard Kelly out, then Captain Pakul handed him a pen and asked him to draw a floor plan of the Metesky home. They wanted to eliminate surprises when they entered the house of a madman.

At 10:00 p.m. the detectives returned to the police station in downtown Waterbury, where a prosecutor and city court judge signed a search warrant. With all preparations in place, Lynch now placed a final call to the crime lab in New York, where Joe McNally, its handwriting expert, had spent the evening comparing the blocky penmanship found in Metesky's Con Ed file with the letters F.P. had sent to the *Journal-American*. They looked almost identical. McNally judged Metesky "a good bet," though a degree of uncertainty lingered. The detectives had suffered too many miscalculations and setbacks to make any assumptions.

The arrest proceeded as it might in an old black-and-white movie. At 11:45 p.m. three unmarked police cruisers crossed a bridge spanning the Naugatuck River and drove into Brooklyn. The cars crept uphill to Fourth Street, their headlights shining through the freezing ground fog blanketing the Naugatuck Valley. The men in the cars did not speak. They looked silently out the windows at factory workers' homes half-hidden in mist. There was no sound in the streets, only the crunch of tires, as if Waterbury were waiting for something to happen.

The cars eased to a stop in front of no. 17. The three-story house, with its pillars and sagging porches, loomed through the fog. The rooms were entirely dark. Lynch and four detectives stepped onto the creaking porch. Two men walked to the rear of the house to head off an escape route, their heads wreathed in their misty winter breath. They prepared themselves for the worst.

Pakul knocked on the weathered door and waited. His men clenched and unclenched loaded revolvers stashed in overcoat pockets. A small vestibule light blinked on. The front door opened. Standing in the wan parlor light was a thickset middle-aged man wearing round gold-rimmed eyeglasses and burgundy pajamas buttoned to the neck under a bathrobe. His gray hair was neatly parted. Could this be him? Could this be the human face behind so much terror?

"George Metesky?" asked Captain Pakul.

"Yes." The man met the midnight visitors with an ingenuous expression. He looked as if he'd just woken from a comfortable sleep.

"These gentlemen are New York City detectives." They flashed their badges. Metesky looked at them blankly. His small, close-set blue eyes glinted with a hint of amusement. Had he gone to bed that night knowing that he might be roused by a knock on the door? "It was almost like he was waiting for us," a detective later said. "His hair was neatly combed; his eyeglasses were spotless, sparkling."

Pakul explained that they were investigating a hit-and-run. They had a search warrant and wanted to look around. The men wiped their feet and filed into a parlor. The surroundings were quaint to the point of creepy—peeling wallpaper, lace curtains, and fading prints. Baby photos and a portrait of Jesus in the manger hung in the hallway. Threadbare rugs covered linoleum floors. The furnishings conveyed a family's efforts to keep up the appearance of a middle-class household.

Metesky asked the officers to speak quietly so as not to wake his sisters. Detective Lynch nodded. He asked if they could see Metesky's bedroom. They found it small, and as orderly as a jail cell with crisply folded pants and shirts. The brass bed was primly made up. Two New York City subway tokens and some flashlight bulbs sat on an oak dresser. On a high closet shelf the detectives found a loaded .38 caliber Smith & Wesson, a snub-nosed revolver easily concealed in holsters or pockets. It must have come as a relief to find it before Metesky could lay his hands on it.

A detective asked Metesky if he ever drove to New York. He nodded. Had he gone through White Plains? He nodded again.

Metesky must have known why the detectives were calling on him in the middle of the night. And they knew that he knew. But for the moment both sides persisted with the fiction of a hit-and-run investigation.

The detectives found a notebook filled with handwriting similar to F.P.'s block lettering. They handed Metesky a pen and asked him to write his name on a yellow legal pad. They watched, spellbound, as the familiar block letters appeared on the page—the G in *George* had the telltale double bars. The Y had its distinctive serif. "This is not then about an auto accident?" he asked. Something about Metesky's bland smile was infuriating.

"Why don't you go ahead and get dressed, George," Lynch said. "We'd like to see the garage."

Here was a moment of truth. So far Metesky had perfectly matched Dr. Brussel's profile—Slavic, middle-aged, medium build, residing with female relatives in Connecticut, history of workplace disputes. The detectives waiting in the hallway knew that Dr. Brussel had also predicted the bomber would dress in a neatly buttoned double-breasted jacket. Sure enough, Metesky stepped from his bedroom wearing sensible brown rubber-soled shoes, red-dotted necktie, brown cardigan sweater, and double-breasted blue suit.

He led them down a gravel driveway, their flashlight beams swinging over the muddy gravel. Metesky unlocked the garage doors and flipped on the lights. The police report would call the garage as "clean and orderly as a hospital operating room." Rows of methodically placed tools hung on a wall beside the $4,000 Daimler sedan Metesky's sisters had bought him with earnings from their modest factory paychecks. The odometer read forty-five hundred miles, enough for thirty round-trips to New York City.

Tucked against the rear wall sat a spotless workbench with a well-oiled metal lathe powered by an extension cord running to the basement of the house. "Here we have the whole story," said Lynch, patting the lathe. It was the second giveaway.

"You're looking for more than an accident," Metesky repeated. He spoke in a soft, unaccented voice with awkward double negatives and other slight grammatical lapses, just as Dr. Brussel had anticipated.

Detective Michael Lynch looked at Metesky. "George, we're from New York. You know why we're here, don't you?"

Metesky shrugged slightly, shook his head. "I really don't."

"We think you do."

The detectives circled Metesky. He glanced from one to the next. "I think I'd better consult an attorney before I say any more."

"Come on, George," Lynch said. "Never mind an attorney. Why are we here?"

Metesky breathed rapidly. His eyes narrowed. His lips curled with a hint of amusement. Finally he said, "I guess it's because you suspect that I'm the Mad Bomber."

"Maybe you are not so mad," Lynch said. "Tell me, George, what does F.P. stand for?"

Metesky exhaled. His frown relaxed. "Fair play." With those two words, barely whispered, the seventeen-year manhunt came to a quiet end.

The sound of men's voices had roused Anna and Mae, who emerged from their bedrooms looking like biddies in a Norman Rockwell painting. They thought that perhaps the men had come at last to give George the money owed him from his long-fought compensation case. They padded down the hallway with sweaters pulled over their nightgowns in time to see their brother led in handcuffs to an unmarked police cruiser.

They stood by the open door clinging to each other and issuing tearful pleas. "George couldn't hurt anybody," they said. "He was a gentleman in every way."

As the cruiser pulled away into the foggy New England night, Metesky looked back at his sisters through the rear window.

PART TWO

THE LAW OF INSANITY

CHAPTER FOURTEEN

INTERROGATION

January 1957

THE DETECTIVES LED METESKY UP A NARROW STAIRCASE IN THE WATER-
bury police station and down a hallway to a bare, windowless room. Like
most interrogation cells, it was arranged to isolate and unnerve. Metesky
sat upright in an uncomfortable chair facing Detective Lynch. Five other
detectives stood against the walls, bleary eyed but alert to the enormity
of the moment.

In crime shows, the coercive pressure of questioning renders suspects
by turns surly, defiant, insulting, and, occasionally, sobbingly remorse-
ful. Metesky responded in no such way. Now that he had confessed, his
demeanor changed from quietly obliging to eagerly forthcoming, like a
biddable job applicant who couldn't wait to tell his story. He turned an
amiable smile on his inquisitor and spoke in soft, well-mannered phrases,
as might an old friend recounting a fishing adventure.

At 1:30 a.m., Detective Lynch began more than six hours of questioning by asking about the first bomb, placed on a Con Ed windowsill in 1940,
and advanced chronologically down a prepared chart of all thirty-two
known bombs, and letters, while jotting notes on a yellow legal pad. As
proof of authorship, Metesky gave Lynch the date and location of fifteen
bombs the police had not found. He referred to them as "units"; he was

visibly uncomfortable with the word *bomb*. His additions brought the total to forty-seven.

"Metesky was hazy as to some of the correspondence," Lynch later reported in a police memo, but he "made full admissions to each and every bomb." He had uncanny recall for dates and locations. "I guess I have pretty much of a one-track mind," he said. "Once I fixed on a place, that's where it had to go. I wouldn't change."

With a roomful of detectives staring him down, Metesky calmly corroborated technical details and particulars of fabrication that only the bomber could know. He spoke of the bombs pridefully, almost lovingly, as an artist might speak of favorite works.

Captain Finney and his squad colleagues had for years puzzled over the bomber's ingenious homemade detonator fuses, particularly those used in the early years of his campaign. The crime lab had repeatedly found a sticky candylike residue. The forensic experts on Poplar Street had tested it and examined it through microscopes, but they could never identify the residue. They could only guess that the gummy substance had something to do with the timing mechanism.

Metesky was eager to explain. He pulled a throat lozenge, or cough drop, from his pocket. "Have you ever seen one of these? If you ever want to trigger a bomb, lozenges are invaluable. I used them as timers, but I had to be very careful." He explained that he used ordinary drugstore lozenges to separate electrical contact points. He would spend hours in his garage shaving the lozenges down to one thirty-second of an inch—as thin as a shaving of cheese. At that width they were delicate. Over and over they broke, obliging him to start over.

Before planting the bomb he would place a drop of water on the lozenge. When it dissolved, which normally took half an hour, the contact points would touch and the resulting electrical connection ignited the bomb. Ka-boom! With that, Lynch offered Metesky coffee and a sandwich. He chuckled softly and said he would prefer throat lozenges.

Starting with the March 1954 blast at Grand Central, the crime lab's forensics men had come across shattered bits of cheap wristwatches. After the sixteenth bomb, Metesky had concluded that the dissolve rate of the lozenges was too fluky. If they softened too fast, he barely had time to escape, as occurred the night he almost got caught at Radio City Music Hall. If they failed to dissolve at all, the bomb sat dormant—a dud.

He devised a new fuse with $5 wristwatches bought in pawnshops or drugstores. "Because it was easier and safer for me," he said. He removed minute and second hands with tiny tweezers. He drilled a hole in the crystal, inserted a wire, and adjusted the hour hand. The countdown could last as long as twelve hours, depending on how far back he pushed the hour hand. When it came around to make contact with the wire, the circuit was completed. The filament in a flashlight bulb ignited, which, in turn, sparked the gunpowder. "It was very easy this way," he said. He also switched from gunpowder siphoned from shotgun shells to the more volatile powder found in revolver bullets.

He was as careful to conceal himself as he was in the fabrication. "I always carried a small piece of cloth with me. I used it to wipe my fingerprints off the bombs and the envelope when I was mailing a letter. I even put the cloth over my hand when I put the letter in a mailbox."

When newspapers failed to report on his early bombings or mentioned them only in brief, Metesky switched to more provocative targets: train stations, movie theaters, and the public library. "I started on the other places to get publicity for the injustices against me."

Lynch asked him how he felt when he read about the injuries he had caused.

"I was sick."

"Nevertheless, you continued to place them," Lynch said.

"I took an oath to keep on placing them until I was dead or caught."

Meanwhile, word of Metesky's arrest got out. At 2:30 a.m. an indiscreet local policeman leaked to the local newspaper, the *Waterbury Republican,* that Metesky had confessed. As the interrogation stretched into its second hour, a *Republican* reporter was joined at police headquarters by George Lezotte, a correspondent for a New Haven radio station, WAVZ, who lived in Waterbury. One by one reporters, photographers, and cameramen arrived from towns all over southern New England. They congregated in the first-floor booking area and took turns badgering Lieutenant Domenic Manello, the desk officer, to let them upstairs. "No photographs," Manello said, "until he's booked."

Every time somebody came downstairs the news cameras were raised and readied, then lowered in disappointment when it turned out to be a detective or clerk.

All the while the phone rang, ceaselessly and insistently, with news outlets begging for interviews and information. William Lamb, the night dispatcher, firmly turned away all callers. "No, we can't tell you anything," he repeated. "Yes, they are questioning someone upstairs. . . . No, I can't let you talk to the New York detectives. They've left orders not to be disturbed."

The Waterbury reporters were accustomed to working in a backwater, subsisting on recaps of speeches at Rotary Club dinners and high school basketball coverage. For these few nocturnal hours they found themselves unexpectedly at the center of the news universe. "Seasoned newspapermen were incredulous when the first word of the story came out," the *Waterbury Republican* wrote on the next day's editorial page, "and as the fantastic yarn expanded to its full proportions their incredulity was replaced by amazement. Imagine sitting on a hot story like this one for sixteen years without even getting a glimmer of what was going on!"

At 3:00 a.m., the detectives put Metesky in a holding cell while they broke for coffee. Captain Pakul came down to speak with the press standing vigil at the foot of the stairs: "There's absolutely no question of it. He's the guy."

After his brief remarks to the press, Pakul allowed an Associated Press photographer upstairs to see Metesky. The next morning, newspapers from Long Island to Los Angeles published the same front-page photographs of Metesky smiling broadly through the bars of his holding cell or reclined on his cot with his hands behind his head. The Mad Bomber, who had menaced the city for so long, looked as mild mannered as a candy-store clerk, complete with thinning hair and receding chin. He looked like "the usher who passes the collection plate in a small-town church," wrote *The New York Times*. "He would be a deacon, probably, and certainly he might lead the weekly sing at Rotary and Kiwanis and, in his spare time, work hard for the Community Chest."

At 4:00 a.m., Captain Finney and five other police officials arrived from New York, trailed by a pack of big-city reporters—Richard H. Parke of *The New York Times,* Joe Famm of *The Mirror,* Guy Richards of the *Journal-American*. They had driven fast through the fog-covered country-side. "I drove up the Merritt Parkway in the middle of the night with a photographer," said Carl Pelleck, a crime reporter for the *Post*. "The fog was so thick he hung out the window with a flashlight."

At 4:30 a.m. the detectives reassembled in the interrogation room. Questioning resumed. This time Lynch pressed Metesky on his motives. In response, he took them back twenty-six years to the morning of September 5, 1931, a Saturday of a Labor Day weekend. Metesky had arrived in the Bronx for his daily shift as a generator wiper at a Con Ed power plant on the banks of the East River tidal straight known as Hell Gate. In tie and jacket, he stood out among the workmen exiting the Cypress Avenue subway stop. Metesky dressed for middle manage-ment, but his job was blue-collar. At the foot of 138th Street, hulking over the whirls and whitecaps of Hell Gate, stood an eight-story redbrick power plant grimed with coal soot. It occupied two city blocks. Four blackened smokestacks cast morning shadows on the Bronx riverfront. Seagulls wheeled in the briny air. The behemoth plant supplied most of the electrical current to America's largest city, a metropolis pulsating with light. It sucked millions of gallons of water from Hell Gate and heated them to a thousand degrees in twenty-one cast-iron boilers fed by burning coal. Sheets of rising steam spun turbines in two giant genera-tors, the biggest in the world.

Metesky was one of the low-caste workers laboring in close contact with the devil-hot furnaces and walls flaking with asbestos. "The work we did [at the power station] was unhealthy" he said. "I had to clean re-actors. Cement dust was everywhere in the air. We came out filthy dirty and coughing at the end of the day. The mask they provided for us was useless."

His grimy and unrelentingly stressful job was facilitated by the technical skills he had acquired as an ordnance officer in the marines. He was lucky to have it. Jobs were scarce in 1931, especially for high school dropouts such as him. Thousands of unemployed auto workers marched on a Ford factory in Dearborn, Michigan, that year. In New York, nearly a million applied for city relief. Immigrants were routinely spat upon or roughed up for stealing jobs that belonged to "real" Americans. It would not have surprised Metesky to be heckled or punched. He grew up in Waterbury, but his parents had emigrated from Lithuania. He had inherited their long vowels and rolling R's, along with their foreign aspect.

Metesky earned a reputation for diligence. The floor boss trusted him to read the meters on high-tension control and generator boards. It was up to Metesky to throw the appropriate switches to avert overloads and keep the electricity flowing to households and offices from Riverdale to the Rockaways. He found a thrill of power in the meters and dials. "You have to know where every single switch in that powerhouse is," he later said. "You have to know what to do if a mistake is made."

Metesky's scrupulous mind-set endeared him to managers, but coworkers found him priggish and cold. He awkwardly dodged eye contact and held himself above the harmless shortcuts and idle banter that helped pass a long shift. Instead he insisted on rigid adherence to procedure, as if he were a self-appointed compliance officer. One coworker described him as "spinsterish."

On the morning of September 5, Metesky tended the churning boilers unaware that one was malfunctioning. A buildup of soot and coal choked the passageways, known as baffles, that conducted the hot air given off by burning coal. The boiler juddered and wheezed as its airways closed off, but the twenty other heaving boilers drowned out the warning sounds. The pressure built like a volcano until it could no longer be contained. Metesky was walking by as the pressure reached the breaking point. The boiler's cast-iron walls shattered in a single violent instant. A

draft of toxic fumes engulfed him. He lurched four steps backward, clutch-
ing his throat. Chemicals singed the capillaries of his lungs with pain like
a thousand needle pricks. His throat burbled. Blood sputtered its way up
his gorge. He coughed hard and long, the hacks and barks growing progressively more violent. One knee, then the other, sank to the cold concrete floor.

Two coworkers, Cavanaugh and Casey, alerted by the blast, found
Metesky lying in a splatter of hacked-up blood. He explained what had
happened between shallow gasps. He got no sympathy from the foreman,
Purdy, who, by Metesky's account, put him to work loading lumber in
the back of a car. "Apparently the coughing and blood were normal occurrences at Con Edison," Metesky said, "because when I told these three
guys, they weren't a bit surprised."

After twenty minutes he collapsed again. "They let me lay there for
two hours. I finally recovered enough to get up." When his shift ended,
he rode the subway back to his mingy boardinghouse room on West
Eighty-Eighth Street. Too weak to rise, he lay in bed racked by bouts of
vomiting as his body labored to expel blood seeping from his lungs. He
could taste its warm thickness as it spilled from his mouth and stained his
bedsheets dark crimson.

Metesky's workdays were over. After a hospital stay in Waterbury,
Metesky moved to a cabin on the grounds of a Tucson sanitarium, where
doctors treated him for tuberculosis with rounds of torturous injections
to his abdominal cavity using syringes as hefty as knitting needles. He
passed the hours between treatments shooting a borrowed pistol at targets set up in the tinder-dry sagebrush behind his cabin. In the evenings
he wrote letters to Con Ed on a portable Remington typewriter parked
on his kitchen table.

His financial situation grew dire. He applied for compensation. Con
Ed responded by paying him 80 percent of his $37.50-a-week salary for
twenty-six weeks after the accident. He also received a group insurance
settlement of $58 a month. After exchanging dozens of letters, Con Ed
cut Metesky off for good with a parting recommendation: he was free to

apply for disability payments with the New York State Workmen's Compensation Board, which guaranteed injured employees compensation and benefits. He could be eligible for as much as $25 a week for as long as he remained disabled.

Before 1914, disabled workers like Metesky had no recourse except the dubious prospect of suing their employer. That changed after a cigarette ignited a fire in the Triangle Shirtwaist Factory, a Greenwich Village sweatshop, in 1911. Most workers escaped down a staircase, but those on the ninth floor found themselves trapped by a locked exit door, a standard sweatshop practice to prevent employees from sneaking unauthorized breaks and pilfering merchandise. Horse-drawn fire engines arrived, but their ladders could reach only to the sixth floor. One hundred and forty-six workers died. Many leaped to their death with clothes aflame. The singed bodies of teenage girls littered the sidewalk. It was the gravest workplace disaster in the US until 9/11. The fire swept in a wave of labor reforms, including a 1914 New York State law guaranteeing injured workers medical care and regular payouts.

For Metesky, the Workmen's Compensation Board turned out to be another dead end. The board rejected Metesky's application because he filed it more than a year after the statute of limitations expired. He suspected Con Ed had strung him along with minor payments knowing that he would soon be ineligible.

Metesky was still partially confined to bed when his money ran out. He had no choice but to check out of the sanitarium and move to a place capable of truly poisoning his psyche: his family home in Connecticut. In that house nothing changed, lending its enclosed world a creepy stillness and immutability—the sour stench of kugelis and pork dumplings, the dispirited rooms burdened by the false cheer of patterned linoleum floors and cut-rate lace curtains, the muffled sound of upstairs boarders, the psychic reverberations of his dead parents lingering among religious mementos and piano sheet music, the memories of a mother who never learned English, doting on her youngest child with Lithuanian endearments, the stern father, a night watchman in a lumberyard, stoically embittered by his failure to advance in America. A house can hold a human presence forever.

Metesky passed entire days in his childhood bed gasping for a decent breath. "My name might as well be on a tombstone," he told his sisters, who sat at his bedside for hours. The comment seemed designed to solicit their sympathy. It worked. They pampered him, just as their mother had, cleaning and cooking and passing him pocket money earned at their factory jobs. Like a child, he surrendered himself to dependence.

In desperation, Metesky turned again to the Workmen's Compensation Board. Three times Metesky appealed. Three times he was denied, sunk by his Con Ed colleagues—Casey, Cavanaugh, and Purdy—who were reported to have testified in a hearing that Metesky had held a bloody handkerchief to his face, but only because he suffered a nosebleed. One stated under oath that Metesky wasn't even at work on the day he claimed to have suffered his injury.

As Metesky described how the three men's testimony punctured his appeals for compensation, the detectives gathered in the interrogation room must have wondered if the furnace explosion ever actually happened, or if hallucinations had seized his mind. Supervisors at the power plant recorded an accident in their daily logs, so something occurred. But maybe a schizophrenic delusion caused Metesky to exaggerate its severity to life-threatening levels. It's also possible that the accident happened just as Metesky described, but his three colleagues lied under oath because they, like most of the shift workers, hated Metesky's smug and superior demeanor. Or maybe they were pressured by management to cover up health risks in a facility full of toxic materials.

Metesky proceeded with righteous anger. He wrote a stream of shrilly indignant letters to Governor Herbert H. Lehman, Lieutenant Governor Charles Poletti, and Industrial Commissioner Elmer Andrews pleading with them to intercede in a clear case of injustice. The outpouring of letters continued—about eight hundred thousand words, by his count—to television stations, newspapers, churches, and Con Ed. "I even tried to purchase space in the press, and even the papers rejected my offers,"

Metesky told the detectives. "I never received so much as one single penny postal card in reply."

When his health permitted, Metesky drove his Daimler down the Merritt Parkway and parked on the Upper West Side of Manhattan. From there he traveled the city by subway. He was jostling about on one such outing, clutching the overhead handrail, when his three former Con Ed colleagues Casey, Cavanaugh, and Purdy—the trio whose testimonies had sunk Metesky's appeals for workman's compensation—appeared to board the train and sit down opposite him.

Metesky was sure he recognized them, though it seems more likely a hallucination. Schizophrenics can go for years suffering modest delusions and a slow unwinding of wits. Their inner disturbance is private and so hidden that it may be imperceptible to those around them. Then, without warning, the schizophrenics can experience a temporary outbreak of psychosis—a psychotic break—in which the world as they know it, as healthy people know it, pitches away beneath their feet and they tumble into a black madness of hallucinations, disconnected flights of thought, and godly voices whispering inside their heads.

Metesky was likely in the throes of just such an episode when he glowered at the three men, real or imagined, on the subway. In his recollection, they were laughing at him. They snickered at his misfortune. The years of suffering and rage came to a boil. In a single galvanic moment Metesky pictured an explosion ripping off his betrayers' right arms, the same arms they had raised in oath at his hearing.

"I figured I would put one bullet through the right arm of each one of them because they raised their right arms when they swore to tell the truth and then lied against me." As if in a movie, the scene unspooling in his head cut to a bullet penetrating the chest of Harland C. Forbes, the president of Con Ed. Lynch and the other detectives may have thought back to the .38 caliber pistol they'd found in Metesky's bedroom.

His rage, long restrained, had finally found expression in violence. His disordered mind hardened with a clarity of purpose. The only proper course was retaliation—against Con Ed and the allied forces of American society. He knew with utter certainty that the conspiracy was directed at him and all the other defenseless men and women. Destiny had selected him to defend them with violence—a righteous violence.

Metesky was a mild man, gentle George. As with Spider-Man or the Hulk, the mysterious alchemy of an industrial accident transformed him into a superhuman defender of justice. Or so he believed.

Bombs were a natural choice. As Dr. Brussel had observed, anarchists and other dissidents frequently deployed them in Eastern Europe. A bomb had also been used as an instrument of vengeance closer to home. In the spring of 1920, when Metesky attended Crosby High School, ten thousand mill workers protesting wage cuts clashed with police in the streets of Waterbury. In July an unexploded bomb was found in the bushes outside a house formerly owned by Police Superintendent George M. Beach.

Metesky had concluded that letters would not be enough: "People pay more attention to the noise of a bomb than to the written word."

Why, Lynch asked, did Metesky stop planting bombs during the war years? He explained that as an ex-marine and a patriot he felt that it would have been wrong.

Captain Finney and the other detectives were surprised that Metesky had confessed so avidly, but it made perfect sense to Dr. Brussel. In a follow-up conversation with Finney, he explained that Metesky "admitted his crimes eagerly in the end because he was positive we didn't know. He wanted us to know about him, and it frustrated him to stay hidden. He may have thought of himself as a kind of benevolent god, but he was aware that this god was never going to be revealed to us in any magical or mystical fashion. He knew he had to communicate with us in order to be revealed."

One last mystery remained to be discussed. Dr. Brussel had theorized that F.P. spurned women because his psychosexual development had been arrested in the oedipal phase. He was unlikely to have a wife or a girl-friend because on some level he was still fixated on his mother. Lynch now gingerly broached the subject with Metesky: Did he have any female friends? Did he even like women? Metesky said yes, women interested him. As if to prove the point he claimed to have had an ongoing affair with a socially prominent Waterbury woman. He couldn't name her, he said, because she was married and their connection would cause a scandal. "She is decent and has always been good to me," Metesky said. "She didn't know anything about the bombs and there is no reason to bring her into this."

As he spoke of his alleged girlfriend, Metesky began for the first time to lose his composure, suggesting that he was either anxiously protective of her or lying about her existence. "You'll hammer away at me and try to force me to tell you" who she is, he said. He began to cough violently, the first time detectives had seen an indication of his illness. One of them put out his cigar. A second fetched Metesky a glass of water. Lynch let the subject drop.

At 5:30 a.m., not yet dawn, Deputy Police Commissioner Walter Arm, a former crime reporter for the *Herald Tribune,* came downstairs to brief reporters gathered at the Waterbury police headquarters. His opening words were "This is the man." He suggested that the newsmen get breakfast. It would be some time, he said, before they brought Metesky down for booking. Instead of heading to a local diner for eggs and toast, the reporters drove like a herd over to Fourth Street to inspect the Metesky house and interview the sisters, who had just returned from dropping off clean underwear and socks for their brother at the police station.

Anna, the older sister, met the reporters in the parlor with eyes red from crying. She mewlingly maintained her brother's innocence. He could not possibly have conducted a secret life, she said. Yes, he spent hours alone in the garage, but he was working on inventions—an electric snowplow and a solenoid pump for which he'd earned a patent. He machined washers and other small parts for use around the house. Yes, he disappeared in his car for entire days, but usually to visit their older brother John, an accountant, and his wife, Gertrude, in Hartford, or so he said.

He couldn't possibly have done the terrible things he confessed to. "He isn't the type," Anna said.

Mae opened the door to an adjoining room and poked her head out to address the reporters. "Go away. The door's open and I'm cold. Oh, God, why don't you go someplace else? I'm sick."

A reporter for the *Naugatuck Daily News,* a local newspaper, called Hartford, hoping to interview Metesky's brother John. Instead, John's wife, Gertrude, answered the phone. "My God, they have the wrong man," she said. "It just couldn't be George. I just don't believe it. He was a good, decent man, and I say the Waterbury police have got the wrong man."

A reporter calling from the *Journal-American*'s newsroom reached John, who said, "His arrest is ridiculous and outrageous. We'll get the best lawyers in the country to defend him."

The reporters were back at the foot of the stairs by the time Metesky came down for booking at 6:30 a.m., their first glimpse of the bomber. Now they phoned the rewrite men preparing stories back in New York. Fifteen reporters fought for the use of six phones.

At 7:00 a.m., Metesky returned to his holding cell and lay down on a cot covered by a canvas blanket. He had answered questions for six hours without losing his cheery composure. Before Metesky dozed off, William Schmitt, the detective who had disassembled one of the bombs by hand, entered the cell. The detectives knew that Metesky was their man, but they still lacked a critical mass of corroborating evidence. As daylight neared, Schmitt was preparing to reenter the house to search for the missing link: bomb parts. When they had knocked on Metesky's door more than seven hours earlier, he had greeted them with a slightly bemused look, as if he were expecting them. If he had anticipated an arrest, he might have booby-trapped his home—a final act of vengeance known to police as "a last laugh."

"George, do you recognize my name?" Schmitt guessed that Metesky had read newspaper accounts of him defusing a live bomb.

"Oh, yes. I worried about you."

"George, we know you made the bombs. Are there any more in the house? Your sisters are still there, and if anything happens to them, it will be on your head."

"You didn't find them, did you?"

"Find what, George?"

The detectives returned to the house at 8:00 a.m. and made their way through the reporters and press photographers gathered out front. For the second time in eight hours they knocked on the door. The sisters met them with more quavery-voiced declarations of George's innocence. They were still in their nightgowns and bathrobes.

"My brother would never do damage to anybody," Mae said. "Don't worry about him."

"We're not worried about him," a detective said.

The gathering of evidence began. First the detectives loaded the metalworking lathe into a car for delivery to the crime lab in New York, along with metal shavings swept from the bench. They collected notebooks found in Metesky's bedroom and the Remington typewriter he used for some of his bomb warnings. "That's the clincher, if we ever needed one," a detective said. "The typefaces are identical."

Then, following the directions Metesky had given Schmitt an hour earlier, five detectives lay on their backs in a pantry off the well-scrubbed kitchen and shone flashlights behind a soapstone laundry sink. Detective John Justy reached into the dirty recess between the sink and the concrete wall, contorting his body to get an extra inch of extension. He grunted as his fingertips brushed something dangling back there. He reached a little deeper and grasped four red wool socks hanging from a water pipe. He handed them, one by one, to Schmitt, who pulled four pipes from the socks along with Timex wristwatches without straps, four penlight batteries, copper wire, a gasket made from a matchbox cover, four Allen wrenches, two iron screws, eight small Allen plugs, eight small brass screws with nuts, five iron nuts, two small springs, two rubber eyedropper bulbs, one brass grommet, and assorted other bomb gear. "Now from these," Lynch said, "I drew an opinion."

The hidden trove of bomb parts erased the last shred of doubt. The bomb squad now had Metesky dead to rights. And just in time. The materials retrieved from behind the wash sink would have made three bombs, his biggest yet, destined for the congested hallways of the Coliseum.

Later that morning Metesky stood handcuffed before Judge Hugh McGill in Waterbury City Court. In his round-rimmed glasses and double-breasted suit, he could have passed for a prosperous small-town businessman. He was surrounded by policemen—and the press. The crowd of reporters, photographers, and cameramen who had stood an all-night vigil in the police station had reassembled among the white columns and oak panels of the courtroom. Judge McGill didn't normally allow press in the courtroom, but bowed to the momentousness of the proceedings. "It seemed the only thing to do," Judge McGill said. "There were so many photographers, reporters, and spectators in the court that it would have been difficult to do otherwise without considerable embarrassment."

The prosecutor began by reviewing the charges. He told Judge McGill that Metesky had agreed to waive his right to an extradition hearing; he would willingly face charges of felonious assault, malicious mischief, and possession of a dangerous weapon in New York City.

"Do you understand these proceedings?" Judge McGill asked.

"I have a pretty good idea," Metesky softly answered.

Metesky's sisters, Anna and Mae, were all but swallowed by the two hundred spectators and members of the press packed into the gallery. It was so crowded they could barely glimpse their brother as he rose to address the judge. When the proceedings concluded, a bailiff led Metesky off to a holding cell. The sisters shyly approached an officer and asked if the court might allow them to see their brother before he was removed to New York. The officer brought them downstairs, where Metesky sat alone in a bare cell. He rose to greet them, his fingers wrapped around the iron bars. The sisters began weeping at the sight of him. Were the accusations accurate? they asked. Was he really the bomber? It was all true, he told them. He was guilty as charged.

Before the bomb squad detectives officially took custody of Metesky from Waterbury officials, he sat in a court anteroom for a five-minute interview with John Tillman, a reporter for WPIX, a New York television station. Asked how he felt after his arrest, Metesky said he "wouldn't call it a relief. It was bound to happen this week. If not today, then later in the week." If he wasn't arrested, he said, he would likely have turned himself in to the *Journal-American*. He undertook the bombing campaign, he said, "because he had no choice." The interview aired at 7:00 p.m. that night on a news show sponsored, coincidentally, by Con Ed.

At 1:55 p.m. detectives loaded Metesky into a police cruiser for the drive to New York. Immediately afterward, a *Herald Tribune* reporter named Earl Ubell placed a call to Dr. James Dr. Brussel's downtown office. In the first of dozens of interviews, Dr. Brussel explained that everything the police had learned about Metesky in the previous twelve hours seemed to match the description Dr. Brussel had given the police more than a month earlier. As he'd predicted, Metesky was "a classic textbook case of paranoia."

CHAPTER FIFTEEN

THE SMILING AVENGER

January 1957

AT 4:30 P.M. ON THE AFTERNOON FOLLOWING HIS ALL-NIGHT INTERRO-
gation, George Metesky stepped smiling from a police cruiser behind
the Centre Street police headquarters in downtown Manhattan. Patrolmen had cleared the cars from the west side of the street and set up wood
barricades to contain the three hundred spectators—half of them press.
Twenty-five cops took up their positions.

Metesky arrived with his right wrist handcuffed to the wrist of grim-
faced detective Jimmy Martin. Detective Lynch gripped Metesky's left
arm. Metesky wore the same double-breasted suit and fedora he had left
home with sixteen hours earlier. Stubble flecked his chin. His blue eyes
sagged with fatigue. But his smile was undimmed. His chubby face shone
with a giddy satisfaction. He basked in the attention he had craved all along.
The *World-Telegram and Sun* called him "the smiling avenger."

"The face might have been that of a successful political candidate
or a winner of a Nobel Prize," Dr. Brussel would write. "Metesky was
smiling. . . . No, not smiling: beaming. . . . He shouted cheerful greet-
ings to the crowds who gathered. . . . Under one arm he carried a neatly
wrapped brown-paper parcel containing a change of underwear. It was
as though he were going on vacation. He seemed to be enjoying every
minute of it."

Metesky treated his perp walk as if it were a red-carpet whirl, turn-ing happily to face the popping of flashbulbs. Reporters and photographers in trench coats stood five deep behind police barricades, some holding boxy black cameras or operating film cameras perched on tripods. "This way, George," the photographers yelled. He looked up to oblige one stra-tegically stationed on the roof of the police shack.

"Are you glad it's all over, George?"

"Yes." He nodded enthusiastically.

"Are you sorry you hurt the people?"

"Yes, I am sorry I hurt the people, but I'm not sorry I did it."

A *Journal-American* photographer handed Metesky a copy of the first afternoon edition. He held it up like a graduate proudly displaying his diploma. The sidewalk gathering snapped him smiling above the banner headline: "Letters to Journal Trap the Mad Bomber." The enormous black headline letters accompanied by a photograph of him crowded news of Eisenhower's second inauguration off the front page entirely. (Strangely, the *Journal-American*'s article jumped to an inside page where it ran along-side an ad that read, "You'll be better off with Con Edison.")

The detectives stood by with rueful smiles. They suffered a few minutes of Metesky's grandstanding, then ushered him down into "the hole," their term for a staircase descending steeply to a basement booking room, where he would be photographed and fingerprinted.

Metesky was still smiling that evening when he stood handcuffed in an ill-lit felony court for the Borough of Manhattan to be charged with assault, malicious mischief, damaging a building by explosion, en-dangering life, and possession of dangerous weapons. He was still clutch-ing the afternoon's edition of the *Journal-American,* as if it were a prized memento.

The long manhunt was over. Within a few hours the city's newsrooms had pivoted from the mystery of the bomber's identity to the question of Metesky's fate. On the day after his arrest the *Daily News* ran a shrill, over-size front-page headline declaring, "Caged Bomber May Get Life." Maybe so, but first the courts would have to determine if he was competent to stand trial. He conducted himself normally in most daily functions, but psychiatrists assigned by the court would surely confirm Dr. Brussel's contention that the bomber was a paranoid schizophrenic. The case had come along at the exact moment when the psychiatrist's role in the judicial process was a point of contention and controversy. Who would determine where the line between sanity and madness stood—the lawyers or doctors? And where exactly did Metesky fall in relation to it?

There was no hint of the struggle to come when Metesky's court-appointed lawyer, a veteran Legal Aid attorney named Benjamin Schmier, who had, coincidentally, defended the bombing suspect Frederick Eberhardt six years earlier, paved the way for an insanity defense by telling Magistrate Judge Reuben Levy that he "saw a man with a psychosis, with a persecution complex.

"You are asking me to act for this defendant," Schmier continued, "and before I can act, I must be convinced that in my legal mind that this defendant understands the very nature of the charges against him and is able to differentiate between right and wrong. I am not sure of that. As a matter of fact, if I were forced to make a statement for the record on that score, I would say it is my humble belief at this time that this defendant is of such a state of mind as to not understand the nature of the charges against him. I would like to be fortified with a psychiatric report, and I think the interest of justice would be served if Your Honor would grant my application."

The judge agreed, saying, "The defendant's actions are indicative of an ostensibly deranged mind." He smacked his gavel and remanded Metesky to Bellevue, a city hospital, for evaluation.

If the prospect of confinement in the notorious Bellevue wards scared Metesky, he didn't show it. He was still smiling when the bailiff led him off in handcuffs.

In the hurly-burly of New York politics, even a success can invite recriminations. Metesky's arrest was followed by a public dispute over who deserved credit for his capture and who should get the blame for an over-long, ineffectual manhunt.

The newspapers found it easy to get behind Alice Kelly, the tall, blonde Con Ed clerk who had found the Metesky file. The *Herald Tribune* called her the woman with the "rare photographic memory." It was suggested that as an exemplar of the spunky New York Irish spirit she should join the reviewing stand at the St. Patrick's Day parade on Fifth Avenue. A vocal Con Ed stockholder proposed that Kelly fill an open seat on the company's board of directors.

At the very least Kelly was expected to receive the $26,000 reward posted by the NYPD and the Patrolmen's Benevolent Association. However, Commissioner Kennedy was the sole judge of the money's disposition, and he was opposed to rewarding anyone associated with Con Ed. So opposed that he considered withholding the prize from Kelly on a technicality: The Board of Estimate had posted the reward for the bomber's conviction. If a court judged Metesky incompetent to stand trial, he would never be convicted.

An hour after returning from Waterbury, Kennedy's spokesman, Walter Arm, gathered the police shack reporters to dispute Con Ed's claim that Alice Kelly found the file. "We haven't got the full version of events yet, but we say it's not so," Arm told reporters in a voice strained with stress and exhaustion from staying up all night. "As far as we know, it was one of our men." He mistakenly insisted that on Friday, January 18, detectives had completed their search of the files at Con Ed's Hester Street warehouse, then, having finally learned of the hidden pre-1940 files, dug into them. On Friday evening, Arm said, Detective Bertram Scott had personally pulled the Metesky file and spotted its telltale language.

Then why, reporters asked, had Scott waited until Monday morning to bring the file to headquarters? Arm lamely replied that he did not yet have "a complete report on the matter."

The next morning Kennedy summoned twenty-three policemen, including Bertram and the four bomb squad detectives who had made the arrest, to headquarters and congratulated them on "excellent work." He promised each man a promotion, along with a $746 raise. As first-grade detectives, they would now make $7,104 a year. In the dingy police shack rooms across the street, reporters laughed. The raises were obviously staged to promote the police department efforts.

Even now, in their hour of success, the police were forced to play defense. Newspapers reminded readers that sixteen years had passed between Metesky's first bomb and his arrest—during which he had planted thirty-two bombs and injured fifteen people. Reporters hinted that if Dr. Brussel had not shrunk the search window for them, the police might never have caught Metesky.

To defray blame, an anonymous police official, later identified as Walter Arm, told the Associated Press on January 24 that Con Ed had impeded the investigation by withholding the pre-1940 records that contained Metesky's file. The police had asked Con Ed "repeatedly for two years to produce records prior to 1940," the source said, and each time Con Ed "claimed it had none." The police had not learned of the secret files, the source said, until they received a tip two weeks prior to the arrest. When they again requested the files, "a series of stalls ensued."

As soon as the police accusation against Con Ed leaked, the fraternity of police shack reporters scrambled across Centre Market Place and raced upstairs to see if the commissioner would corroborate the charge. He refused to let them into his office. They encamped in the hallway with no sign of dispersing. The commissioner is busy, they were told. The reporters suspected his schedule was not the problem; he just didn't want to answer questions that might prove embarrassing. Finally, after an hour, a press photographer took a picture of the reporters standing beside Kennedy's closed door. The picture would appear in that afternoon's papers, the reporters told the commissioner's assistant, unless he saw them now. Within minutes the commissioner threw open the door.

The reporters crowded around Kennedy, using the edge of his desk to write on. He began by reiterating the leaker's contention, saying, "We were informed that 1940 files were the earliest that Consolidated Edison had. The obvious question this raises is, Why were the earlier files not searched? The impression given to me by men who investigated the situation was that such files were not in existence."

Not surprisingly, a Con Ed spokesman responded by saying the utility had fully cooperated. If there was a delay, he said, it was caused by the need to vet the stacks of thick files with Con Ed lawyers. He challenged the anonymous source to step forward: "If any charge is to be made, let them take off their masks. Let the man making the charges identify himself and tell us what the charges are. We are not police. We sell electricity. When the police asked for information, or names, or access to files, we gave it."

Con Ed president Harland C. Forbes phoned Kennedy to say that he wanted to make plans for "straightening out this confusion by going over the matter jointly." The two men met the next day at police headquarters. Afterward Kennedy reluctantly granted a press conference to twenty or so reporters. In a rare moment of public humiliation, he conceded that Con Ed's version of events was correct. He acknowledged that Deputy Commissioner Arm's contention that Bertram Scott had found the file was made on incomplete information by exhausted detectives.

Now the reporters circled Kennedy's desk like sharks quickened by the scent of blood. They stepped up their questioning while scribbling Kennedy's responses in spiral-bound notebooks. One asked why sixty hours had elapsed between Kelly's discovery and Scott's errand to pick up the file. Kennedy didn't have an answer. "It was only a ten-minute ride to the Con Ed offices," another said. "Why did Scott wait until Monday morning?"

Kennedy answered, unconvincingly, that Scott hadn't picked up the file on Friday night because Metesky was "one of a number of leads" the police were working on at the time.

Reporter: "This was not good police work, was it, Commissioner?"

Kennedy: "Police were working for five or six years and did not know of such a file. We have no power over Con Ed to force them to give over their files—to know that there was such a file."

Reporter: "Are you satisfied with the police work in this case?"

It was one query too many. A dark cloud passed over Kennedy's face, and he strained to maintain his bearing: "A man has been arrested who was at liberty for sixteen years. His dangerous potentialities have been nullified. I think the facts speak for themselves."

Con Ed countered by arranging for Kelly to meet with reporters. A pretty blonde with a ready smile, she was the popular favorite to win the $26,000 reward, especially now that Kennedy had confirmed that she had, in fact, found the file. He was obliged to acknowledge her contribution to Metesky's capture, but it galled him to think that a Con Ed employee would pocket the reward money after the company had hid its files from his men.

In the end, Kennedy's frustration was groundless. After the rift between Con Ed and the police had turned ugly, Kelly disavowed any claim to the prize. She privately told a deputy police commissioner that her mother, a woman of steadfast Catholic principles, considered the reward blood money and urged her not to accept it. Publicly Kelly said, "I was just assigned to . . . pull these cases out and that's why I feel . . . that this business of people talking about a reward, and all that sort of thing—I have no more right to that than the man in the moon." All she wanted, she said, was to get back to the routine clerical work that had piled up on her desk since she was assigned to the bomber search. The $26,000 was never awarded.

The police were unable to prove that Con Ed deliberately hid files from them, but detectives assigned to the case privately expressed suspicions that the company did so for fear that the files would reveal a succession of illnesses caused by conditions in the power plants. "They knew that we had detectives in Albany looking over all the old compensation files," Detective Edward Lehane told a magazine more than twenty years later. "There was some indication, I believe, that they were getting close up there in Albany. So they knew the goddamn net was closing. That's when Con Ed suddenly came up with it."

Con Ed had explaining to do, given that the company had repeatedly told Captain Finney and his detectives that it had destroyed all employee records dated before 1940. The Metesky file proved that was untrue. A company lawyer now claimed that their initial statement referred only to litigation cases. It was, Forbes said, a misunderstanding.

The *Journal-American* faced no such recriminations. The newspaper, like its competitors, was suffering from the early onset of print's decline, but for one glorious moment it basked in an unequivocal triumph engineered almost single-handedly by Berkson. The publisher led the way as pressmen, copyboys, and editors celebrated day and night at Moochie's Saloon. They pressed in among the longshoremen and fishmongers to raise sloshing pints of Piels and Ballantine as congratulatory telegrams poured in from FBI director J. Edgar Hoover, Governor Averell Harriman, and Mayor Robert Wagner. William Randolph Hearst Jr., in a boastful front-page column, called the bomber coverage "one of the great journalistic coups of the past generation." Even the paper's afternoon rival, the *World-Telegram and Sun,* commended their "esteemed compeers at the *New York Journal-American* for some first-class newspaper work. . . . The fog surrounding the final hours of the chase cannot obscure the excellent job they did."

If that weren't enough praise, NBC aired a thirty-minute fictionalized version of the *Journal-American*'s role in the manhunt. Berkson was played by Whitfield Connor, a Shakespearean actor with a string of Broadway credits.

In an editorial published the day after Metesky's capture, Berkson said, "We intend to abide by the promises that we made to him in our exchange of letters, namely that his grievances will be aired fully and fairly and that he will receive the full benefits of our American system of justice."

Between trips to Moochie's, Berkson followed through on his promise by persuading Bart J. O'Rourke, one of the city's most respected labor lawyers, to conduct a pro bono investigation of Metesky's compensation case. His first job would be to determine if the Workmen's Compensation Board would be willing to reopen Metesky's original claim. If they did, Metesky could be owed as much as $15,000.

The *Journal-American* would benefit from the effort, even if Metesky did not. By retaining O'Rourke, Berkson kept the Metesky story in the headlines, with the *Journal-American* playing the role of a magnanimous central player. Berkson also inoculated himself against any accusations that he had manipulated Metesky simply for the newspaper's gain.

After studying the files sent down from Albany, O'Rourke concluded that the board was within its rights to reject Metesky's appeal, filed in 1934, because he submitted it after the two-year statute of limitations. Still, a wily veteran lawyer such as O'Rourke could sniff out a potential loophole. What if, as seemed likely, the Bellevue doctors pronounced Metesky insane? Would that not excuse his late filing in the eyes of the law? O'Rourke also suggested that Metesky's case was part of a widespread practice by Con Ed and other companies to cheat injured employees by doling out small sums from a special fund for a year or so, after which the employees no longer qualified for workman's compensation.

In the days after Metesky's arrest, reporters followed up the loose strands of the story, including expressions of relief from his victims. "Thank God, now [Metesky] can't hurt anybody else," said Abraham Blumenthal, the postal worker whose left leg was injured when a shard of glass severed a blood vessel a month earlier at the Paramount Theater in Brooklyn. "I'll never forget that man, that's for sure. He had the whole city in a panic. Everyone was afraid to go to a movie or make a call from a phone booth. Now the city will be at peace again."

His wife, Ruth, added, "I wasn't hurt seriously but I've been too frightened to go anywhere since."

With the fear receding and details of the manhunt wrapped up, reporters shifted their focus to the riddle of Metesky's mental condition and the pressing question of whether his derangement would excuse him from prosecution. How crazy was he, anyway? Too crazy to stand trial?

At Metesky's arraignment, Magistrate Judge Reuben Levy said that he "saw a man with a psychosis, with a persecution complex." Psychiatric terms such as these might sound familiar, but for the most part the public did not understand them. Nor did reporters. The phone in Dr. Brussel's downtown office began to ring. He became the unofficial psychiatrist to call for explanations. He held forth, even though he had never met Metesky in person—not yet anyway.

On January 26 he appeared on a local television news show, *Eye on New York,* to explain that Metesky's paranoia stemmed from the repression of unresolved psychosexual issues dating back to early childhood. Dr. Brussel predicted that there would be no cure for Metesky: "I doubt if shock therapy would affect him, and he's not a fit candidate for formal psychoanalysis." For one thing, analysis required patients to trust their doctors. Paranoids such as Metesky would only view doctors with suspicion, and they would never amend or adjust their thinking. "Nothing you can say will make the paranoiac change his mind," Dr. Brussel would later write. "He can marshal all kinds of compelling evidence to support his central premise. His delusion is rooted in reality in such a way that it baffles efforts to dispel it. He'll walk down a street with you and say, 'See, I told you I'm always being followed—why, there's a man right behind us now, following me!' And you look back, and sure enough, there's a man behind you. You can't argue the man away. He's there, he's real. The difference lies in your interpretation of reality. You figure the man just happens to be going your way. The paranoiac is convinced the man has some sinister purpose."

The job of plumbing the reaches of Metesky's mind fell to a panel of Bellevue psychiatrists. Metesky passed the short, dark days of late January in an open Bellevue ward waiting for them to rule on his state of mind: Was he competent to stand trial, or wasn't he?

CHAPTER SIXTEEN

MR. DEATH

January 1957

JAMES D. C. MURRAY STEELED HIMSELF IN HIS LAW OFFICE ON THE THIRTY-seventh floor of the Woolworth Building, a Gothic spire rising above City Hall Park. At seventy-four, his neatly parted white hair was thinning, and chronic migraines sapped his vigor. As he aged into his seventies, the nervous tension of oncoming trials induced periodic headaches. "It feels as if some diabolical demon sticks a red-hot poker through your eye and out the side of your head," he said.

Murray had plenty of cause for tension. For fifty years he had represented hundreds of the most detested defendants—a procession of rapists, kidnappers, mobsters, crooked cops, and more than a hundred accused murderers. He defended a babysitter who drowned a three-year-old, a butler accused of murdering his wealthy employer, a man who raped and killed a fourteen-year-old girl, and a couple who starved their adopted son to death.

For these unenviable assignments Murray was paid modestly, if at all. "When I stop working," he said, "my natural habitat will be the alms-house." He once smuggled one of his own suits out of his closet so a penniless client could wear it to court. He kept the loan a secret from his wife, confessing only when she set out to accuse the dry cleaner of stealing.

He stood up for the hopeless cases, one after another, with masterly skill and a soft voice sweetened with Irish lyricism. He was deservedly known as the champion of lost causes. (The only lawbreaker he refused to defend was Fritz Kuhn, a leader of the German American Bund, a Nazi organization.) At one stretch, in the 1920s, he won forty-three straight felony acquittals. "He is a superb stage director," an acquaintance said. "He keeps the jury's interest and sympathy focused on the defendant. He is never aggressive or noisy—never invites you to admire his smartness."

Nothing about Murray was intimidating. A grandfatherly figure, he was gentle and melancholic. He came to court wearing bookish horn-rimmed glasses, sober black suits, and drab ties secured day after day with the same clip. He never shouted or pounded the defense table. He never speechified. Nonetheless prosecutors watched him with apprehension. He might be quiet, but he was shrewd. "You can't turn your back on Murray for a second," said a prosecutor. "He's like a cat. He jumps as soon as he sees an opening."

He had a gift for the destroying phrase dropped with keen timing. But his aspect was cool. Over fifty years of exposure to cases of heartbreak and tragedy, he only once allowed himself to show uninhibited emotion in court. In 1942, he defended a seventeen-year-old boy who pled guilty to killing a man. For four years the man had abused the boy's widowed mother. Murray stood before the judge, his cheeks shiny with tears, to ask that the boy's sentence be suspended. Murray would have been disappointed, he said, if his own son had not acted the same way under the circumstances. The judge granted the suspension.

Murray was man of inflexible habits. He spent his days in court or consulting with clients, then, without deviation, boarded the 5:20 train to Rockville Centre, a bedroom community near the south shore of Long Island. "I don't like the city," he said. "I hate crowds. I don't like people. I detest courtrooms."

He refused to take work calls at home, and he never shared the particulars of his cases with his family. His wife learned whom he defended only by reading the *Journal-American* and the *Herald Tribune*. "She doesn't know whether I'm a street sweeper or a lawyer," he said, "unless she reads the paper."

Murray had no hobbies or pastimes. He didn't play cards or watch baseball. "I've never been to a nightclub or a racetrack in my life," he said. "The last movie I saw was maybe twenty-five or thirty years ago. I don't read crime or fiction. I go to bed at nine o'clock every night while my wife watches television as late as she can—maybe to four in the morning."

Family was his only diversion. Every Saturday, without exception, Murray took his family, including ten grandchildren, to lunch at the same neighborhood restaurant. He often ate with his youngest grandchild on his lap: "After we're through, you can tell what the menu was by studying my shirtfront. It abounds with circumstantial evidence."

Murray never fully explained why he agreed to defend murderers and rapists, except to say that he "was born with a constitutional pity for those in trouble." In his view, the man or woman on trial was always an underdog, no matter the circumstances. "He is but an individual, and opposing him is the organized might of society. The forces of law are set in motion to destroy the defendant; the only one who can stand between him and destruction is his lawyer."

He often agreed to take on defendants that he personally despised out of sympathy for their families: "I always remember that it isn't the man in the death house who suffers. He may have a fine brother, sister, or a wife and children. Although they are blameless, they go on suffering for years."

Murray may have agreed to represent Metesky for his sisters. The afternoon after their brother's arrest, Anna and Mae put on their best church dresses and drove the Daimler across the Naugatuck River to the downtown Waterbury office of Harry F. Spellman, a prominent local attorney and a former New Haven County prosecutor. The sisters had by now accepted that their mild-mannered brother was the bomber, though they refused to blame him for his actions. "It is possible that he may have been so upset and aggravated by his suffering that this perhaps bothered him mentally," Mae said. "But if George did anything wrong, he is not responsible."

Responsible or not, he would need counsel. They were determined to hire the best possible lawyer, no matter the cost. "What we have," they told Spellman, "we are more than willing to give to George. We will even sell the house to help him, and we will go live in the poorhouse." Spellman agreed to help, but urged them to retain Murray, another Waterbury native, as lead attorney.

Murray's upbringing was only marginally different from Metesky's. His father was a $5-a-day mechanic in a Waterbury metal-rolling mill. When Murray was young, explosions in a local dynamite factory left dozens of workers dead or crippled. The widows and survivors received almost nothing. The courts were controlled by the mill owners, so there was no legal recourse. Families became destitute. "Those things impressed me," Murray said. "As I grew older, I began to conclude that the benefits of law were only for the well-to-do, and the poor didn't have a chance." Yes, Murray told Anna and Mae, he would defend their brother.

The next afternoon Murray sat in his comfortably worn office in the Woolworth Building, once the tallest building in the world, where he had worked for twenty-seven years. It was nothing like the modern offices of the young go-getter law firms in midtown glass towers, with their polished chestnut desks and rolling cocktail carts. A light scattering of dust lay across Murray's glass-fronted bookcases, containing rows of leatherbound law journals. Tufts of stuffing spilled from the ripped seams of a pair of black leather club chairs. Framed pictures of his grandchildren sat among disordered piles of files. Murray sat at his mahogany desk, flicking his cigarette ash and gazing at the majestic necklace of lights strung across the Brooklyn Bridge. He rubbed his throbbing temples. His powers might be waning, but he would have to summon strength for the coming fight.

Murray's first step was to make sure Metesky never went to trial. On January 24, two days after the arrest, Murray set out with Spellman to appraise their client's condition for themselves. They walked through a menacing spiked iron gate at First Avenue and Thirtieth Street to a nine-story redbrick building with a short curtilage of lawn hard against the East River. Prison bars covered the windows. Its macabre aspect reflected its reputation as place of straitjackets and bodies contorted in anguish.

The Bellevue psych ward was a grim municipal madhouse, a city-run asylum housed within one of America's oldest public hospitals. In unforgiving New York, Bellevue was a place of last resort for the addled, anguished, and lost. This was where cops brought handcuffed bridge jumpers and florid psychotics found wandering the streets, scratching their faces and muttering at the moon. The halls rang with yelps and howls.

Murray and Spellman arrived at three fifteen. They had to wait while attendants took Metesky upstairs for an electroencephalogram, a brain-wave recording used to study schizophrenia. Ninety minutes later Murray found Metesky waiting by the door to a locked second-floor prison ward painted off-white and furnished with plastic chairs. The ward contained ten lockup rooms with no furniture, only mats on the floor, for violent patients. Metesky was wearing the hospital uniform of blue wool pajamas and slippers with a knee-length pinstriped bathrobe. He sat on a bench opposite the two lawyers and blinked nervously at them. Three guards stood nearby in case he attempted suicide.

If Metesky entertained thoughts of ending his life, he didn't share them. On the contrary, he might have been the only patient to enjoy detention in Bellevue. The guards described him as a "most happy fellow" as he awaited his fate. He showed not the slightest inclination to violence or conflict. After a lifetime of secrecy and seclusion, he worked the drab open wards like the mayor of Bellevue, chatting and joking about the weather and tele-vision shows with the twenty-five other patients on his ward, a group that included murderers, armed robbers, and other violent criminals. In the coming days he became the ward's unofficial checkers champion. He cheer-fully alerted nurses when patients required medications, or when they con-tracted a fever or a headache, though nurses may have detected a trace of condescension in his voice when he did so. "He thinks he's a hero and ex-pects somebody to put a laurel wreath on his head," an attendant told re-porters. "He doesn't view his plight with any apprehension."

Murray spoke quietly with Metesky for forty-five minutes, explaining that New York State normally allowed offenders such as him to stand trial only if a panel of psychiatrists judged them sane enough to understand the charges and assist in their defense. If the psychiatrists found them incapable of doing so, judges ordinarily declared the defendants incompetent and committed them to an asylum for the criminally insane. The court made the final ruling on fitness to stand trial, but the psychiatrists were essentially the arbiters of insanity, even though *insanity* was not a term generally used within the psychiatric field.

In the judicial world, psychiatrists were ascendant. A few years earlier they'd played only a marginal consulting role. Back then courts ruled on insanity based on the defendant's ability to tell right from wrong. The litmus test for sanity was morality, not science. Did the mother who drowned her toddlers grasp the horror of her deed? If she felt no bite of guilt or remorse—if she was unaware that she'd done wrong—she was judged incompetent for trial.

This right-and-wrong standard, known as the McNaughton Rule, dated back 114 years to an English common-law rule that spared a defendant if he "did not know what he was doing was wrong." The rule was named for Daniel McNaughton, an intensely private twenty-nine-year-old Scottish woodworker who, in 1843, imagined that the British government was conspiring against him. "They followed me to France, into Scotland; in fact, they follow me wherever I go," he said. "I can get no rest from them night or day. In fact, they wish to murder me."

He heard God's whispered warnings that Robert Peel, the prime minister, was the devil in disguise. McNaughton had persuaded himself that if he killed Peel, all of Europe would revere him as a savior. Like Metesky, he had been a solitary man, unmarried, who felt sure that a violent stroke of vengeance would earn him glory.

McNaughton stalked Peel for days, loitering outside the government offices in Whitehall so frequently that guards questioned him. He trailed Peel's carriage as it ferried the prime minister along the gloomy winter streets of London. On the afternoon of January 20, McNaughton waited outside Peel's home in the Charing Cross neighborhood with two pistols stashed in his waistcoat. At 3:30 p.m. a man with a top hat stepped from the doorway and walked south. McNaughton drew his pistols and shot the man in the upper back, just below the shoulder blade. He then stepped onto Peel's doorstep and demanded that passersby bow down to him. "I have ridden Europe of a monster," he yelled. In fact he had shot the wrong man. The figure who now lay bleeding in the street was Edward Drummond, Peel's private secretary and a distant relative of Henry VIII's. Drummond died five days later at his home in Grosvenor Square.

At McNaughton's trial, his defense lawyer showed that McNaughton was "laboring under an insane delusion." The jury found him "not guilty on the ground of insanity" and sentenced him to life in an asylum.

The decision met with strident objections from London newspapers, which accused the court of letting McNaughton off easy. Queen Victoria, who had survived an assassination attempt three years earlier, wrote Peel to express disapproval. She feared that leniency would lead to more assassinations. In response, the House of Lords asked twelve eminent judges for a statement clarifying exactly what mental condition absolved a defendant of responsibility for a crime. The judges said defendants would be excused from trial if they were "laboring under such a defect of reason, from disease of the mind, as to not know the nature and quality of the act . . . or, if he did know it, that he did not know he was doing what was wrong."

The American courts adopted the rule, and it endured for a century as the litmus test for criminal insanity. If a person committed a violent crime without understanding that society forbids the act—without comprehending its ghastly brutality—he or she was excused from trial. The thin line between sanity and madness was firmly established, at least until now.

The judge with the greatest influence on Metesky's future would never face him in a courtroom. David Bazelon was the leonine white-haired chief of the United States Court of Appeals for the District of Columbia, the second most influential court in the country. In one pivotal case after another he asked penetrating questions while peering down from the bench with half-glasses perched on the end of his nose. More often than not those questions tested convention. His court was considered the country's most liberal, far to the left of the Supreme Court. Bazelon was its most liberal member.

Bazelon was an activist judge, but hardly an outsider. He was a well-connected member of the capital's liberal intelligentsia. He met once a month to discuss law and policy with an old-boy clique of left-leaning Washington big shots—a group that included Justice Earl Warren and Thurgood Marshall, then a civil rights lawyer—over simple family-style lunches served in the back room of a wholesale liquor warehouse lined with framed black-and-white portraits of politicians and athletes.

He was known in particular for defending the disadvantaged, a concern that came from personal hardship. He was the youngest of nine children. His father, a grocer in Superior, Wisconsin, died when Bazelon was two, leaving his family penniless. Bazelon was the only member of his family to attend college. He paid his way by moonlighting as a movie usher.

Bazelon was fond of saying that brains meant nothing without heart. He accordingly made a career for himself as judge who looked out for the urban poor and downtrodden. He tended to absolve offenders of blame, casting them instead as victims of substandard living conditions. Most wrongdoers, he believed, were decent characters corrupted by inadequate upbringings. The judiciary's job was to rehabilitate, not incarcerate. Bazelon studied psychology to better understand the causes of defendants' behavior. He became conversant enough to lecture in psychiatry at the Johns Hopkins School of Medicine, and he taught a course on the legal aspects of psychiatry at George Washington University. Colleagues considered him an intermediary between the bench and the couch.

"[Bazelon] observed that most 'blue collar' crimes were committed by persons who had deprived, abusive, or traumatic childhoods," wrote Ralph Slovenko, an expert in forensic psychiatry. "Because they were 'ill' by what he considered to be psychiatric standards, Bazelon felt these persons should be treated instead of punished."

In Bazelon's view, the McNaughton Rule reflected the old morality and crude psychology of Victorian England. It didn't utilize Freudian insights; in fact, Freud was not born when McNaughton took effect. The growing consensus in liberal-thinking law circles was that McNaughton's rigid, antiquated right-and-wrong standard should give way to a more enlightened rule that would allow doctors to weigh in with a modern understanding of the underlying mental illnesses that led to crime. Not surprisingly, Bazelon was on the lookout for ways to give psychiatrists more say in insanity cases.

Bazelon found his opportunity in the sad case of Monte Durham. The navy had judged Durham unfit for service and discharged him at age seventeen. He spent the next six years shuttling in and out of mental hospitals, where doctors diagnosed him as psychotic. Between incarcerations he dabbled in petty crime. In 1951, when Durham was twenty-three, the DC police caught him breaking into a Georgetown home. The court rejected Durham's insanity defense because, in its estimation, his lawyer had failed to prove that he could not distinguish right from wrong. He was found guilty and sentenced to a term of three to ten years.

Bazelon qualified to hear Durham's appeal because his court then had criminal jurisdiction in the District of Columbia. He promptly pronounced Durham's original trial inadequate because the lower court had not allowed a psychiatrist called as an expert witness to present his full testimony. Bazelon's court then overturned the earlier verdict. The opinion, written by Bazelon himself, replaced McNaughton with a new test, the so-called Durham Rule, which held that a person was not responsible for a crime if his or her actions were the "product of a mental disease or defect." Gone was the Victorian discussion of right and wrong. The Durham Rule cast criminal behavior as a sickness. And sickness was best evaluated by psychiatrists, not lawyers.

The Durham Rule was welcomed as a leap forward. It gave psychiatrists room to address the basis of a defendant's behavior in a full, nuanced manner. Dr. Karl A. Menninger, the dean of American psychiatry, described it as "more revolutionary in its total effect than the Supreme Court decision regarding desegregation." The American Psychiatric Association said that Bazelon "has removed massive barriers between the psychiatric and legal professions."

When the commendations died down, doubts crept in. In practice Durham began to look unworkable. Psychiatrists on the stand dissected intricate emotional problems with impenetrable terms such as *reduplicative paramnesia* and *dissociative fugue*. For every psychiatrist testifying for the defense, there was one for the prosecution. They constantly contradicted each other. No one seemed to know what the definition of insanity was, or who would decide.

Lawyers and psychiatrists had always viewed each other with suspicion. Now their antipathy grew into open hostility. Jurists worried that psychiatrists might be too sympathetic to defendants, and too eager to forgive them. Psychiatrists suspected the courts were not truly interested in understanding the accused and their motivations, only in expedient punishment. "The prosecutor and the medical expert is not a co-operative relationship in search of the truth, but a sort of joust, a boxing bout with few if any holds or fouls barred," wrote Dr. Gregory Zilboorg, a prominent historian of psychiatry.

Metesky came before the court at this moment of dispute between two powerful fields. After Murray met with Metesky at Bellevue, he declined to tell reporters waiting for him outside if he would adopt the insanity defense, saying, "This was simply the first in a series of consultations."

The three Bellevue psychiatrists charged with evaluating Metesky spent weeks asking about his family history and the surging resentment leading up to his bombing campaign. During their long sessions, held in a room off the open ward, they found him to be "alert, cooperative, and eager to oblige in answering questions." He cheerfully described his fantasy of shooting the president of Con Ed in the heart and, for the first time, revealed a plan "to get back at people" by manipulating Con Ed power switches in such a way that New York would suffer a citywide blackout. He spoke with a "glow of ecstatic fervor" as he described his planned "martyrdom."

Session after session, through the short, dark days of late January and early February, the psychiatrists kept probing. Why did Metesky hide his vendetta from the sisters who had sacrificed so much for him? How did he decide to use bombs to fight injustice? Did he feel remorse over the injuries he caused?

The psychiatrists also interviewed Metesky's sister Anna, who, when pressed, acknowledged that her brother had always been strangely solitary, even as a young boy. He never once brought a friend home from parochial school, never went on a date. He showed no interest in girls at all. He was oddly uncommunicative, even with his own family. Anna could not recall his sharing anything about his two tours of duty with the Marines except that he showed his sisters photographs of Dominicans with their heads cut off.

In the twenty-two years since he had returned home from the Tucson sanitarium, Anna and her sister, Mae, had noted with concern how mistrustful their brother had grown. He complained that acquaintances were exchanging information about him behind his back and muttered to himself about imagined slights. "We attempted to get him to see a doctor, but he refused," Anna said.

On January 30, a grand jury indicted Metesky on forty-seven counts. If convicted on all counts, he could receive a maximum sentence of 815 years in prison. The next day Metesky arrived with all the fanfare of a visiting dignitary. He rode in a prison van flanked by police cruisers with flashing lights. The caravan pulled up to the New York County Court of General Sessions at 100 Centre Street, where felonies were tried. Metesky stepped from the van, shackled and guarded by fifteen patrolmen. It was "a police production worthy of Hollywood," the *World-Telegram and Sun* wrote. "There were enough cops on hand to have awed a

Dillinger." Metesky posed on the courtroom steps for two full minutes with flashbulbs popping before police escorted him to a detention pen.

The security was so tight that Murray, at first, could not enter to explain the day's proceedings to his client. "I went to go into the detention pen," Murray later said, "and there were twenty heavy-hooved cops, and they slammed the door into my face. I had to go get the clerk before they let me in."

After Murray finally met with Metesky, the judge summoned the accused. "George Metesky to the bar," the court clerk said. "Bring him out, Captain."

Bailiffs escorted Metesky from a detention cell into the courtroom, where he stood at the bar in his dark overcoat, a blue-striped shirt, and maroon tie. He rested his hat on the rail. He stared vacantly at the judge with a look of confusion.

"Are you George Metesky, alias George Milauskas?" the clerk asked. "Yes, sir."

"You are indicted for the crime of attempted murder, and so forth. How do you plead?"

Metesky seemed not to understand the question. Murray stepped in to propose that the pleading be postponed until the psychiatrists had completed their examination, and that Metesky stay on at Bellevue in the meantime. A brief conversation followed in which Karl Grebow, an assistant district attorney, asked if Murray was, in fact, asking for a postponement so that he could go on vacation. "Not me," Murray said. "I had a vacation once. In 1935."

The judge agreed to postpone the arraignment until February 21, by which time the psychiatrists would presumably have submitted their report. "Okay, let's go," a guard told Metesky. He picked up his hat and headed back to the van for the return ride to Bellevue.

Murray wanted to emphasize Metesky's craziness to more easily get him excused from a trial. After the court session adjourned, he stopped to give reporters a graphic description of his client's state of mind: "He has delusions of grandeur and claims he is the savior of soulless corporations.

He shows no sorrow for his acts and keeps saying, 'I'd do it again.' . . . His sisters told me that he'd watch a funeral on television and laugh like the dickens. Other times he would be very dejected and go to bed for periods of up to eighteen hours without speaking to them."

On February 19, Metesky, still smiling but noticeably ashen after nearly a month of confinement, stood handcuffed to a corrections officer in the Kings County Courthouse in downtown Brooklyn, where that borough's district attorney was pursuing his own charges against Metesky stemming from the December bombing at the Paramount Theater. Metesky was in the rare position of facing concurrent charges in neighboring jurisdictions, Manhattan and Brooklyn, that would have to be reconciled, though nobody knew exactly how. The Brooklyn judge, like his Manhattan counterpart, postponed the proceedings for the psychiatric report.

By penal regulation, Metesky was required to be rephotographed at police headquarters. "Gee whiz," he told the two police photographers. "I thought I'd get a Manhattan cocktail after this was all over. Boys, I need one bad."

By mid-February impatience set in. Was Metesky mad or wasn't he? The question was confounded by his seemingly ordinary demeanor. He behaved normally most of the time, and he was clearly capable of shrewd, dispassionate reasoning. He had behaved normally, enough at any rate, to enlist in the Marines and get jobs without raising suspicions. *The New York Times* compared him to Dr. Jekyll and Mr. Hyde—angelic around family while conducting a secret life as a bomber.

"This fellow is smarter than a Supreme Court justice," Murray said by way of explanation for the long delay. "If a blithering idiot gets into the psychopathic ward, the doctors can report on him in ten days or so. But there is probably no limit as to disagreements on Metesky."

The scheduled hearing date came and went and still the psychiatrists deliberated inside Bellevue's dark-brick building. The whispered consensus in the city's judicial chambers was that Metesky would be declared insane, but the certainty ebbed with each passing day.

Finally, on February 28, Judge John A. Mullen of the New York

County Court in Manhattan could wait no longer. In a fit of judicial impatience he abruptly called an unscheduled hearing. "If the written report is not ready, tell Bellevue to send one of its psychiatrists along with Metesky, to report to me orally on his mental condition," Judge Mullen ordered.

The various players scrambled for the courtroom. Reporters and bailiffs hurried to their places. Bellevue attendants told Metesky to change out of his hospital garb and into his double-breasted suit, and they hustled him downtown in a police van. Murray was trying a manslaughter case in the Bronx. By necessity, he sent an associate, Irving Greenberg, in his place. Dr. John Cassity, one of the Bellevue psychiatrists, rushed to the office of Karl Grebow, an assistant district attorney, who had to be summoned from another courtroom. Together they burst into the courtroom.

Judge Mullen was a throwback to Tammany Hall days, an old-school jurist with the hard features of a Dickensian magistrate. Mobsters called him Mr. Death because he meted out the toughest sentences. Please, anybody but Mullen, they told their lawyers. Anybody but Mr. Death.

Judge Mullen, the mouthy curmudgeon, had spent his life sentencing criminals in a city beset by crime. He was notorious for lashing out at the softhearted progressives, the reformers who had come into influence with Mayor Wagner. Eleven years earlier, while sentencing two seventeen-year-olds who had shot and killed a sixteen-year-old bystander during a gang skirmish, Mullen had made headlines by accusing former mayor Fiorello La Guardia of "coddling" Harlem street gangs. Gangs throughout the city, Mullen told the boys, "had been broken up by the use of nightsticks by policemen who were permitted to do their duty and use force, the one thing young thugs like you boys here before me respect."

Now sixty-eight, Mullen's bald head was mottled with age spots. His blue eyes shone when anger gripped him, which was often. "The judge looks very much like the Hollywood conception of a shrewd Irish football coach," a court reporter for the *New York World-Telegram* once wrote.

Mullen bristled at the long delays caused by the plodding psychiatric deliberations. The holdup was, he believed, further evidence that the judicial system was bogging down with fuzzy-minded reforms, bureaucratic flab, and weakness. A 1953 study showed that the average time elapsed between arrest and final sentencing in New York State was more than two years. By comparison, British courts disposed of cases within two weeks.

Mullen hated postponements, and he hated what he saw as a judicial culture degenerating into laxity. He belonged to a small but outspoken group of judges who wanted to block violent criminals from exploiting lenient insanity provisions. Four years earlier a twenty-nine-year-old Air Force veteran named Bayard Peakes applied to present an incoherent thirty-three-page paper proving the existence of eternal life at a meeting of the American Physical Society, which sponsors research on physics. He titled the paper "So You Love Physics." Karl K. Darrow, secretary of the society and an accomplished physicist, not surprisingly mailed Peakes a rejection letter. In response he bought a .22 caliber automatic pistol and a box of bullets. On the morning of July 14, 1952, he showed up at the society's offices, in a laboratory building at Columbia University, with the intention of killing Darrow. When he found that Darrow was out, he aimed his pistol at the only available target, a pretty eighteen-year-old stenographer with reddish-blonde hair. She was at her desk reading the first of three unopened letters from her fiancé, a Marine Corps private stationed in Korea. Five shots struck her, three of them in her chest, one in her right hand, and one in her right forearm. "I just shot a girl," Peakes said to a passerby as he left. "Call an ambulance." She died within hours.

Two weeks later, Peakes, like Metesky, was brought from Bellevue to the Court of General Sessions for arraignment. He pleaded not guilty to the first-degree murder charge by reason of insanity. In a bitter outburst, Judge Saul S. Streit, a tall, somber-faced jurist, noted that psychiatrists at the Veterans Administration had diagnosed Peakes as a dangerous schizophrenic, but the air force nonetheless discharged him to roam free. Streit called Peakes's release "rank negligence" and "utter disregard of public safety."

"No institution, state or Federal, is justified in releasing, discharging or paroling an insane person with a predisposition to criminal, assaultive or homicidal tendencies," Streit said. "It is just a question of time as to when and where some of them may explode." He cited twelve cases of deranged people who had committed violent crimes after their release from psychiatric facilities, including a Brooklyn man who stabbed four people to death and a Bronx girl who fatally shot her mother with a .22 caliber rifle. Judge Streit said he found these cases after "just a cursory examination" of his files. He had no doubt "that there are thousands of such discharged and paroled lunatics at large; it is just a question of time as to when or where some of them may explode."

To Judge Mullen, the Peakes case captured everything misguided about the liberalized judiciary. To make matter worse, Peakes's lawyer was none other than James D. C. Murray, the man who now spoke for Metesky. Judge Mullen's fear was that Metesky might be committed and later released to plant bombs all over again.

A scowl afflicted Judge Mullen's face as he entered the wood-paneled courtroom and climbed the steps to the bench for the Metesky arraignment. He gaveled the court to order and stared implacably as Greenberg, Murray's stand-in, argued that he was unfamiliar with the case and therefore unqualified to represent Metesky. What's more, he said, the report on Metesky's mental condition was still unfinished.

After a long, uneasy pause, Judge Mullen asked Greenberg if he had anything else to say. Greenberg stood flummoxed and speechless behind the defendant's table as Dr. Cassity took the stand. The psychiatrist explained that though Metesky's comportment was calm and agreeable, the Bellevue team believed him to be a paranoid schizophrenic. He detailed Metesky's homicidal fantasies and delusional belief that his bombings safeguarded mankind from malignant forces.

"Did Metesky understand his actions?" Judge Mullen asked.

"I do not think that he knew the nature and quality or significance," Cassity answered.

Mullen squinted and stroked his chin. "Did he know, in your opinion, that exploding a bomb was exploding a bomb?" Or did he think "he was eating apple pie?"

"Yes, I think he knew that."

Mullen's voice grew louder, as if to drive home a point. "Do you think that he knew that that was against the accepted rules of conduct in the society in which he lived?"

"No, I don't think so."

"Did he tell you he was eating cake to get even with society?"

"No, he didn't tell me he was eating cake."

Reporters seated in the press gallery noticed the lawyers stiffen in surprise. The proceeding had taken a strange turn. Judge Mullen's queries, delivered so stridently from the bench, expressed his disdain for the psychiatrists who were, under Durham, supposed to play the crucial role in evaluating Metesky's state of mind. Even more surprising, Judge Mullen's line of questioning focused on Metesky's ability to distinguish right from wrong, suggesting that he would revert to the McNaughton definition of insanity. Was it possible that Judge Mullen would use Metesky to turn back the judicial clock?

Judge Mullen now shifted his gaze to Metesky, who stood smiling wanly at the side of the courtroom. With a nod to Greenberg, Judge Mullen demanded that the defendant enter a plea. Greenberg jumped to his feet. His face burned and his voice became shrill. Metesky could not enter a plea, Greenberg insisted, until the psychiatric report was finalized and submitted. To do so would be a miscarriage of justice. Again Mullen demanded a plea. Again Greenberg refused.

Judge Mullen shrugged. As judge he would enter a plea of not guilty on the defendant's behalf. He then ordered Metesky to stand trial for his crimes. The courtroom fell silent. It appeared Metesky would not be excused on account of insanity after all.

Judge Mullen's voice broke the shock of silence. "What the doctors say about sanity is one thing. I have formed an opinion. The report is no deterrent at this stage of the game. All delays in cases of this sort are unwise. No harm will be done to the defendant until he is tried and convicted by a jury of his peers. A great deal of disservice to the community can be done by dragging this case along." With that Judge Mullen confirmed that his courtroom had no use for psychiatrists. Dr. Cassity looked as if he might explode, then hung his head in frustration.

Talking to reporters outside the courtroom, Judge Mullen said, "It is my opinion that he does know the nature and quality of his acts." In other words, under the McNaughton Rule Metesky would be considered fit for trial.

For Metesky, the hearing was only further proof of the powerful forces allied against him. He later accused Judge Mullen of conspiring with Con Ed. "He is obviously being paid off by them in his public office in some manner." Con Ed, Metesky said, should be on trial, not him.

For five weeks, Metesky had been confined at Bellevue, where, in Judge Mullen's view, psychiatrists had coddled him while asking their ineffectual questions. Enough was enough. Judge Mullen now ordered Metesky to the Manhattan House of Detention, the grim downtown Tombs, on White Street, where he was put on twenty-four-hour suicide watch in a special eighth-floor ward, though he had done nothing to indicate that he might harm himself. The warden was unwilling to take chances with a high-profile inmate, so guards stripped Metesky of his necktie, belt, and shoes and placed him in a solitary cell. The bright overhead light stayed on all night.

Within hours Anna Kross, the progressive-minded city commissioner of correction, set to work discharging Metesky from the Tombs. "He's a sick man," she said, "and we have no facilities to give him psychiatric care."

She would need a court order to transfer Metesky back to Bellevue. She tried to reach Judge Mullen, but he made himself unavailable. She then conferred with Judge Nathan R. Sobel, a county court judge in Brooklyn, who agreed to sign a court order, but only with Judge Mullen's consent.

Told of Kross's efforts to move Metesky, Judge Mullen said, "She had better not." He had already made it clear that he would not tolerate any more delays or interference.

"I'm going to do what I think is right as the commissioner," Kross told the press in response. The next day she sent Metesky back to Bellevue in open defiance of Judge Mullen, and on the flimsy authority of the February 19 arraignment in which a Brooklyn judge seconded Judge Mullen's directive that Metesky be sent to Bellevue.

Judge Mullen, now sounding contrite, downplayed the run-in. He denied any "tension" with Kross. He said he had simply tried to jump-start the stalled proceedings: "I remanded the defendant in order to break his stay in Bellevue, to prevent his indefinite stay there for 'observation.' I don't believe in letting people hibernate in the psychopathic ward, or be used as guinea pigs by psychiatrists when they may be menaces to the public and more properly confined in penal institutions."

As Metesky rode uptown, escorted as always by dark-suited detectives, the six-page single-space psychiatric report was at last hand delivered to Judge Mullen's chambers. Signed by three psychiatrists, as the law required, it stated their consensus that Metesky, as a paranoid schizophrenic, was incapable of understanding the charges against him and therefore belonged in a mental hospital, not a prison. "While generally compliant in his demeanor, both on the ward and in our examinations, it is our feeling that this is merely a façade and that his inner feelings are smoldering with intense hostility based upon definite delusional ideas. . . . The examiners are of the opinion that he is a suitable case for commitment to a mental hospital for the mentally ill."

This assessment made no difference to Judge Mullen. He was the curmudgeonly face of a gathering backlash against the Durham Rule, now three years old. Mullen and a bloc of other conservative judges feared that Bazelon's liberalized definition of insanity would contribute to what the legal scholar Jerome Hall called "the growing cult of irresponsibility" and would, in effect, allow psychiatrists to take over the administration of criminal justice.

The Durham Rule was a high-minded concept when Bazelon framed it, but it had proven messy in practice. Instead of the simple, understandable rule that had endured for more than a century, juries and judges now grappled with murky psychiatric theories and their confusing nomenclature of abreaction, manifest content, and signal anxiety.

Mullen had had enough. With the Metesky case he would take a firm stand. He was determined to dismiss the psychiatric report as a consulting opinion of small consequence, a bit of testimony without binding authority. Besides, Bazelon's federal court had no direct control over state courts. It was time to make clear, once and for all, that judges, not doctors, ruled the courtroom.

A quarter mile from Judge Mullen's courtroom, on the far side of City Hall Park, James Murray sat rubbing his temples in his book-lined law office. His headaches had only grown worse as he looked ahead to the inevitable face-off with Judge Mullen—two warhorse Irish lawyers on a collision course. There was no avoiding the confrontation.

The showdown came on March 22. Murray stood in a crowded courtroom and accused Judge Mullen of ignoring the law by holding the hastily convened February 28 hearing before receiving the psychiatric report and, worse, misapplying a legal standard. Instead of concentrating on the psychiatrists' diagnosis—the accepted requirement for competence to stand trial—Judge Mullen had addressed whether Metesky grasped the nature of his actions, a standard normally used to determine innocence by reason of insanity once a trial was under way. "The law is right there," Murray said to Judge Mullen. "It's as plain as the nose on my face."

Murray said that he had "been around a long time, maybe too long, and never in my experience has there been a valid and legal proceeding in a case before written Bellevue reports were submitted."

Leaning over the bench with his wrinkled face twisted in a sour pinch, Judge Mullen said he was "not interested in how long you've been around." He pointed a crooked finger at the defense lawyer and twice called him

"Murray," dispensing with the nicety of the honorific "Mr.," as if they were two Irish kids scrapping in the alley.

Murray answered that the opinion of a lawyer with more than fifty years of experience should count for something.

With loudening voice Judge Mullen said he didn't care how long Murray had practiced. He reminded Murray that a judge was not legally required to follow the psychiatric report.

Murray now matched Judge Mullen's angry pitch, demanding that the judge withdraw from the case on grounds of prejudice. By sending Metesky to the Tombs before the psychiatric report was complete, Murray said, the judge had "already determined the issue and expressed an opinion." Mullen had clearly concluded that Metesky was fit for trial despite his obvious impairments. "You had no authority," Murray added, "to do what you did."

Judge Mullen then denied Murray's request for a ten-minute recess, saying, "I'm anxious to proceed. Time is passing on a matter that should be brought to a conclusion."

Judge Mullen refused to step down, but he agreed to nullify the hasty hearing he had conducted on February 28 and hold a new one. It was a qualified victory for Murray, who had earned a chance to keep his client from standing trial. Throughout the proceedings Metesky sat quietly in a wooden box reserved for defendants. As the proceeding broke up, he had to be roused from sleep, his forefingers stuck in his mouth.

The events in Judge Mullen's courtroom had no direct influence on the Brooklyn court where Metesky also faced indictment. The possibility arose of what Murray called "a rather bizarre conflict" if the two courts reached different verdicts. "One county is looking for the torso," he said, "and the other county is looking for the head."

Fortunately for Metesky, the Brooklyn judge was more sympathetic. Earlier in his career Judge Leibowitz had on four occasions worked as a defense lawyer for Al Capone, so he knew how to finesse a conflict. "Out of courtesy and respect" he postponed his proceedings until the question of Metesky's competence resolved itself in Judge Mullen's courtroom. But before adjourning, Judge Leibowitz made clear where he stood on the matter: he fully acknowledged the Bellevue report and warned that he would "proceed in the manner provided by law."

Two days later Metesky was back in Judge Mullen's courtroom for a formal inquiry to determine, once and for all, his fitness to stand trial. Dr. Albert LaVerne, an associate professor of psychiatry at Fordham University and one of the psychiatrists examining Metesky, was testifying when Judge Mullen interrupted to demand that the psychiatrist use "plain English." LaVerne, a thin man with a mustache and widow's peak, insisted he was using appropriate language. After a few more interruptions, he glared up at Judge Mullen and said, "I cannot permit you to put me in a position where I am not permitted to speak in the language of my discipline."

In questioning LaVerne, Murray repeatedly referred to Metesky's "delusions." Judge Mullen interrupted to ask Murray to use the word *thoughts* instead of *delusions* so that everyone could understand what he meant.

"*Delusion* is kindergarten English," Murray said.

"Maybe I'm not out of kindergarten," Judge Mullen answered.

"Well, I don't know about that, but I am."

"Well, maybe you'll help me out."

Despite Judge Mullen's objections, the three Bellevue psychiatrists testified, unanimously and unequivocally, that paranoid delusions deranged Metesky's mind. Their assertions bore out, once more, Murray's contention that Metesky belonged in an asylum, not jail. So Murray must have felt confident when he rose and asked for the court to officially accept the report.

Judge Mullen, who had been uncharacteristically quiet, looked at Murray and yelled out, "Your motion is denied!" It appeared that Mullen had waited all day for his chance to deflate Murray. Then, with a gloat, Judge Mullen demanded to know how Metesky pleaded.

Metesky had sat through the proceedings looking indifferent. He absentmindedly rolled and unrolled a sheet of paper in his hands and measured the thumb of his right hand against his left-hand fingers. Now, after a baffled look at Murray, Metesky stood and said, "Not guilty." He would be going to trial, and almost surely to prison for the rest of his life.

It was the first time anybody could recall a judge disregarding an undisputed medical opinion. "To try an insane person makes the court ridiculous," the *Journal-American* wrote in an editorial. "This is a case for doctors, not for lawyers and judges. If the guy is what he seems to be, a hospital, not a courtroom, is definitely indicated." In response, Judge Mullen told the press that juries disregarded testimonies all the time. By the same reasoning, why couldn't a judge disregard the testimony of psychiatrists?

Judge Mullen had gained the upper hand, but not for long. On Saturday afternoon, April 6, Metesky was sitting in his austere private cell on the second floor of Bellevue when he began coughing. Three weeks earlier doctors had collected sputum cultures that showed that tuberculosis bacteria, long dormant, were active again in his lungs. Doctors had quarantined Metesky to prevent him from infecting others. There would be no more checkers in the open ward.

Now the tuberculosis erupted with a sudden nonstop hacking that gushed up mouthfuls of frothy blood. Woozy and weak, Metesky lay on his cot with blood streaming from his nose and from the corners of his mouth. He coughed up an entire pint of blood, which spilled onto the bed and linoleum floor. His blood pressure plummeted and his heart raced as it struggled to deliver oxygenated blood to his anemic body. He shivered and slipped into shock. Metesky accepted that he was dying, and he made no effort to alert a nurse. He bled for hours before an orderly found him and scrambled immediate treatment. Asked why he hadn't called for help, Metesky said, "It's no use living. I deserve to die."

Doctors stabilized Metesky. They kept him isolated with minimal activity, but they warned that the strain of a trial would likely induce a fatal hemorrhage. And the presence of a contagious tubercular patient in court presented a grave public-health risk. The prospect did not deter Judge Mullen. He continued to impanel a jury.

Murray had originally set out to spare his client from prison. Now he was racing to save his life by heading off a trial before it began. Two days after Metesky's relapse, Murray asked for a private conference with Judge Leibowitz, Mullen's Brooklyn counterpart, in his chambers. With the Brooklyn district attorney's blessing, they made plans to fast-track a competency hearing, thereby preempting Judge Mullen's New York trial. The law required Metesky's presence at the hearing, but he was too weak for courtroom attendance. Judge Leibowitz could not conduct the hearing at Bellevue because it was in Manhattan, and therefore within Judge Mullen's jurisdiction. So an ambulance was arranged to take Metesky to a Brooklyn hospital.

On April 10 a makeshift courtroom was set up in a room normally used for Ping-Pong in the prison wing of the Kings County Hospital. Attendants wheeled Metesky in on a gurney rigged with an oxygen tank and a bag of intravenous fluid. His skin was the gray-white of a fish belly. He breathed heavily through a surgical mask. Nurses hovered. The judge advised all present that Metesky was contagious, and he invited them to wear hospital gowns and masks for protection.

Murray began by establishing how far Judge Mullen, across the river in Manhattan, had strayed from normal procedures by rejecting the psychiatric report. "How many reports would you say you have signed for the Court of General Sessions where you have made investigations pursuant to the order of the court, approximately," Murray asked Albert LaVerne, one of the examining psychiatrists.

"I would say two or three thousand," Dr. LaVerne answered.

"How many of those two or three thousand reports have been rejected by the Court of General Sessions? . . ."

"I can't recall a single one at this time."

Dr. LaVerne then testified that Metesky was unable to participate in his defense because "it is not possible for him to shut off the spigot of fury and hatred."

"Of the thousands of schizophrenics that I have had the opportunity of examining and seen," LaVerne continued, "in my opinion he's one of the most dangerous to society, and one of the most psychotic that I have ever seen."

"In other words," the judge asked, "it is your position, Doctor, that . . . if Mr. Murray was to consult with this man in preparing his defense, he would be talking to a crazy man, an insane man?"

"That is correct. In the back of his mind is the feeling that Mr. Murray is aiding and abetting the great conspiracy to frustrate him from exposing Con Ed."

"As he lies there now"—Judge Leibowitz pointed at the shrouded figure on the gurney—"would you say that he is dangerous?"

"Undoubtedly. Very dangerous."

"If we were to let this man loose tomorrow, do you think he would place another bomb?"

"Undoubtedly."

"If Metesky were to confer with Mr. Murray, would the attorney be conferring with an insane man?"

"He would." Dr. LaVerne paused.

Everyone looked to the far side of the room where Metesky convulsed with coughing. His harsh barking was followed by the wet gurgle of blood. A blue pallor came over his face. Nurses wheeled him into the corridor and pressed an oxygen mask to his face. The coughing slowly subsided.

Dr. LaVerne was a psychiatrist, but he also practiced as a medical doctor with a specialty in tuberculosis. With Metesky removed from the room, Judge Leibowitz asked Dr. LaVerne how long Metesky might live. "That, Your Honor, is a question which no doctor can answer," Dr. LaVerne said. "He doesn't have too much more to go. . . . I imagine it is a question of weeks."

Antibiotics did not seem to help. Tuberculosis now infected two-thirds of Metesky's lung tissue. He would either bleed to death or choke to death on his own blood. It was impossible to know which might happen first.

"If these procedures are prolonged much longer," Dr. LaVerne added,

"Your Honor may have a corpse, rather than a defendant, on which to make a decision."

"I agree with you," Judge Leibowitz said. "I don't think there is any purpose in keeping a desperately ill man here."

On April 18, Judge Leibowitz delivered his opinion: George Metesky was "medically insane." He committed him to Matteawan State Hospital, an upstate asylum for the criminally insane.

With a deft bit of legal maneuvering, Murray had derailed Judge Mullen's hell-bent plan to hold a trial, no matter what. However, Judge Mullen could in theory still bring Metesky back from Matteawan at any time to stand trial. Judge Leibowitz said he would not "share the responsibility for this man's welfare in such an event."

To discourage Judge Mullen from persisting, Judge Leibowitz made an implicit plea: "One would be less than human not to be sympathetically moved by this pitiful condition of this hopeless, incurable man—incurable both mentally and physically. The doctors have told the court that his days on earth are numbered." Knowingly or not, Leibowitz borrowed the phrase Metesky had used in his first letter to the *Journal-American*: "My days on earth are numbered."

CHAPTER SEVENTEEN

MATTEAWAN

April 1957

LATE ON THE MORNING OF APRIL 19, 1957, GEORGE METESKY LAY wrapped in blankets in the back of a New York City Department of Correction ambulance as it wound its way up Asylum Road in the Hudson Valley town of Beacon, New York. He was accompanied by three guards and a doctor. The ambulance was equipped with an oxygen tank and two pints of blood plasma in case Metesky hemorrhaged. A mask covered his face.

Metesky had suffered a night of violent coughing at Kings County Hospital in Brooklyn. It was unclear if he could survive the seventy-mile drive, but in the end doctors pronounced him well enough to go. Before his 9:30 a.m. departure, Metesky, with a weak smile, told a Roman Catholic priest that he "had made peace with the world." He had just enough strength to raise a hand as an Associated Press photographer snapped a picture for the next day's newspapers.

Shortly before noon, the ambulance slowed as it passed through a chain-link fence topped with coiled razor wire and rolled to a stop in front of the redbrick turrets and steel-barred windows of Matteawan State Hospital for the Criminally Insane where more than a thousand afflicted souls with little hope of relief or release passed their days in open, high-ceilinged wards.

The long-term prospects were far from Metesky's mind. A doctor and three guards gingerly wheeled his gurney from the ambulance to a special third-floor tubercular ward housing forty patients, where he was expected to die within a week or so.

No sooner had Metesky arrived in failing condition than Judge Mullen began plotting to haul him back to Manhattan to face the pending charges. He considered Metesky's transfer to Matteawan further evidence that psychiatrists now wielded more influence than judges in questions of criminal insanity, and that psychiatrists too often used their sway to excuse offenders such as Metesky from facing responsibility for their actions. "Three weeks ago Metesky was able to stand trial," Judge Mullen said, hinting that accounts of Metesky's illness were exaggerated. "I don't know what's happened since then. . . . This court has the power to call Metesky from Matteawan at any time if it decides to do so."

Judge Mullen consulted with Frank Hogan, the Manhattan district attorney, who, like Metesky, was a Waterbury native. On April 20, the day after Metesky arrived, Hogan called the Matteawan superintendent, Dr. John F. McNeill, to express Judge Mullen's interest in returning Metesky to the courtroom. McNeill explained that Metesky was bedridden and incapable of attending a trial. He had lost twenty pounds in the weeks since his tubercular outbreak. He could barely walk to the bathroom, let alone sit in a courtroom for hours at a stretch. The next hemorrhage, should it occur, would likely kill him. Besides, his contagiousness would present a grave public health hazard. Hogan reported the conversation to Judge Mullen, who asked that Hogan check back with McNeill in the late summer or early fall. Judge Mullen refused to drop the case, even as Metesky lay on his deathbed.

Metesky spent the following weeks confined to a cot, laboring for every breath and sweating through the nights under heavy wool blankets. His plump figure withered to an apparition. The smirk undimmed by three months of hearings and handcuffs had now gone out of him, gone for good. He told nurses and doctors that he would soon be off their hands. He said it with certainty.

But as summer greenery brightened the Fishkill mountains, Metesky's condition improved by increments. The antibiotic dihydrostreptomycin gradually took hold and turned back the bacteria. He confounded all expectations by stabilizing and strengthening. He could breathe again without incessant coughing.

As Metesky recovered, he rose from bed to find himself in an institution where madness was often seen as a form of wickedness, as it was in previous centuries, and treated with consequent brutality. After lights-out, two night-shift guards regularly came for a tubercular patient named Paul Simulick. "The Mutt and Jeff team, I called them," Metesky would write to a reporter. "They used to take him out around midnight and beat him up. They hit him with wet towels. The poor guy would holler like hell. They would do this almost every night. It terrorized the other patients; they could hear him screaming and getting hit."

Simulick eventually killed himself. "He just couldn't take it anymore," Metesky said.

Matteawan was nominally a psychiatric hospital. Doctors treated patients with Thorazine injections and insulin shock, just as they would in a conventional psychiatric hospital. Patients were assigned therapeutic work shifts in gardens and carpentry shops and invited to pass the hours playing cards or tennis.

Like many asylums of its day, Matteawan resembled a grand hotel. Doctors had no effective treatment for mental illness when Matteawan was built in 1892. All they could do was erect massive brick buildings with towers and turrets out in the fresh air and sunshine, where patients would live free from the stress of ordinary life. A belief in the salubrious effects of wholesome outdoor play generated the popular image of the lunatic gamboling across a lawn with a butterfly net.

In reality, Matteawan functioned as a prison. Its founding purpose was "the isolation of dangerous and vicious patients." The patients were also inmates. Because they all had violent histories—40 percent had faced murder charges—the hospital was rigged with an alarm system and encircled by a fourteen-foot fence. A special police force patrolled the grounds.

Until Metesky, the hospital's most famous resident had been Harry Thaw, who spent five years in Matteawan after fatally shooting the architect Stanford White on the rooftop of Madison Square Garden. A year after Metesky arrived, the hospital admitted Izola Curry, a black woman who had stabbed Martin Luther King Jr. at a Harlem book signing. Like Metesky, she was diagnosed as a paranoid schizophrenic.

Matteawan was a holding pen more than a place for healing, a penitentiary with indeterminate sentences. The only sure way to leave was to die. Because patients had not gone to trial, they had no release dates. Quarantined in the upstate hills, they were the judicial system's forgotten population. They were out of sight, and out of mind. The desperation of dead-end sentences led to a disturbing number of suicides and a lot of attempted escapes, including Harry Thaw, who dashed through an open gate and into a waiting limousine. Afterward officials initiated a permanent twelve-man armed patrol.

By Christmas, Metesky's tuberculosis had gone into remission. He transferred to the psychiatric ward, where he read the newspaper in high-ceilinged wards with elaborate tile work and generous windows admitting a wealth of light. He strolled among expansive acreage designed by Frederick Law Olmsted, where patients played tennis and threw iron rings, known as quoits, at targets.

It was nearly impossible to leave Matteawan, but it looked as if Metesky might be the exception. Hogan, like a patient predator, periodically mailed Superintendent McNeill letters inquiring about Metesky's health. To each letter McNeill responded that Metesky's physical health was revived but his mental condition was no better. "He's still paranoid," McNeill said. "I think he's a permanent case. . . . He hasn't changed his views. He's depressed most of the time. He rarely speaks to the other patients. He insists he got a bad deal—that he is being persecuted and prosecuted." McNeill reminded Hogan that Judge Leibowitz of Kings County, Brooklyn, had committed Metesky to Matteawan. By state law Leibowitz retained jurisdiction over the case. It was Metesky's schizophrenia, not the tuberculosis, which had caused Judge Leibowitz to send Metesky to Matteawan.

Until hospital psychiatrists saw significant improvement in Metesky's mental condition, McNeill could not recommend his release to Judge Leibowitz.

So Metesky stayed on. Eight months into his sentence, news came that the Workmen's Compensation Board had rejected the appeal filed by Bart O'Rourke, the labor lawyer retained by Seymour Berkson to reopen Metesky's original claim for benefits. O'Rourke had argued that the board could not hold Metesky responsible for submitting his claim after the two-year deadline because, as three Bellevue psychiatrists had attested, he was mentally incompetent. "If this is true, it is a reasonable hypothesis that during the time he was required to file a claim . . . he was psychotic," O'Rourke said. The board disagreed, saying O'Rourke had not provided sufficient proof that Metesky was insane in the year after his accident. Once again, the board denied the claim. With that, Metesky's long offensive against Con Ed came to an end.

For the next fifteen years Metesky proved a model inmate. He fastidiously followed hospital rules, rarely causing trouble for patients or staff. The order and routine of Matteawan suited him. He wrote his sisters weekly letters, attended chapel, and listened daily to music and the news on radios provided in the wards. His one act of disobedience was to refuse to wear the striped prison uniform. Instead he wore his double-breasted suit, neatly buttoned, as if to demonstrate that he was perfectly sane.

"I'm perfectly all right—I'm not insane," he told McNeill. "I belong outside. I still feel I was justified in what I did."

As Dr. Brussel had predicted, Metesky never responded in the slightest to treatment. He was convinced that the authorities would pronounce him sane at any moment and release him. He never tried to escape, as Harry Thaw did, but he repeatedly attempted to secure his freedom by a writ of habeas corpus. He waged a lengthy legal campaign, not unlike F.P.'s years of letter writing.

Dr. Brussel occasionally visited Matteawan to interview patients who had applied for transfer to noncriminal mental institutions. On one trip he asked to see Metesky. It was the first and only meeting between the bomber and the psychiatrist who put the police on his trail. "He was calm, smiling and condescending," Dr. Brussel wrote. Metesky told Dr. Brussel of his plans to be discharged and then deprecated his bomb-making skills. The devices were never powerful enough to cause much damage, Metesky said.

Was it possible, Dr. Brussel asked, that during all that time Metesky had actually suffered from mental illness? Was it possible that he really was a paranoid schizophrenic, as Dr. Brussel had concluded?

"He didn't become angry," Dr. Brussel wrote. "He was the patronizing and successful paranoiac who, as God, could appreciate and magnanimously forgive his children's mistake. He smiled at me. With a wave of his hand he said, 'It could have been, it could have been. But I wasn't.' Then he bowed graciously and left the room."

EPILOGUE

THE TARGET OF THE SIXTEEN-YEAR MAD BOMBER MANHUNT turned out to be as mild mannered as a small-town clerk. But he pulled into his dark orbit a constellation of outsize personalities—a polymath psychiatrist who supervised lobotomies and shot himself up with Demerol, a foreign correspondent turned publisher trying to keep his afternoon newspaper afloat, a rigid law-and-order police commissioner with a weakness for Puccini. They came together for one anxious season, then dispersed, as characters do, to follow diverging paths.

For Dr. James Brussel, the 1957 Christmas season was a gratifying stretch. With Metesky committed to Matteawan, the interview requests from newspapers and radio and television stations tapered off, leaving Dr. Brussel with an afterglow of renown. The extemporaneous profile he wrote a year earlier had not led police directly to Metesky's door, but it had provided the critical break in New York's longest manhunt. His portrait of the mystery bomber—Slavic, friendless, single, fastidious, chronically unemployed, irascible, given to delusions of self-importance— allowed detectives to narrow the search frame and concentrate their efforts on a specific type. Just as important, Dr. Brussel had provided a geographic target for the manhunt. He also decisively changed the course of the investigation by convincing the police to publicize his profile. Exposure would, he promised, help lure F.P. into the daylight, which is exactly what happened as F.P. began his correspondence with the *Journal-American*.

The resulting newspaper coverage planted the basic facts of the case in the public's mind. Without them Alice Kelly could not have recognized the threatening remarks in the Metesky file.

Dr. Brussel brought flesh and form to a fugitive who for more than a decade had no more shape than a shadow. He gave F.P. an inner life, a bio, a backstory. He made the terrorist understandable. His profile helped lead detectives to F.P.'s door; it also had an electrifying effect on law enforcement. He had shown that a psychiatrist could deduce personality patterns, motivations, and future behavior from physical evidence—and do so with startling accuracy. His prediction that F.P. would be wearing a double-breasted jacket when caught was his tour de force, a bit of bravado that paid off. Dr. Brussel acknowledged that it had been a hunch, a prophecy that he couldn't entirely explain. It was a mystery even to him.

"Everybody has a hunch occasionally," he would write. "It is a common experience and sometimes an embarrassing one, for it's hard to explain a hunch. The strange flash of intuition feels true; you're almost sure, somewhere inside you, that it is better than just a guess. But how do you convince anybody else?"

After Dr. Brussel's first wife, Audrey, died of a heart ailment, he lived alone on the grounds of the Creedmoor psychiatric hospital, attended by a mental patient named Annie whom he employed as a housekeeper. In 1957, Dr. Brussel married an attractive widow, also named Audrey, and moved with her to an apartment on Twelfth Street in Greenwich Village. (By then one of his parakeets had died. At Audrey's insistence, the surviving bird did not come with them.)

Dr. Brussel was raised in Brooklyn, and he had lived in state-owned housing for most of his adult life. Greenwich Village, by contrast, was the heartbeat of the city's downtown cultural life. He and Audrey lived a few blocks from the Village Vanguard, where Miles Davis played his audacious improvisations, and the Cedar Tavern, where Robert Motherwell held manic discussions with fellow painters. Dr. Brussel could not plausibly be described as bohemian; he wore a suit every day, and he liked nothing more than to fly first-class. Still, he fit comfortably in Greenwich Village, where psychiatrists were esteemed as secular priests and creative spirits flourished all around.

Though Jewish, Dr. Brussel would celebrate Christmas with Audrey and her two children, John and Judy Israel. A few days later they would leave for Jamaica. Relaxed in anticipation of the coming holiday, Dr. Brussel unwound with the newspapers on Christmas Eve.

It was impossible to read the papers that day without confronting the details of a murder committed the previous evening a few miles from Creedmoor hospital, Dr. Brussel's former home and still a focus of his professional life. A matronly forty-four-year-old widow named Mary Nerich had attended a Christmas party after work. She rode the bus home about 9:00 p.m., then walked down a side street leading to the modest house she shared with her sister and brother-in-law in the quiet neighborhood of Queens Village. She never made it home. She was found on the blood-pooled sidewalk with more than a dozen stab wounds. "I read about it in *The New York Times*," Dr. Brussel said, "felt a pang of shock and sorrow—and then, like almost everybody else, turned my attention back to the approach of Christmas and the New Year."

By now Dr. Brussel may have accepted that the Metesky case was an isolated chance to test his theory of reverse psychology, and that he might never have another. Then, on the day before Dr. Brussel left for Jamaica, a gruff-voiced Queens homicide detective named Captain McCarthy phoned Dr. Brussel's office. Captain Finney had referred him. "I've heard a lot about you from other men in the department," McCarthy said. "We have a case here that's giving us some trouble, and I wonder if I can ask for your help."

A week after the murder the police still grasped for leads. Mrs. Nerich had no enemies, and the evidence bewildered the police. All they knew was that somebody had stabbed her through her coat using a penknife or some other small blade, then stole $45 in cash and a driver's license from her purse. The stabber had used her lipstick to write "Fuck Mary" on the side of her purse and on a nearby house before tossing the bag away and vanishing down the dark streets. Two neighbors reported seeing a man walking slowly up and down the sidewalk, as if waiting for somebody. Whenever he passed under a streetlamp, they said, he removed his hands from his coat pocket and looked at them.

"The community is getting nervous, demanding action," Captain McCarthy said, "and the commissioner calls me several times a day to find out why we're getting nowhere."

Brussel silently constructed a picture of the killer in his mind while Captain McCarthy waited on the line. "Physically, this is a skinny kid," Dr. Brussel said after lengthy consideration. "Not over five three in height or, say, a hundred twenty pounds in weight. A puny, unattractive, unloved, angry, frightened little schizophrenic. Probably has acne. Lives near the street where Mrs. Nerich was found. He has no friends, hangs around home with his mother—if she's still there—watches TV, reads comic books. He may be in high school, where he's barely making the grade or on the point of flunking out."

On the morning of January 4, Dr. Brussel was drinking coffee and reading *The New York Times* in the lobby of his hotel in Jamaica. An article tucked on a back page reported that the police had caught Mrs. Nerich's killer, a sixteen-year-old boy who lived near his victim, just as Dr. Brussel had predicted. Also consistent with Dr. Brussel's profile, the murderer was a sallow, withdrawn kid with a D average and a bad case of acne.

"You solved the case by telephone, without even visiting the scene of the crime," Captain McCarthy later told Dr. Brussel. "Just sitting there in your office, you gave a picture of the killer. . . . I still don't understand how the hell you did it." Dr. Brussel's answer was Freudian insights, deductive reasoning, and intuition.

The outcomes weren't always so clear-cut. Detectives came to Dr. Brussel's Broadway office late one afternoon in September 1963, this time with crime-scene photographs of a double murder. A few weeks earlier, in the last hot days of August, two young women, ages twenty-one and twenty-three, roommates and recent college graduates, had been stabbed sixty times collectively with a kitchen knife and the jagged edge of a broken soda bottle in their East Eighty-Eighth Street apartment.

A third roommate came home from her publishing job to find the bodies lying on a bedroom floor bound together by strips of bedsheets. One was naked, her body eviscerated.

Murder of this grotesque nature would shock any neighborhood, but all the more on a sedate stretch of the Upper East Side. Gay Talese, reporting for *The New York Times,* wrote that the news had "injected fear into a neighborhood that rarely knows it, and whose residents have long paid high rents to avoid it."

The detectives reviewed the evidence with Dr. Brussel. "Never before or since have I seen anything that filled me with such horror and pity," he later wrote. "I didn't eat dinner that night."

After a deliberative pause, Dr. Brussel said that the killer, like Metesky, was a paranoid schizophrenic. He would know the girls from parties or from work, though they may not have noticed him. A young man, under thirty-five, he worked in advertising or some other creative field and was well built and fastidiously dressed.

In late April 1964 a detective called Dr. Brussel to say that the police had made an arrest, and the suspect had confessed.

"He confessed?" Dr. Brussel asked. The killer he pictured would not confess. Metesky had eagerly divulged his history because he wanted the world to admire his grand campaign against injustice. But in this case the murderer's drive for revenge was highly sexual, and he would not wish to share it. "Describe this man to me."

George Whitmore Jr., a nineteen-year-old black man living in Brownsville, Brooklyn, was childish, borderline retarded, sloppy in personal habits, a messy dresser, barely literate. The police had picked him up loitering in a Laundromat and booked him on flimsy evidence: his wallet contained a photograph of a white girl who resembled one of the victims.

"He isn't your man, confession or no confession," Dr. Brussel said.

Sure enough, within weeks Whitmore recanted, claiming that the police had bullied the confession from him. The murders had occurred on the same day that Martin Luther King Jr. delivered his "I Have a

Dream" speech from the steps of the Lincoln Memorial. In the gathering atmosphere of racial activism, the NAACP and the American Civil Liberties Union came to Whitmore's defense, portraying him as a victim of police mistreatment. The police never read Whitmore his rights and he was not given access to a lawyer for nearly twenty-four hours. In light of these embarrassing omissions, the police dropped the case against him.

Weeks later, with the public demanding action, the police arrested Richard Robles, a frail heroin addict who was eventually convicted of murder in the first degree. (Fifty-three years after the killings, Robles remains in prison.) Again, Dr. Brussel was unconvinced. The suspect who truly matched his profile was a foppish young magazine writer who had left fingerprints on the girls' mailbox. Suspiciously, he moved to Europe immediately after the murders. "The case was officially closed," Dr. Brussel wrote. "In my mind it's still open."

Dr. Brussel's relationship with the NYPD soured when he refused to endorse Robles's guilt. "I suspected they would not consult me again for years," he said, "perhaps never again." His growing reputation for profiling nonetheless assured that investigators outside New York would solicit his help.

In February 1964, Dr. Brussel received a cablegram at his hotel while vacationing in Malindi, a beach resort seventy miles north of Mombasa, Kenya. It was an invitation from John S. Bottomly, assistant attorney general of Massachusetts, to join a task force of forensic psychiatrists, medical examiners, and others to discuss a series of murders by a fugitive known as the Boston Strangler. Dr. Brussel answered by return cablegram: TAKING THE NEXT SUBWAY OUT OF AFRICA.

Eleven women had been strangled in Boston and its suburbs since June 1962. Most were molested and choked with articles of their own clothing in shabby walk-up apartments without sign of struggle—no broken windows, no jimmied locks—suggesting that they unwittingly welcomed the strangler into their homes. A low-grade hysteria beset the city. The Boston Strangler was not the first serial killer, but he was among the first reported on by the growing field of television news. From Brockton to /

Brookline, residents opened doors more cautiously. They stockpiled hand-guns and enrolled in self-defense classes. Women varied their routes to and from work, and they carried knives and pepper spray in their handbags. Some women kept their bedroom lights on all night or slept over with friends. "We were desperate for clues," said a Boston homicide detective.

On April 10, Dr. Brussel flew to Boston and took his place among a dozen eminent doctors, psychiatrists, and pathologists, a dream team, as-sembled around a conference table on the third floor of an old brown-stone owned by Boston University. "I hope you can do your Mad Bomber trick for us here, Dr. Brussel," Bottomly said.

"I'll do what I can," Dr. Brussel answered.

Bottomly was a tall, no-nonsense lawyer appointed by an ambitious young attorney general, an African American Republican among en-trenched Irish Democrats. He had announced that his office would take over the manhunt. His first act was to put Bottomly in charge.

Bottomly assembled the Medical-Psychiatric Committee, as he called it, to help stymied Boston detectives think of alternatives to conventional investigative practices, which had so far turned up nothing. The com-mittee's mandate was to use what Bottomly called "unusual methods" to find the strangler before he killed again. (In his enthusiasm for unusual methods, Bottomly had hired a Dutch psychic named Peter Hurkos, who, he claimed, discovered his gift after falling on his head from a ladder twenty-one years earlier.)

With his experts gathered, Bottomly showed photographs of two groups of murder victims: the first five were grandmotherly types. The next six were younger, and far more attractive. The killer had arranged all of them in grotesque postures with legs splayed apart and stockings, bras, and belts cinched around their necks and neatly tied with a bow. "I went home to New York feeling sad and angry and baffled," Dr. Brussel wrote. "The photographs we had been shown . . . haunted my imagi-nation."

Dr. Brussel spent the next three weeks searching for some organizing pattern. "Somewhere in this terrible saga of death and sex was a single thread of meaning," he wrote. "I knew it was there, but couldn't put my finger on it." The flash of intuition that had helped crack the Metesky case still eluded him by the time he flew back to Boston for the follow-up. The men around the table nodded in consensus as one after another asserted that at least two stranglers had to be at work, maybe three or four. The wide span in victims' ages suggested as much, as did the disparity in sexual violations: only the younger women had been raped.

Without quite intending to, Dr. Brussel grunted in disagreement. All eyes turned to him, followed by an uneasy silence. Now he would have to voice a dissenting opinion. During the meeting the crucial pattern had come to him. "The ideas that had been milling about in my head suddenly fell into step. The pieces of the pattern abruptly arranged themselves and locked together. I had it!"

Dr. Brussel cleared his throat and proposed, as calmly as he could, that there was a single strangler. "What has happened to him, in two words, is instant maturity," he said. "In this two-year period, he has suddenly grown, psychosexually, from infancy to puberty to manhood. . . . He had to commit these murders to achieve this growth. It was the only way he knew how to solve his problems, find himself sexually, and become a grown man among men."

The first five victims, all matronly older women, were found without semen in their vaginas, Dr. Brussel pointed out. The strangler had molested them with his fingers and probed them with blunt objects found in their apartments, as might a curious boy with no sexual experience. On some level he was still an adolescent and wouldn't dare have sex with the women; he wouldn't know how. These older women were stand-ins for his mother. He had wanted to punish her—maybe for denying him love—and took it out on these surrogates.

The strangler eventually shifted his sexual attention to women closer to his own age and began having sex with them, probably after they died. "He was taking steps toward his manhood and sexual potency," Dr. Brussel explained, "but he hadn't gone the whole distance yet." He had a typically schizophrenic ambivalence toward them. He desired them, but he punished them. He loved them, but he wanted to kill them. He expressed his hatred by biting them or stuffing underwear in their mouths. His last victim, nineteen-year-old Mary Sullivan, was found with semen in her mouth and a broom handle shoved in her vagina. He mocked her by leaving a greeting card at her lifeless feet reading, "Happy New Year."

The committee listened politely, but its members unanimously rejected Dr. Brussel's interpretation. "Go ahead, Doctor," one of them said. "Hang yourself."

So Dr. Brussel continued: The strangler was a paranoid schizophrenic. He strangled his victims so forcefully that they died instantly, so he was probably an athletic, well-proportioned man in his late twenties or thirties. Strangling was a favored murder method in southern Europe. The killer therefore was likely of Italian or Spanish descent.

"Is that it?" someone asked.

Dr. Brussel stood up and looked around the room. "One more thing. I don't think he'll be caught by ordinary detection. . . . He'll be found eventually but this will happen because he has voluntarily told his story. You see . . . I think he has finished."

"Finished?"

"Yes. He's been seeking two things: to grow up sexually, and to avenge himself for his mother's rejection of him or whatever caused his hang-up. I believe he has succeeded on both counts. . . . From now on he'll get his sexual satisfaction from conscious women, in a more or less normal fashion."

Before the group adjourned, Dr. Brussel issued a closing prediction: "He may want to tell of his success, even if he talks to only one other person. . . . Now that he has made himself mature, he may want people to know."

Through the summer and fall of 1964 Boston braced for the next strangling. It never came. Maybe the strangler left town to escape the manhunt, homicide detectives said. Maybe his tortured state of mind had caused him to kill himself. Or maybe, as Dr. Brussel suggested, he was done with killing.

Shortly after nine thirty on the morning of October 27, 1964, a newly married twenty-year-old Cambridge coed was dozing in bed after her husband had left for his teaching job. She awoke to find a man standing at her bedroom door. He stepped to the bed and pressed a knife blade to her throat. "Don't make a sound," he said, "or I'll kill you." He tied her arms and legs to the bedposts with her husband's pajamas and stuffed her panties in her mouth. He kissed and fondled her for an hour, then fled as abruptly as he had arrived, saying, "I'm sorry," on his way out.

Within hours she had described the intruder to a police sketch artist—slicked-back dark hair, dark eyes, and a prominent nose. A Cambridge detective identified the suspect in the sketch as a prolific sex offender named Albert DeSalvo, a husky onetime handyman and former army middleweight boxer with a gentle manner and a magnificent head of wavy dark hair. He fit Dr. Dr. Brussel's profile: ruggedly built and of Italian descent.

DeSalvo was a burglar and con man who had talked his way into dozens of women's apartments. The police brought him in for questioning, then released him on bail. He was eventually arrested for a string of unrelated sexual assaults and committed to Bridgewater State Hospital, south of Boston, a facility for the criminally insane. While there he confessed to killing the eleven women, and two more that the police had not yet connected with the Boston Strangler, in a private interview with F. Lee Bailey, the celebrated defense attorney. "He had reached a point," Bailey wrote, "where he was bursting to talk." As Dr. Brussel had surmised, the strangler was unable to keep his sexual feats to himself.

Bailey made sure that DeSalvo's admission was inadmissible in court. As a result, he was never tried for the thirteen killings, though in 1967 he was sentenced to life imprisonment for robbery, and for the other series of sexual attacks. The first defense witness F. Lee Bailey called at DeSalvo's trial was Dr. James Brussel, who had twice interviewed DeSalvo in prison. Dr. Brussel gave the court a clinical explanation for DeSalvo's freakish sexual practices. Bailey hired Dr. Brussel as a defense witness, despite his seat on the district attorney's consulting committee. "He seemed more knowledgeable than anybody else in the case," Bailey said, "on my side or theirs."

(DeSalvo was stabbed to death in prison in 1973, at age forty-two. He had recanted his confession shortly before his death. However, a 2013 test showed that semen found on the body of Mary Sullivan, the Boston Strangler's last victim, matched DeSalvo's DNA.)

To gain footing in those early days, profiling had to be sold by a performer, and Dr. Brussel knew how to put on a performance. He had a head for science and a showman's touch. His charisma and confidence swept detectives—and juries—along with him as he made nimble leaps of deduction. By the 1970s Dr. Brussel was known as the father of the emergent field of profiling. The press variously called him the "Prophet of Twelfth Street," "Sherlock Holmes of the Couch," and "the Psychiatric Seer." The Metesky case, more than any other, had established him as a folk hero of criminology.

"At times I was almost sorry I had been so successful in describing George Metesky, for I had to live up to that success," he later wrote. "It wasn't always easy and sometimes it was impossible. There were times when I made mistakes. There were times when I simply lacked enough information to build an image of the criminal. There were times when the law of averages let me down: I'd diagnose a man as a paranoiac and imagine him as having a well-proportioned physique and then he'd turn out to be among the 15 percent of paranoiacs who are not so built. Yes, there were cases on which I failed. But I continued to succeed often enough so that the police kept coming to me."

Dr. Brussel was irrepressibly inventive, even in his later years. He had a thriving sideline profiling on behalf of police departments around the country, and he wrote eight books, including *Instant Shrink: How to Become an Expert Psychiatrist in Ten Easy Lessons,* which made basic psychiatry understandable for lay readers—a precursor to the *for Dummies* series. He wrote about the dangers of sunburn, high blood pressure, and other common ailments in popular magazines and discussed them on radio call-in shows and in an outpouring of published letters to newspaper editors. Had he been born a generation later, Dr. Brussel could easily have hosted a daytime television show devoted to health issues.

He also wrote a crime novel, *Just Murder, Darling,* about a husband who bludgeons his wife's lover to death with a tire iron and frames her for the murder. As a profiler, Dr. Brussel could slip into the criminal mind-set, and it came naturally to him as a crime novelist as well. "A man has to be paranoid to turn out something like that," he said. "So I guess I am. I have a dirty, rotten no-good mind, and my wife and I laugh about it all the time."

In 1969, Dr. Brussel, by then sixty-four, briefly returned to national notice at the trial of Robert F. Kennedy's assassin. Defense lawyers hired a San Diego psychologist named Dr. Martin M. Schorr as an expert witness. Schorr submitted a written report describing the accused killer, Sirhan Sirhan, as afflicted by an oedipal hatred for his father. Schorr read part of his report into testimony:

> By killing Kennedy, Sirhan kills his father, takes his father's place as the heir to his mother. The process of acting out this problem can only be achieved in a psychotic insane state of mind. . . . He finds a symbolic replica of his father in the form of Kennedy, kills him, and also removed the relationship that stands between him and his most precious possession—his mother's love.

Schorr later admitted that he had lifted passages, in some cases word for word, from *Casebook of a Crime Psychiatrist,* a 1968 memoir Dr. Brussel had written about six investigations he had participated in, including the Metesky manhunt.

Dr. Brussel's *Casebook* would figure prominently in profiling's evolution. A handsome young FBI officer named Howard Teten read the accounts with intense interest. He had developed his own crude profiling methods as a crime-scene analyst in San Leandro, California, before join-ing the FBI. In 1973 he visited Dr. Brussel at his Greenwich Village apart-ment. Teten came as an apprentice seeking knowledge from the master.

Teten offered to pay Dr. Brussel a fee, whatever his hourly rate as a psychoanalyst might be, to share his techniques—the mix of Freudian the-ory, deductive reasoning, and intuition that had served him so well in the Metesky case and others. The FBI couldn't afford his rates, Dr. Brus-sel said, so he'd help Teten for free.

"While [Brussel] was for all intents and purposes retired at that time, he was most gracious and was quite willing to discuss his approach to profiling," Teten would recall. "Over the next year or so I visited him on several occasions, examining the similarities and differences in our ap-proaches."

Even before meeting with Dr. Brussel, Teten had created a profiling division within the FBI, initially known as the Behavioral Science Unit. This semisecret experiment was conducted from a windowless room six stories below the FBI Academy in Quantico, in rural eastern Virginia. Teten began by assisting police with some of the five thousand or so mur-ders that went unsolved each year. He helped detectives throughout the country determine what sort of person they were looking for by match-ing crime-scene evidence with patterns of behavior documented in abnormal-psychology classes and textbooks—the same technique Dr. Brussel had initiated. If the Behavioral Science Unit had hung a founding father's oil portrait over its mantel, it would have been the gaunt counte-nance of Dr. James Brussel.

By the 1980s, Teten's basement skunkworks had established itself as a national clearinghouse for crime data and forensic analysis, translating au-topsies, crime-scene photos, and other evidence into profiles of striking accuracy. Police precincts could call on its services twenty-four hours a day, 365 days a year. And they did so with growing urgency as violent crime increased, particularly serial crime by deviant offenders such as John Gacy and Ted Bundy. According to FBI profiler Robert K. Ressler, the upswing resulted from "the kind of society we had become: mobile, in many ways impersonal, flooded with images of violence and of heightened sexuality."

The debate over profiling's legitimacy persisted long after Dr. Brussel's death, in 1982. In a 2007 article in *The New Yorker,* Malcolm Gladwell argued that profiling, like fortune-telling or astrology, is written in such broad language that it can validate almost any conclusion one cares to draw from it. In Gladwell's view, Dr. Brussel was a con man with a Freudian degree. By way of evidence he cited a list of minor mistakes Dr. Brussel made. Metesky was a few years older than Dr. Brussel had predicted, for example, and he suffered from tuberculosis, not heart disease. (Dr. Brussel had, by his own admission, eliminated tuberculosis as a possibility because antibiotics had proven effective by the late 1950s. He had not considered that Metesky, as a paranoid schizophrenic, was inclined to discount the advice of doctors.)

"Brussel did not really understand the mind of the Mad Bomber," Gladwell wrote. "He seems to have understood only that, if you make a great number of predictions, the ones that were wrong will soon be forgotten, and the ones that turn out to be true will make you famous. The Hedunit is not a triumph of forensic analysis. It's a party trick."

Profilers working today readily acknowledge the fallibility of their methods. For all their study of behavioral traits, they still cannot point to the specific identity of an offender as their television counterparts do. Nonetheless, by combining accumulated data—the location of a crime, its organization, how the offender behaved before and after an event—with solid criminological judgment, profilers succeed at a far greater rate than they would without this expertise. "By studying thousands of cases, profilers educate their gut instincts, which allows them to see patterns in behavioral nuances," said Jim Clemente, a retired FBI profiler and expert on serial murders and sex crimes. "We don't perform magic. We let our subconscious do multiple calculations for us. We learn to rely on it in cases where the average cop hits a dead end."

Today profiling plays a prominent role in the pursuit of all serial offenders. It has also become a preoccupation of popular culture. In the late 1970s a quiet, bearded former Associated Press editor named Thomas Harris audited classes and met with FBI agents at Quantico, Virginia, where he learned about the agency's semisecret efforts to profile killers and sex offenders. "What I try to do with a case is to take in all the evidence I have to work with . . . and then put myself mentally and emotionally in the head of the offender," said John Douglas, one of the profilers Harris consulted over the years. "I try to think as he does. Exactly how this happens, I'm not sure. . . . If there's a psychic component to this, I won't run from it."

Harris applied what he had learned at Quantico to his writings. His bestselling 1981 novel, *Red Dragon,* and its sequel *Silence of the Lambs,* introduced the world to Hannibal Lecter, a psychiatrist and homicidal cannibal, and Will Graham, the profiler who tracked him. Like Dr. Brussel, Graham succeeded because he could get inside the mind of a madman and follow his logic.

"It's the way you think," Graham's FBI supervisor tells him in *Red Dragon.*

"I think there's a lot of bullshit about the way I think," Graham replies.

"You made some jumps you never explained."

Harris almost single-handedly created a profiling genre that stormed the bestseller lists and commands prime-time programming. In televisions shows such as *Criminal Minds* and *Law & Order,* profilers come off as scientist-wizards who, thunderstruck by clairvoyant visions, pluck serial killers out of the crowd. "They make profiling seem like a magic wand that, when available to police, instantly solves the crime," wrote Robert K. Ressler. "Profiling is merely the application of sound behavioral science principles, and years of experience, gained in part by evaluating crime scenes and evidence, and also by interviewing incarcerated criminals, with the goal of pointing the police toward the most likely category of suspects. Profiling never catches a criminal. Police do that."

Real-life profilers such as Ressler and their fictional counterparts both descended from Dr. Brussel. He was the first to draw outsize deductions about serial criminals from granular bits of evidence. No less important, he knew how to sell his conclusions with self-assurance and showmanship.

As the fascination with profiling grows, paranoid schizophrenics like Metesky have also become a familiar type in movies and on television—unbefriended men with long-simmering rage and elaborate plans for revenge.

The *Journal-American* rode a surge of popularity in the weeks after Metesky's arrest. Circulation shot up by more than one hundred thousand, though the paper's upsurge would not be enough to sustain it in the face of Walter Cronkite, David Brinkley, and the ascent of television news. Advertising bled away, and a dustup with *Time* magazine diminished the *Journal-American*'s recent glory. Berkson and Hearst sued Time Inc. for libel after *Time* published an article, headlined "Bombs Away," suggesting that the *Journal-American* had withheld the contents of Metesky's first letter from the police in hopes of engineering his surrender on their own. The aspersion was unfounded; Berkson had, in fact, consulted with Commissioner Kennedy immediately after the letter's arrival.

It's easy to imagine Berkson's reaction to the charge. He prided himself on propriety and rectitude, even if his employers at Hearst headquarters often did not share those values. It must have galled him all the more that *Time,* an uptown Ivy League outfit, wrote about the downtown *Journal-American* as if it were holding its nose.

The lawsuit bounced around until June 25, 1959, when an appellate court dismissed it. "Unless this article can fairly be read as charging a crime, it is not libelous per se," the court ruled. "We are of the opinion it cannot fairly be read in that sense."

Berkson did not live to see the lawsuit's resolution. He spent Thanksgiving of 1958 in San Francisco with Eleanor and their son, Bill. Berkson stayed on to attend a Hearst board of directors meeting after Bill returned to Brown University. Years earlier doctors had warned Berkson of a frail heart, a condition no doubt aggravated by a punishing appetite for work. He addressed the ailment with long walks through the New York streets and nightly single shots of bourbon. While in San Francisco he suffered a heart attack, requiring emergency surgery. Unable to travel, he convalesced at Saint Francis Memorial Hospital, where he passed the hours dictating memos and reading the Boris Pasternak novel *Doctor Zhivago,* newly translated from the Russian, sent by Bill. Berkson wrote his son a thank-you letter on hospital stationery, saying he admired the book's "gripping intensity."

He added, "You are a man now and much more mature than most lads your age. If the worst had happened I at least had the feeling of tranquility that your mother had a strong and stalwart son at her side and that this would help to tide her over."

On January 2, Berkson, accompanied by his wife, Eleanor, checked out of the hospital and moved into a suite in the Mark Hopkins Hotel. He planned to convalesce there for a few days before returning to New York. He died in his hotel suite three days later when a second heart attack struck. He was fifty-three years old.

"It is a mad era and the madness is among the great as among the simple people . . . ," wrote Berkson's friend the columnist George Sokolsky, who was himself in the hospital when he learned of Berkson's death. "A newsman, like Seymour Berkson, was on top of all this and it worked him and he was everlastingly in search of a story until his heart grew tired and gave out."

Eleanor died forty-four years later, at age one hundred. Among her papers, Bill found a stack of letters that she had written to Berkson after he died.

Three years after Berkson's death, New York newspapers were thrown into disarray. Seventeen thousand employees—reporters, photoengravers, rewrite men, copyboys, photographers—went on strike. New York had always been a newspaper city, saucy with boldfaced gossip and gutter politics, box scores and acid theater reviews. It was hard to imagine the city getting by without them. But habits evolve. Gradually, almost imperceptibly, through the winter months of 1962, readers shifted their attention to the evening news broadcasts. When the newspapers and unions reached a settlement in March and tabloids and broadsheets once again rolled off the presses, many readers didn't come back.

Television news sealed its supremacy in the days after John F. Kennedy's assassination. Americans glued themselves to their sets on November 22, 1963, as the impossible reports came from Parkland Memorial Hospital in Dallas. Fifty-one million homes watched the three networks in communal shock and mourning as Air Force One touched down at Andrews Air Force Base with the slain president's body aboard. They watched the live coverage that Sunday as Jack Ruby thrust his snub-nosed revolver into the assassin's gut in the Dallas police headquarters. They were watching still as the black-veiled widow and her two children walked in the funeral cortege. "As the day of the assassination and the three days of memorial pageantry for John Fitzgerald Kennedy unfolded in Washington," Robert Caro wrote in *The Passage of Power,* the fourth volume of his biography of Lyndon Johnson, "America sat before its television sets watching it as if the country was gathered in one vast living room: a nation that was, for those four days, a single audience—in a way that had never happened before in history. " It was hard for newspapers to compete—especially hard for afternoon papers such as the *Journal-American* because their late-day editions competed head-to-head with the evening news broadcasts.

The *Journal-American*'s final days dwindled down like a slow death. After months of rumors, word came that Richard Berlin would finally get his way: the paper would print its final issue on April 23, 1966. Rewrite men went through the motions that afternoon, banging out stories about a group of doctors speaking out against birth control pills; about a fourteen-year-old Bronx girl who faked her kidnapping in order to spend time with her boyfriend; about a circus acrobat gravely injured during the first public performance of a trick she had practiced for two years; and about the last-place Yankees' demoralizing loss to the Baltimore Orioles.

Editors put the final edition to bed. Then the bottles came out from desk drawers. The phones rang with questions from other newspapers. Nobody picked them up. The staff stood around their metal desks in the open newsroom drinking from plastic cups pilfered from the cafeteria. Moochie's Saloon sent over buckets of ice.

The staff drank in dispirited silence. "No one in management had the stomach to make a speech," wrote William Hearst Jr., who came downtown for the wake. "The occasion was simply too tragic."

The *Journal-American* was a grubby operation, but the staff loved it as one might love an unkempt hound. For most of them, the paper was an extended family. As the night wore on, a reporter named Gus Engelman began to weep. Stan Blair, a reporter from the Brooklyn bureau, came over and wrapped a reassuring arm around Engelman's shoulders. "Well, buddy," Blair said, "this is it." Then he cried, too.

An editor typed out a farewell editorial, promising that the paper would live on as part of an improbable merger with the *World-Telegram* and *Herald Tribune*. "We think this will be a glorious beginning, not a sorrowful end. We are sure you'll agree." (As promised, a merged evening paper, the *World Journal Tribune,* would hit the newsstands in September, but it lasted only eight months.)

Late into Saturday night and Sunday morning the reporters and copy editors, typographers and press operators, cursed their unions. They cursed Walter Cronkite. Most of all they cursed the Hearst suits who failed them— particularly Richard Berlin, the chief executive officer who had eyed the *Journal-American* like a vulture since succeeding William Randolph Hearst in 1951. An eavesdropper in the newsroom that night would surely have heard reporters and editors drink a toast to Seymour Berkson, the Fifth Avenue publisher with a tabloid touch who delivered the paper's brightest moment: the correspondence with a mystery bomber.

As the 1950s drew to a close, forensics solidified its place in policing's arsenal of crime-fighting tools. Howard Finney's advocacy of the field, and his shrewd leadership of the crime lab and the bomb squad in the Metesky case, put him on the national map of crime-prevention leaders. In 1961 the City of Buffalo hired him as police commissioner with a special mandate to reform a thirteen-hundred-man department debased by corruption and inefficiency.

Buffalo was accustomed to backslapping, look-the-other-way police officials. Finney moved quickly, some said ruthlessly, to remake the department. He demoted or reassigned more than sixty detectives and put fifty additional patrolmen on the streets. The gambling, liquor, and vice squads were disbanded, replaced by a central bureau staffed by younger, college-educated policemen. Finney launched a barrage of raids on gambling dens and swept the streets of teenage gangs and the homeless. He was moving a little too fast for some people's comfort.

"I am *not* here to discuss political issues," he told the Buffalo City Council with his usual implacable demeanor. "I do *not* consider law enforcement a political issue." His exchange with council members, sometimes heated, elicited both cheers and boos.

He resigned less than two years into the job. "I'm smoking three packs of cigarettes a day, drinking a gallon of coffee, working ten to twelve hours a day, and they don't want [the reforms]," he said. Finney returned to New York to become executive director of the Harbor Waterfront Commission, a watchdog agency founded to fight corruption and organized crime on the docks. He later went into private law practice. He died in 1983.

On the hot summer morning of August 24, 1967, Abbie Hoffman, the mop-haired Yippie ringleader, and fourteen sidekicks threw money at traders and clerks from a visitors' gallery two stories above the floor of the New York Stock Exchange. The traders grabbed at the fluttering bills. Some of them looked up and gave Hoffman the finger. When the head of security asked who authorized their visit, the Yippies said George Metesky.

A decade after Metesky had receded from public notice, the Yippies, a militant hippie offshoot, had adopted him as a patron saint, occasionally signing his name on violent manifestos. Hoffman wrote his 1967 book, *Fuck the System,* using George Metesky as a nom de plume. A sequel, *Steal This Book,* contains step-by-step instructions on assembling pipe bombs with a flattering attribution to Metesky.

Hoffman wrote Metesky in Matteawan to say that the Yippies stood ready to deploy their guerrilla tactics on his behalf. Their kinship with Metesky went unreciprocated. He was aware enough to know that their involvement might hurt his cause at a time when he was trying to regain his freedom by navigating an elaborate judicial process, and he wrote back to discourage them. "They were ready to go and demonstrate on my behalf," he said. "I told them, 'Better soft-pedal it. You're liable to make it worse for me.'"

The Yippies' yearning for anarchy and dissent never factored into Metesky's agenda. He had no political motives, only a paranoid's delusion of conspiracy. He was not a radical or a Communist, nor did he ever use anarchist sloganeering.

Metesky's crusade did not subside during sixteen years spent within the thick masonry walls of Matteawan. As his health improved, his old rage returned. He railed against the treatment of patients left to languish for indefinite confinement in the obscurity of the Hudson Valley hills. While other patients passed the days playing tennis or gardening, Metesky, dressed in his double-breasted suit, wrote longhand letters to public officials complaining of the abusive conditions, and of his unjust imprisonment. He would escape not by bolting through the gates, as Harry Thaw had in 1913, but with a long, grinding campaign to prove his sanity. "They tried to drive me insane," he said. "But the more I realized what they were doing, the more determined I was to fight my way out."

Metesky was convinced that the entire legal-bureaucratic apparatus—district attorneys, judges, state psychiatrists—conspired to prolong his incarceration. "It is indeed a shameful situation, where people who are badly in need of correction themselves are busily pointing a finger at me with their own slimy hands," he wrote to District Attorney Frank Hogan.

In November 1963, he mailed a series of fuming letters to judges and prosecutors accusing his own lawyer, James Murray, of fumbling his case and stealing $19,108 under the pretext of reimbursement for ongoing efforts to get the charges dropped. After Metesky's confinement in Matteawan, a state judge had appointed Murray as a "committee of one" to oversee his client's finances. "I became fully convinced," Metesky wrote Hogan, "that I was betrayed and abandoned by my attorneys."

Metesky's point of view was paranoid, to be sure, but there were legitimate reasons to reconsider his custody. He had an unblemished record of good conduct, and as he repeatedly reminded officials, he had been detained for years without a trial. Metesky also complained, understandably, that the state was holding him in a limbo without due process. Like many Matteawan patients, he faced a life of detention without having been convicted of anything. He demanded to be put on trial for his crimes or be released.

For a while it looked as if he might get his way. In January 1964, Metesky petitioned the trial court in Dutchess County asking for a writ of habeas corpus. He argued that his detention in Matteawan violated his civil rights and asked to face trial on seven counts of attempted murder and other criminal charges pending against him. "I made this application in order to tell the Court that I am sane," he said, "that I understand the nature of my charges, and that I am able to confer with counsel." As a matter of routine, the judge solicited the opinion of a Matteawan psychiatrist, who advised that Metesky was still mentally impaired. The judge promptly dismissed the petition.

Metesky was by now well schooled in legal procedures. He quickly drafted his own neatly handwritten appeal to an appellate court, arguing without a lawyer's assistance that the trial court had denied him the right to cross-examine the Matteawan psychiatrist who testified to Metesky's continuing mental impairment. The issue bounced around for two years, but New York's highest court, the Court of Appeals, eventually reversed the denial and returned Metesky's petition to the trial court.

On December 15, 1966, Metesky, now accompanied by a lawyer, was granted his long-sought hearing in a Poughkeepsie courtroom. He had spent almost a decade writing letters and studying law journals in order to establish that he was sane. Sane enough for trial. Sane enough to leave the cranks and crackpots of the Matteawan wards behind. Sane enough to prove, at last, that his persecution had been real, and not some delusion, as doctors insisted. In clear and cogent testimony he explained that he had drafted the habeas corpus petition and maneuvered the complicated appeals process on his own, proof that he was of sound mind.

Once again he was sunk by Matteawan psychiatrists, who testified that he still evinced "inappropriate emotional reaction, expressed delusional ideas. Illogical thinking. Misrepresentation of real occurrences. Impaired judgment and lack of insight." Two months later the trial court judge dismissed Metesky's petition, saying he "failed to establish that he possesses the requisite appreciation of the nature of the crimes with which he is charged."

So after all his elaborate legal exertions, his handwritten petitions and briefs, Metesky landed back where he started—in the open wards of Matteawan with the bullying guards and high arched windows darkened by bars. The hours and days spent reading legal texts had not won him a single concession. It looked as if he would languish in Matteawan forever.

Metesky wanted to clear his name, but most urgently he wanted to escape Matteawan's terrors. On January 3, 1970, a 240-pound patient suffered a violent outburst and attacked three guards while Metesky stood by. "When I seen the charge of the ward knocked down and helpless and another officer knocked senseless, and the third officer trying to dial for help . . . I decided that outside help was urgently needed," Metesky later wrote. He pounded on the locked metal door of the ward so hard that his hands were black-and-blue for days. Within minutes "the ward was swarming with 'blue shirts,' who after a tussle were able to subdue the patient who was still going strong despite being hit on the head with a chair."

Metesky persisted. In November 1970 he tried yet another tack, filing a petition in the trial court of New York County against District Attorney Frank Hogan, seeking the dismissal of the original 1957 indictment against him. It was a Hail Mary pass, a long shot. Metesky wrote a digressive brief accusing Hogan of conspiring with Matteawan to keep its patients locked up without due process and characterizing the hospital psychiatrists as crazier than the patients. Not surprisingly the district attorney filed a statement claiming that his office was unable to proceed with the charges as long as psychiatrists judged Metesky mentally incompetent. Once again, the court denied his petition.

After a decade of setbacks and frustrations, Metesky's oddball single-handed legal maneuverings had exhausted themselves. He would likely remain in Matteawan without hope of ever absolving himself before a jury.

Unbeknownst to Metesky, the civil rights activism of the 1960s was kicking up a sea change in judicial thinking that would soon work in his favor. A series of reform-minded court decisions recognized that hospitals for the criminally insane such as Matteawan could not hold patients indefinitely without due process, and that the courts must recognize the constitutional rights of the criminally insane guaranteed under the Fourteenth Amendment.

In the winter of 1971 a thirty-year-old lawyer, Kristin Booth Glen, with support from liberal advocacy groups, filed a class action lawsuit on behalf of Metesky and other Matteawan patients claiming that their open-ended detention without trial violated their constitutional right to equal protection under the law. "I was fearless, and I was absolutely charged with the rightness of my argument," she said. "I knew I was right. I was outraged that people could be held forever. If they were tried, many of them would have been released years earlier."

A federal district court in New York City agreed. A year later the

Supreme Court unanimously upheld the decision, saying criminal defendants judged too mentally ill to stand trial could not be committed to asylums operated by the Department of Correction unless juries determined them to be "dangerous."

Metesky's case had gone to the highest court in America, and he had won. Despite his impairments, he had, at last, prevailed.

"Matteawan will no longer be a dumping ground for people about whom there are suspicions, but no hard proof," Glen said. "These people have neither been found guilty of crimes nor found dangerous by a jury."

In compliance with the ruling, Metesky and 275 other patients were transferred to hospitals run by health officials, not corrections officers, where administrators emphasized treatment, not punishment. By coincidence, Metesky landed at Creedmoor Hospital in Queens, one of the state hospitals supervised by Dr. Brussel. Seven months later the Department of Mental Hygiene pronounced Metesky fit for discharge, provided he make regular outpatient visits to a clinic near his home. After seventeen years of incarceration his righteous anger had dimmed to an ember. F.P. was gone for good, leaving only gentle George.

One legal issue remained: the pending charges against Metesky. Fortunately for him, a 1971 law provided that inmates held in a facility for the criminally insane were eligible for release when they had been confined for two-thirds of the maximum sentence they could have received at trial. In Metesky's case, the gravest charge, a murder conviction, could have brought a twenty-five-year term. Two-thirds of that term, or sixteen years and eight months, had lapsed. Accordingly, on December 12, 1973, a state trial judge dismissed the forty-seven-count indictment against him, clearing the way for his release. "Many of us had sleepless nights because of the terror you were causing," the judge told him. "I expect there will be no repetition."

"I think the judge is right," Metesky answered. "There won't be any repetition."

A front-page *New York Times* story published on the day of his release quoted Metesky as saying that he had no intention of returning to violence.

When the reporter asked if he still held a grudge against Con Ed, Metesky said, "I think it's best not to talk about that just now."

After seventeen years of confinement, Metesky, now seventy, walked out of the criminal courts building. "Free at last," he said, waving his release papers at waiting reporters.

Age had shrunk Metesky's body and his eyes looked flat behind heavy black-framed glasses. After his release he boarded a Greyhound bus for Waterbury. He sat alone near the front, an overnight bag and black valise filled with legal documents resting on the seat beside him. He watched through rain-splattered windows as the remembered landscape—the low brown winter hills of western New England, the worn brick warehouses, the dark cut of the Naugatuck River—came into view. At nightfall he stepped onto the sagging porch at 17 Fourth Street. The house looked the same, except that it now stood in the shadow of a highway. He rang the doorbell.

A light switched on. Mae, now seventy-five, came to the door in a heavy plaid jacket and beret. She smiled. "Hello, George."

Anna had died ten years earlier.

Metesky had turned down a marriage proposal from a woman who corresponded with him while he was in prison. "I finally told her if I have to make a choice," he told a reporter, "it will be caring for my sister."

For the next two decades Metesky lived as any retiree might. He looked after Mae and listened to an ancient radio in the parlor. He read historical fiction and did crossword puzzles, many of which were no doubt composed by Dr. Brussel. His favorite TV show was a detective program called *The F.B.I.* On Sundays he drove a '74 Dodge downtown to attend mass at St. Patrick's. "George was very faithful to his church attendance, faithful to Mass and the sacraments," Father Shea, the pastor, said.

Metesky was the picture of a broken-down old man walking with a cane, gentle if a bit grumpy. "In a suit he looks like Senator Metesky, in a polo shirt he looks like a retired porter," one visitor wrote. "The last thing he looks like is an insane criminal."

Metesky gradually receded from public consciousness, but his name came up every time a serial killer made headlines, as if he were the founding father of violent schizophrenia. In a sense he was. Investigators concluded that both the Son of Sam and the Unabomber fashioned themselves after Metesky, at least to some extent. When a bomb killed eleven at the TWA terminal at LaGuardia Airport in December 1975, Metesky urged the perpetrator to surrender, saying, "They never stop coming after you."

Metesky died in 1994 at the age of ninety. He was buried beside his sisters on a sloping cemetery hill. In the end, the tubercular bomber had outlived all of his pursuers.

ACKNOWLEDGMENTS

THIS BOOK WAS ASSEMBLED FROM THREE YEARS OF RESEARCH, DURING which I traversed an unusually varied landscape of subjects—psychiatry, forensics, crime prevention, bomb technology, newspaper history, and the legalese of criminal insanity. Writing about these topics often felt like traveling among foreign countries. I'm all the more grateful to the guides who pointed the way.

As always, sincerest thanks go to my excellent agent, Joy Harris, for her thoughtful advice and skillful handling of *Incendiary*'s conception, and all that followed. Andy Martin and Charles Spicer saw the potential from the beginning and spread their infectious enthusiasm. An author knows when he's in good hands. I'm grateful as well to April Osborn, Sarah Melnyk, Paul Hochman, Joseph Brosnan, and Steve Boldt

Thanks to Donna Wemple, a shrewd reader, who took an early version of *Incendiary* to the beach. I extend thanks as well to Crary Pullen for her diligent photography research.

I wish to acknowledge the archivists and librarians who welcomed me into their specialized realms: Jeff Roth, manager of the *New York Times* archive, cheerfully dug among his warren of filing cabinets on my behalf. I'm grateful for his expertise and energy. Thanks also to Arlene Shaner of the New York Academy of Medicine for granting me access to its gemlike library on Fifth Avenue. I express gratitude, as well, to the Briscoe Center at the University of Texas, which made available its extensive newspaper archive, including morgue clippings inherited from the *New York Journal-American*. Jeffrey Kroessler was kind enough to arrange several visits to the library at the John Jay College of Criminal Justice.

Sincerest thanks to those professionals who patiently answered questions from an unschooled outsider to their field: Dr. Park Dietz, an accomplished forensic psychiatrist, was kind enough to discuss Dr. Brussel's contribution to his field. Jim Clemente, a retired FBI profiler, was extraordinarily generous with his time. Mark Torre, commanding officer of the NYPD bomb squad, kindly invited me into the squad office to discuss its history. Bill Berkson took great care in helping me toward a more nuanced and accurate account of Seymour Berkson's unusual career as editor and publisher. Likewise, Judith Gutmann and John Israel both welcomed me into their homes to discuss the quirks and genius of Dr. Brussel, their stepfather. F. Lee Bailey agreed to read and comment on text describing Dr. Brussel's role in the Boston Strangler case. The Honorable Kristin Booth Glen answered questions about the class action lawsuit she filed on behalf of Matteawan patients detained without trial. Stephen Petrus, a historian at the Museum of the City of New York, helped me understand the city politics of the 1950s.

Thanks also to those retired reporters who recounted the golden age of New York newspapers: Mike Pearl, Marilyn Bender, Mickey Carroll, Frank McLoughlin, and Nicholas Pileggi.

Lastly I'd like to thank my family. My daughters, Evie and Cricket, must wonder what their father does all day. Here's the evidence, for better or worse.

If you have comments or questions about *Incendiary,* please tweet me at @michaelcannell.

SOURCE NOTES

Preface

vii "the age of anxiety": W. H. Auden, *The Age of Anxiety: A Baroque Eclogue* (New York: Random House, 1947).

viii "Seldom in the history of New York": Associated Press, "Police Hunt for Mad Bomber," *Wellesville Daily Reporter,* January 22, 1957, 8.

Prologue

2 "the greatest individual menace New York City ever faced": "The Mad Bomber," *New York Journal-American,* December 27, 1956, 1.

2 "the most agonizing challenge of modern times": Ibid.

3 "greatest manhunt in the history of the Police Department": Emanuel Perlmutter, "Kennedy Orders Wide Manhunt for Movie Bombing Perpetrator," *New York Times,* December 4, 1956, 1.

3 "the bombs and the letters: these were all the police had": Dr. James A. Brussel, *Casebook of a Crime Psychiatrist* (New York: Bernard Geis Associates, 1968), 11.

3 "was a short, stocky man": Ibid.

4 "They fidgeted, they sighed, they exchanged glances": Ibid., 13.

4 "Any one of the people I saw below": Ibid., 11.

4 "He seemed like a ghost": Ibid., 28.

ONE: Angel of Justice

11 "He's the perfect example of a man": Jamie James, "The 'Mad Bomber' vs. Con Ed," *Rolling Stone,* November 15, 1979, 47.

TWO: Bomb Squad

13 "It is a little flirtation we play with the unknown": Newspaper Enterprise Association, "Unexpected Death Is Work Area of City Bomb Squad," *Rhinelander Daily News,* January 31, 1957, 14.

14 "Woe upon you if you do not resolve": "The Black Hand Scourge," *Cosmopolitan Magazine,* June 1909, 31.

15 "doors of this country would be closed to Italians": "Joe Bruno on the Mob," joebrunoonthemob.wordpress.com/2012/04/16/joe-bruno-on-the-mob-the -black-hand/.

15 "He knew every manner and custom": "A Great Detective's Fight Against the Black Hand Society," *Washington Post,* July 19, 1914, 42.

16 "The United States has become the dumping ground": "Blames Immigration for the Black Hand," *New York Times,* January 6, 1908, 14.

16 "Probably not": "Petrosino Buried with High Honors," *New York Times,* April 6, 1908, 1.

18 "as harmonious as the stars in their courses": *Your World of Tomorrow,* pamphlet, New York World's Fair, 1939.

19 "many people were having drinks": "Crowd Unaware of Bomb Tragedy," *New York Times,* July 5, 1940, 2.

19 "It was his day off": Mary Hosie, "Victim Answered Call to Fair on His Day Off," *Brooklyn Eagle,* July 5, 1940, 1.

20 "It's the business": Philip Messing, "Cops Killed at 1940 World's Fair to Be Honored," *New York Post,* May 25, 2015, 5.

24 "Every infernal machine is different": Joseph Carter, "Wanted: The Man Without a Face," *Collier's,* February 3, 1956, 21.

24 "There's plenty of tension anytime": "Police Bomb Expert: Peter Joseph Dale," *New York Times,* December 26, 1956, 22.

24 "It's hard, dangerous work": Jack Alexander, "Bomb-Squad Cop," *Saturday Evening Post,* September 19, 1959, 46.

25 "One of these days I'm going to be scraping you": Ibid.

25 "The good man upstairs": "Police Bomb Expert," 22.

26 "Everybody along the street would be in danger": "If Parcel Ticks, Shell Is Found, It's Time to Call In Bomb Squad," *New York Herald Tribune,* August 1, 1951, 17.

27 "I really sweated on that one": "His Job Is Dynamite," *Cue,* June 28, 1952, 12.

28 "This defendant is a particular source of annoyance": "Sugar Bomb Suspect Is Sent to Bellevue," *New York Times,* November 8, 1951, 19.

28 "This arrest is an outrage": Ibid.

29 "a stick of dynamite": "Bomb Is Exploded in Union Square I.R.T," *New York Herald Tribune,* November 29, 1951, 1.

THREE: Mr. Think

32 "I've read that a man with a hammer": James, "'Mad Bomber,'" 47.

33 "I just couldn't go in and confess": Meyer Berger, "Twisted Course of Mad Bomber Vengeance," *New York Times,* January 25, 1957, 18.

FOUR: Reverse Psychiatry

36 "It is an ordinary human face": Brussel, *Casebook*, 3.

38 "further evidence of the desire": New York State Department of Mental Hygiene, *Annual Report of the Creedmoor State Hospital* (Utica, N.Y.: State Hospital Press, 1952), 17.

39 "He was a man who was not happy": John Israel, interview with author, September 24, 2013.

39 "I've never fired my .32 Iver Johnson": James A. Brussel, "Gun-Carrying Doctors," letter, *Brandon* (Florida.) *Sun*, June 20, 1974, 4.

40 "psychotic with symptoms of hallucinations": James A. Brussel, "Mary Todd Lincoln: A Psychiatric Study," *Psychiatric Quarterly*, January 1941, 7.

40 "The wild epileptic": James A. Brussel, "Psychosomatics," *Psychiatric Quarterly*, April 1949, 367.

41 "There are hazards involving other patients": James A. Brussel, "The Best in the Treatment and Control of Chronically Disturbed Patients," *Psychiatric Quarterly*, January 1951, 55.

41 "For those in the movement": Jeffrey A. Lieberman, *Shrinks: The Untold Story of Psychiatry* (New York: Back Bay Books, 2015), 69.

42 "Psychoanalysis was in the air": Anatole Broyard, *Kafka Was the Rage: A Greenwich Village Memoir* (New York: Vintage Books, 1997), 45.

42 "When you sat down with him": Israel, interview with author.

43 "not a single personality but two": Walter Langer, *The Mind of Adolf Hitler: The Secret Wartime Report* (New York: Basic Books, 1972), 212.

43 "compensate for his vulnerability": Ibid.

43 "the most plausible outcome": Ibid.

44 "There was no head left on the body": Brussel, *Casebook*,106.

45 "reverse the terms of the prophecy": Ibid., 4.

45 "It was simply my way own way of applying": Ibid.

45 "throws himself into the spirit of his opponent": Edgar Allan Poe, "The Murders in the Rue Morgue," xroads.virginia.edu/~hyper/poe/murders.html.

46 "Like all other New Yorkers I'd been following": Brussel, *Casebook*, 28.

FIVE: Poplar Street

49 "It was in the booth next to mine": *People of the State of New York v. George Metesky*, New York County Court of General Sessions Grand Jury, January 28, 1957.

49–50 "I felt an explosion and something pushed me in the head": Ibid.

50 "He has been described as poker-faced": Associated Press. "New Man Heads Troubled Police Force," *Danville Bee* (Virginia), June 28, 1962, 2B.

53 "That velvet collar should be smeared with blood": Jack Alexander, "Independent Cop—Part II," *New Yorker*, October 10, 1936, 30.

54 "The dealers acted as if we were crazy": "Bomber Leaves a Tangled Trail," *New York Journal-American,* December 31, 1956, 4.

55 "I personally have taken the watch-timing mechanism": Joseph Carter, "Wanted: The Man Without a Face," *Collier's,* February 3, 1956, 56.

56 "The *G* was a *C* with two horizontal lines": Bruce Miller, *Curiosity's Cats: Writers on Research* (St. Paul: Minnesota Historical Society Press, 2014), 206.

57 "I kept after Holland": Ibid., 220.

58 "The detectives who read the note": Carter, "Wanted," 23.

58 "This is a well-constructed mechanism": "Police Files Tell Weird Details of Bomber's History," *New York Journal-American,* December 30, 1956, 6.

59 "The firing device was so intricate": Miller, *Curiosity's Cats,* 207.

59–60 "Some people feed cats": Brussel, *Casebook,* 52.

61 "We're sorry about this, sir": James, "'Mad Bomber,'" 47.

61 "I was so frightened I could hardly speak": "The Mad Bomber's Story Reveals Odd Personality," *New York Journal-American,* January 20, 1957, 7.

SIX: Up from the Streets

66 "the verge of becoming a community of violence and crime": Paul Crowell, "City Crime-Ridden, Adams Declares in Pleas for Police," *New York Times,* August 2, 1954, 1.

67 "Before this hot August Sunday is over": Ibid.

69 "Your boss is one of the pleasantest disappointments": E. W. Kenworthy, *New York Times Magazine,* August 14, 1955, 34.

70 "You thought twice before you used a phone booth": James, "'Mad Bomber,'" 47.

71 "stand together and give our utmost": Charles G. Bennett, "Kennedy New Police Head; Nielson Is Chief Inspector," *New York Times,* August 3, 1955, 1.

71 "There is in his tone none of the over-meticulousness": "All Cop Commissioner," *New York Times,* February 14, 1956, 21.

71 "Oh, yes": Murray Schumach, "Kennedy Took Night Study Route for High School, College and Law," *New York Times,* August 3, 1955, 15.

71 "I didn't catch anything": Wayne Phillips, "Portrait of Our No. 1 Cop," *New York Times,* November 15, 1959, 16.

71 "My people came from Ireland": Associated Press, "New York's Top Cop Is Tough," *Salina Journal* (Kansas), April 29, 1959, 13.

72 "never bothered anybody": "'All Cop' Commissioner," 21.

72 "There were three cops on our post": "Strong Arm of the Law," *Time,* July 7, 1959, 14.

73 "Tsk, tsk, tsk": "Portrait of Steve Kennedy—an Unusual Cop Who's Now Boss," *World-Telegram and Sun,* August 2, 1955, 7.

74 "A policeman's gun is his cross": Don Murray, "New York's Toughest Cop," *Saturday Evening Post,* September 8, 1956, 25.

74 "New York's finest career officer": Phillips, "Portrait," 16.

74 "When the rest of the boys were out": "Stephen P. Kennedy Obituary" (unpublished), *New York Times,* undated.

74 "night study pallor": Helen Dudar, "The Long, Lonely Climb," *New York Post,* November 20, 1955, 2.

74 "Nobody will ever know": Phillips, "Portrait," 16.

74 "I was a law enforcement officer": Sidney Fields, "Only Human," *New York Daily Mirror,* November 20, 1955, 43.

75 "Steve has come up through the ranks": Schumach, "Kennedy Took Night Study Route," 15.

75 "All Kennedy wants is to swing the big stick": Phillips, "Portrait," 16.

76 "Kirk called me the next morning": "Eye on Dr. Sam," New York *Daily News,* January 23, 1955, 5.

77 "Dr. Sam Sheppard, who goes on trial tomorrow": Dorothy Kilgallen, *New York Journal-American,* October 18, 1954, 3.

77 "The case is not closed": "Sheppards' Criminologist Takes Clues Home to Study," *New York Herald Tribune,* January 27, 1955, 5.

78 "He said that Sam's story was consistent": F. Lee Bailey, *The Defense Never Rests* (New York: Stein and Day, 1971), 61.

78 "There are relatively few new ideas about fighting crime": Bennett, "Kennedy New Police Head," 1.

79 "I examined it, and I didn't know": *The People of the State of New York v. George Metesky,* Grand Jury of the County of New York Court of General Sessions, January 28, 1957.

79 "It was an accident": "Police Bomb Expert: Peter Joseph Dale," *New York Times,* December 26, 1956, 22.

80 "I only saw him from the rear": "Recalls Bombing at Grand Central," *New York Journal-American,* December 27, 1956, 6.

80 "People were running in every direction": "Bomb Blast in Penn Station," *New York Journal-American,* February 21, 1956, 1.

81 "I know that gadget so well": "Army to Explode Madman's Bombs," *New York Journal-American,* December 26, 1956, 1.

81 "His face remains a blank no matter": Carter, "Wanted," 56.

82 "It is one thing to live in a cloud of fear": Charles Delafuente, "Terror in the Age of Eisenhower," *New York Times,* September 10, 2004, 12.

82 "If ever there was an argument for scientific police work": "The Mad Bomber," *New York Journal-American,* December 27, 1956, 8.

83 "I didn't realize what the object was": *People of the State of New York v. George Metesky.*

83 "I've used that sort of pipe before": Murray Schumach, "Pipe Bomb From R.C.A. Building Blasts Guard's Home in Jersey," *New York Times,* August 5, 1956, 64.

84 "I was saved by the grace of God": "Rockefeller Center Escapes a Bombing," *New York Herald Tribune,* August 5, 1956, 1.

84 "Left to this evidence": "The Most Wanted Casts His Shadow," *New York Journal-American,* December 26, 1956, 1.

SEVEN: The Paramount

86 "Suddenly I heard a report like a grenade": "Blast Hurts 7 in B'klyn," *New York Journal-American,* December 3, 1956, 1.

87 "The shock and terror of what happened": "Explosion Victim Glad He's Caught," *New York Journal-American,* January 22, 1957, 3.

87 "new audacity, born of apparent desperation": Jess Stearn, "Bomber's Portrait in Script," New York *Daily News,* December 11, 1956, 3.

88 "an outrage that cannot be tolerated": Perlmutter, "Kennedy Orders Wide Manhunt," 1.

88 "Alert every member of the force": Ibid., 47.

88 "In those days a nightlong poker game": Arthur Gelb, *City Room* (New York: Putnam's, 2004), 153.

89 "Nobody wanted to go in with stuff": Nicholas Pileggi, interview with author, January 29, 2016.

89 "Passant would yell out": Ibid.

90 "I like to see things grow": Mary and Rory Doyle, "Bullets," an unpublished article, 1.

91 "At first we requested that no publicity": Morris Kaplan, "13 Bomb Threats Harry City in a Day," *New York Times,* December 5, 1956, 80.

92 "After 16 years of being secretive": Stearn, "Bomber's Portrait in Script," 3.

93 "Europe's foremost expert on identification": Ibid.

EIGHT: "It Will Be Buttoned"

95 "That the human mind works at all": Brussel, *Casebook,* xii.

96 "I felt that my profession was being judged": Ibid., 13

97 "I don't know what you expect me to do": Don DeNevi, John H. Campbell, Stephen Band, and John E. Otto, *Into the Minds of Madmen: How the FBI Behavioral Science Unit Revolutionized Criminal Investigations* (Amherst, N.Y.: Prometheus Books, 2003), 62.

97 "tough, clever man": Brussel, *Casebook,* 11.

97 "I'd seen that look before": Ibid., 13.

98 "scientific types": Michael M. Greenburg, *The Mad Bomber of New York* (New York: Union Square Press, 2011), 213.

98 "They showed one thing very plainly": Brussel, *Casebook,* 14.

98 "People sometimes ask what proportion": Ibid., 80.

99 "a chronic disorder of insidious development": Ibid., 30.

99 "could have been wrong": Ibid.

99 "They are not infallible": "The Man Who Killed Two Career Girls," *New York Journal-American,* October 13, 1963, 1.

99 "trying to screw up the courage": Brussel, *Casebook,* 32.

100 "was almost certainly a very neat, proper man": Ibid., 33.

101 "but he twists it around so that wherever a wire runs": "Psychiatrist Depicts the Bomber," *New York Herald Tribune,* December 27, 1956, 1.

101 "He marshals all kinds of compelling evidence": Ibid., 31.

101 "This pact is a secret between him and God": "Psychiatrist Depicts the Bomber," 1.

102 "He would always have to give the appearance": Joel Seldin, "Bomber a Woman? Idea Called Silly," *New York Herald Tribune,* December 28, 1956, 11.

102 "have confidence only in themselves": Ibid.

102 "For a long while, as the three police officers": Brussel, *Casebook,* 33.

102 "There was a certain stilted tone in the letters": Ibid., 34.

103 "He's a Slav": Ibid., 41.

103 "The misshapen *W* might not have caught": Ibid., 35.

104 "Something about sex seemed to be troubling": Ibid., 36.

104 "To talk about these things now": Ibid.

104 "The bomber obviously distrusted": Ibid., 39.

104 "Something about the bomber's method": Ibid., 36.

105 "He wants nothing to do with men": Ibid.

105 "What is his illness?": Ibid., 42.

106 "all of my physical, mental and financial sufferings": Ibid., 54.

106 "Had I thought about it a little more carefully": Ibid., 43.

106 "What are you going to do with what I've given you?": Ibid.

107 "When he went into a store": Ibid., 45.

107 "but he wasn't sure whether everybody else knew": Ibid., 44.

107 "a mail carrier, a local merchant, a fellow employee": Ibid., 45.

107 "They'll drive us crazy": Ibid., 46.

108 "Captain, one more thing": Ibid.

NINE: "Keep out of This"

110 "It is similar to that used in the atomic bomb": "Tell of Talk in Library with Suspect," *New York Journal-American,* December 26, 1956, 1.

110 "He fell in alongside of us": Ibid.

111 "That looks like the bomber's work": "Mad Bomber Hits Library," *New York Daily News,* December 25, 1956, 2.

112 "We're completely stymied": "5 Bomb Warnings Keep Police on Go but Yield No Clue," *New York Times,* December 26, 1956, 1.

112 "You can call him mad, a crackpot, and a psychopath": "Army to Set Off Bomber's 29th," New York *Daily News,* December 26, 1956, 2.

112–13 "We treat every one as if it were the real thing": Joseph Kahn, *Parade* magazine, February 10, 1957, 19.

113 "They made something happen": "Hoaxers Tormented Bomb Squad with 160 Calls in December, Then Shifted to School," *New York Times,* January 23, 1957, 18.

113–14 "The public can cope with the known": Ibid.

115 "Under no circumstances do I want any member": "Push Bomber, Could Be a Woman," New York *Daily News,* December 27, 1956, 2.

115 "The Mad Bomber yesterday sent his Christmas greeting": "Mad Bomber Hits Library," 2.

115 "The bomb squad, the Police Bureau of Technical Service": Philip J. Meagher, "16-Year Search for Madman," *New York Times,* December 25, 1956, 1.

115 "in the hope that the psychiatrist might work up": Ibid.

116 "The news story didn't contain all my predictions": DeNevi, Campbell, Band, and Otto, *Into the Minds,* 63.

116 "Is this Dr. Brussel, the psychiatrist?": Brussel, *Casebook,* 53.

TEN: The Publisher

118 "Let it latch onto an exposé": "Hearst Wooptedo," *Newsweek,* December 13, 1948, 58.

119 "No one had more fun covering the heartache and happy times": William Randolph Hearst Jr., *The Hearsts: Father and Son* (New York: Rinehart, 1991), 283.

119 "This may be dated": "Seymour Berkson, Publisher of J-A," *New York Journal-American,* January 5, 1959, 1.

119 "He had fine features": Bill Berkson, interview with author, September 15, 2015.

120 "If he cared about anything": Ibid.

120 "If you're going to be a writer": Ibid.

120 "He is slim and dapper and quite active": Damon Runyon, "Brighter Side," *New York Journal-American,* October 25, 1938, 7.

121 "There was a lot of laughter in the house": Berkson, Interview with author.

123 "Seymour was one of the most dynamic creatures": Bob Considine, *It's All News to Me* (New York: Meredith Press, 1967), 89.

123 "that I sometimes answer 'Hello' in face-to-face": Associated Press, "Paul Schoenstein, 71, Dead: Ex-editor, Pulitzer Winner," *Bridgeport Post* (Connecticut), April 15, 1974, 28.

124 "He beat death by three hours": "New York Superman," *Time,* October 2, 1978, 96.

124 "No city editor dare sit back and gloat": Paul Schoenstein, *Coronet,* January 1953, 91.

125 "As a stab in the dark, we decided to write him": Associated Press, "Newspaper Plea Helped to Solve 'Mad Bomber' Case After 16 Years," *Oregon Statesman,* January 23, 1957, 3.

125 "There was a no-nonsense spit-on-the-floor": Mickey Carroll, interview with author, December 30, 2014.

125 "I felt like throwing up": Marilyn Bender, interview with author, June 24, 2014.

126 "I never had the nerve to try the meatballs": Hearst Jr., *Hearsts,* 295.

126 "His natural volume was a yell": Mike Pearl, interview with author, December 30, 2014.

128 "Keep your eyes open and your mouth shut": "Seymour Berkson, Publisher of J-A," 1.

128 "Every time we find a real bomb": "The Mad Bomber," *New York Times,* December 30, 1956, 49.

129 "We can't just barge into these places": Jess Stearn, "A Day in the Hunt for the Bomber," New York *Daily News,* January 20, 1957, 28.

129 "check brown-eyed people, they're no good": "Tips on Bomber Funny and Tragic," *New York Journal-American,* January 13, 1957, 13.

129 "Not only that": Ibid.

129 "But since his wife was some ten years older": Brussel, *Casebook,* 56.

130 "Not a few times I sat in the rear of an unmarked police car": Ibid., 60.

130 "to a T": Ibid.

130 "As I read, I could feel my heart pound": Ibid.

130 "That ended it": Ibid.

130 "I want to do my duty as a citizen": Ibid, 61.

130–31 "Why couldn't I stumble over his file?": Ibid.

131 "Once more, I made a flying trip uptown:" Ibid.

131 "While we were following down such leads": Ibid.

131 "a prankster's holiday": Jess Stearn, "A Day in the Hunt for the Mad Bomber," New York *Daily News,* January 20, 1957, 38.

131 "The way we work, ninety percent of our calls": Carter, "Wanted," *Collier's,* 23.

132 "It's a screwball's delight": "His Job Is Dynamite," *Cue,* June 28, 1952, 12.

132 "It's amazing how suspicious people": Stearn, "Day in the Hunt," January 20, 1957, 28.

132 "A man called here today with a complaint": Ibid.

132 "He's plain crazy": "Tips on Bomber Funny and Tragic," 13.

133 "a startling new avenue of investigation": "Mystery Man Drops Dead During Mad Bomber Probe," *New York Journal-American,* December 29, 1956, 1.

134 "Their task was endlessly complicated": Ibid.

134 "Our policy is to arrest these people": Alexander Feinberg, "Firm Penalty Due for Bomb Cranks," *New York Times,* January 1, 1957, 23.

134 "I didn't believe the man could turn down": Brussel, *Casebook,* 53.

134 "Now listen carefully": "Test-Blast 3 Bombs; Madman's 2 Go Off," New York *Daily News,* December 29, 1956, 6.

136 "The purpose is to split the bomb": "Bomb Found in Broadway Movie," *New York Journal-American,* December 28, 1956, 6.

137 "It looks as if both were real bombs": Ibid.

137 "The question now is, Where do we go": "Police Files Tell Weird Details of Bomber's History," *New York Journal-American*, December 30, 1956, 6.

137 "The Mad Bomber is a man with a diabolical": "Bomber Mystery Baffles Hitchcock," *New York Journal-American,* December 30, 1956, 7.

137 "All of us are schooled by TV": Ibid.

138 "He is a killer type": "Test-Blast 3 Bombs," 6.

138 "I can't tell you how many nights": Edward Condon, "Infernal Machines," *American Spectator,* June 1993, 44.

139 "There was a lot of fear": Delafuente, "Terror in the Age of Eisenhower," 12.

142 "We were in the awkward position": "The Journal's Role—Step by Step—in Capture of Elusive Bomber," *New York Journal-American,* January 22, 1957, 2.

143 "I always help the police": Alexander Feinberg, "Bomb Disrupts Subway Travel," *New York Times,* December 31, 1956, 15.

144 "We solicit the aid and cooperation": "Mystery Man Drops Dead," 1.

ELEVEN: The Truce

145 "For all we know": Associated Press, Francis Stilley, "One of New York's Greatest Manhunts Spreads in Effort to Catch 'Mad Bomber,'" *Lincoln Star* (Nebraska), December 30, 1956, 13.

146 "All those bomb-scare headlines": "Fox Plans Movie on 'Mad Bomber,'" *New York Times,* January 3, 1957, 27.

146 "By now, we suppose": "Notes and Comments," *New Yorker,* January 12, 1957, 17.

147 "a new lead had triggered the outburst": "Bomber Hunt Break Hinted in Cop Flurry," *World-Telegram and Sun,* January 9, 1957, 1.

148 "That German *G*": Stearn, "Day in the Hunt for the ," January 20, 1957, 28.

149 "a little deranged": "Bomber Hunt Focuses on Ex-State Aid," *World-Telegram and Sun,* January 12, 1957, 1.

149 "I'll get even for this": "Con Edison Records Give Clue," *Long Island Star Journal,* January 12, 1957, 1.

150 "For all we know, we may have": Stearn, "Day in the Hunt," January 29, 1957, 28.

153 "He had conceived himself as God": Brussel, *Casebook,* 26.

154 "big, smiling man with a jolly air": "Clerk Described Bomber," *New York Journal-American,* January 12, 1957, 13.

155 "We never did quite make it": Ibid.

155 "As matters stand": Stearn, "Day in the Hunt," January 29, 1957, 28.

155 "If an injustice has been done": "State Promises Review of Case," *New York Journal-American,* January 16, 1957, 1.

156 "We wish to assure 'F.P.'": Ibid.

TWELVE: The Dead Files

160 "As I pulled this typewritten letter": Associated Press, "'Glad I Did It' Says Mad Bomber as 16-Year Reign of Terror Ends," *San Bernardino County* (California) *Sun,* January 23, 1957, 5.

160 "Yes. This is it": Associated Press, "'Mad Bomber' Seized, Locked Up in Bellevue Hospital for Study," *Anderson Herald* (Indiana), January 23, 1957, 1.

162 "This sounds an awful lot like our man": Brussel, *Casebook,* 67.

THIRTEEN: Fair Play

164 "I'd knock on the front door": "Sisters of Mad Bomber Admit They Coddled Him," *New York Journal-American,* January 22, 1957, 1.

164 "Gangs used to break into the lumberyard": "Metesky's First Bombing Turned Out a Dud," *New York Journal-American,* March 23, 1957, 4.

165 "What are you boys doing?": Brussel, *Casebook,* 10.

165 "I hear him out in that garage of his": Ibid.

166 "an unstable person": Police memorandum, April 15, 1957, Detective Mike Lynch, Twenty-Fourth Squad, interview with George Metesky.

167 "These gentlemen are New York City detectives": James, "'Mad Bomber,'" 46.

167 "It was almost like he was waiting": Ibid.

168 "This is not then": Police memorandum, April 15, 1957.

169 "Here we have the whole story": "George Did It," *Time,* February 4, 1957.

169 "You're looking for more than an accident": Mark Sheehan and Ed Butler, Associated Press, "Catch 'Mad Bomber,'" *Winona* (Minnesota) *Daily News,* January 22, 1957, 1.

169 "I really don't": Ibid.

169 "We think you do": Ibid.

169 "I guess it's because": Ibid.

170 "George couldn't hurt anybody": "Sisters of Mad Bomber," 1.

FOURTEEN: Interrogation

174 "Metesky was hazy as to some of the correspondence": Meyer Berger, "About New York: Twisted Course of 'Mad Bomber' Vengeance Traced in a Deeply Complex Personality," *New York Times,* January 25, 1957, 18.

174 "Have you ever seen one of these?": "Metesky Tells How Lozenges Set Off Bombs," *New York Journal-American,* January 27, 1957, 3.

175 "Because it was easier and safer": Ibid.

175 "It was very easy this way": Ibid.

175 "I always carried a small piece of cloth with me": Interrogation of George Metesky at police headquarters, Waterbury, Connecticut, January 22, 1975.

175 "I started on the other places": "Investigate Con Edison Bomb Role," *New York Journal-American,* January 25, 1957, 5.

175 "I was sick": Interrogation of Metesky at Waterbury police headquarters.

176 "Seasoned newspapermen were incredulous": "The Mad Bomber," *Waterbury Republican,* January 24, 1957, 16.

176 "There's absolutely no question of it": Robert W. White, " 'Mad Bomber' Captured at His Waterbury Home," *New York Herald Tribune,* January 22, 1957, 1.

177 "the usher who passes the collection plate": Richard H. Parke, "Sisters Shocked, Loyal to Brother," *New York Times,* January 23, 1957, 20.

177 "I drove up the Merritt Parkway": Carl Pelleck, interview with author, February 4, 2016.

177 "The work we did [at the power station] was unhealthy": "Tells of Injuries at Power Plant," *New York Journal-American,* January 24, 1957, 5.

179 "Apparently the coughing and blood": "Mad Bomber Reveals How Resentment Grew to Hate," *New York Journal-American,* March 21, 1957, 4.

179 "They let me lay there": Associated Press, " 'Bomber' Unburdens Details of His Employment Injury," *Bridgeport Post* (Connecticut), January 25, 1957, 13.

181 "My name might as well be": Sheehan and Butler, "Catch 'Mad Bomber,' " 1.

181 "I even tried to purchase space": Report of psychiatric examination of George Metesky, March 1, 1957, in files of New York County Supreme Court, *The People of the State of New York v. George P. Metesky,* indictment no. 321/1957, courtesy of Municipal Archives.

182 "I figured I would put one bullet": Meyer Berger, "Twisted Course of Mad Bomber Vengeance," *New York Times,* January 25, 1957, 18.

183 "People pay more attention": Miller, *Curiosity's Cats,* 205.

183 "admitted his crimes eagerly in the end": Brussel, *Casebook,* 98.

184 "She is decent": Dom Frasca, "Bomber Reveals Fear of Capture," *New York Journal-American,* January 26, 1957, 4.

184 "You'll hammer away": Ibid.

184 "This is the man": Sheehan and Butler, "Catch 'Mad Bomber,' " 1.

185 "He isn't the type": "Coddled Bomber, Sisters Admit," *New York Journal-American,* March 22, 1957, 55.

185 "Go away": "Sister Doesn't Understand Alibi: 'They Made Me Do It,' " *New York World-Telegram and Sun,* January 22, 1957, 1.

185 "My God, they have the wrong man": "Mild-Mannered Waterbury Man Confesses to Being Mad Bomber Who Plagued Manhattan for 16 Years," *Naugatuck Daily News,* January 22, 1957.

185 "His arrest is ridiculous": "Kin Refuse to Believe He's Guilty," *New York Journal-American,* January 22, 1957, 1.

185 "George do you recognize my name?": Greenburg, *Mad Bomber of New York,* 159.

186 "Oh, yes": Ibid.

186 "George, we know you made": Ibid.

186 "My brother would never do damage": "Sisters Claim Brother Could Not Be 'Bomber,'" *New York Journal-American,* January 22, 1957, 1.

186 "We're not worried": Ibid.

186 "That's the clincher": "Letters Lead to Bomber's Capture," *New York Journal-American,* January 22, 1957, 2.

187 "Now from these": Testimony of Detective Michael Lynch, New York Police Department, Grand Jury of the County of New York Court of General Sessions, *The People of the State of New York v. George Metesky,* January 28, 1957.

187 "It seemed the only thing to do": "Judge May Have Set Precedent on Court Photos," *Naugatuck Daily News,* January 22, 1957, 1.

187 "Do you understand these proceedings?": Ibid.

187 "I have a pretty good idea": Ibid.

188 "wouldn't call it a relief": "Bomber Heard on Con Ed TV Show," *New York Herald Tribune,* January 23, 1957, 5.

188 "because he had no choice": Ibid.

188 "a classic textbook case of paranoia": Associated Press, "'Mad Bomber' Called Classic Case of Paranoia," *Port Angeles* (Washington State) *Evening News,* January 23, 1957, 1.

FIFTEEN: The Smiling Avenger

189 "the smiling avenger": "Metesky Moved to Matteawan," *New York Journal-American,* April 19, 1957, 1.

189 "The face might have been that": Brussel, *Casebook,* 70.

190 "Are you glad it's all over": "'Mad Bomber' Booked, Sent to Bellevue," *New York Herald Tribune,* January 23, 1957, 1.

191 "You are asking me to act": Transcript of court appearance, *The People of the State of New York v. George Metesky,* City Magistrates' Court of the City of New York Felony Court, Borough of Manhattan, docket no. 1226, January 1957, courtesy of Municipal Archives.

191 "the defendant's actions are indicative": Ibid.

192 "We haven't got the full version": "Con-Ed and Cops Wrangle over Who Gets the Credit for What," New York *Daily News,* January 23, 1957, 4.

193 "repeatedly for two years": "Bomb-Hunt Delay Laid to Con Edison by Police Sources," *New York Times,* January 25, 1957, 1.

193 "we were informed that 1940 files": Associated Press, "Police Blame Firm in Mad Bomber Case," *Kingston Daily Freeman* (New York), January 25, 1957, 1.

194 "If any charge is to be made": "Hunt for All Data on Bomber Case," *New York Journal-American,* January 25, 1957, 1.

194 "straightening out this confusion": George Carpozi, "See Insanity Plea for Mad Bomber," January 26, 1957, 1.

194 "It was only a ten-minute ride": Harrison E. Salisbury, "Police Give Clerk Bomb-Clue Credit," *New York Times,* January 24, 1957, 23.

194 "one of a number of leads": "23 on Bomb Case to Be Promoted," *New York Times,* January 24, 1957, 19.

194 "This was not good police work": Salisbury, "Police Give Clerk Bomb-Clue Credit," 23.

194 "Police were working for five or six": "Bomb-Hunt Delay Laid to Con Edison," 1

195 "A man has been arrested": Salisbury, "Police Give Clerk Bomb-Clue Credit," 23.

195 "I was just assigned to": "Bomber Reward Might Go Begging," *New York Times,* February 16, 1957.

195 "They knew that we had detectives in Albany": James, "'Mad Bomber,'" 47.

196 "one of the great journalistic coups": William Randolph Hearst Jr., "Editor's Report: Journalism at Its Best," *New York Journal-American,* January 27, 1957, 1.

196 "We intend to abide by the promises": "Editorial: The Mad Bomber," *New York Journal-American,* January 23, 1957, 26.

197 "Thank God, now [Metesky] can't hurt": International News Service, "Injured Victims Express Relief," January 23, 1957.

198 "saw a man with a psychosis": Transcript of court appearance, *The People of the State of New York v. George Metesky,* docket no. 1226, January 1957.

198 "I doubt if shock therapy": *Eye on New York,* CBS, interview with Dr. James A. Brussel, January 26, 1957.

198 "Nothing you can say will make": Brussel, *Casebook,* 31.

SIXTEEN: Mr. Death

199 "It feels as if some diabolical": William F. Longgood, "Lawyer for the Defense," *Saturday Evening Post,* November 2, 1957, 26.

199 "When I stop working": "James D. C. Murray, Defender in Major Criminal Cases, Dies," *New York Times,* October 15, 1967, 85.

200 "He is a superb stage director": Longgood, "Lawyer for the Defense," 26.

200 "You can't turn your back": Ibid.

200 "I don't like the city": Ibid.

200–01 "She doesn't know whether": Ibid.

201 "The last movie I saw": Unpublished advance obituary of James D. C. Murray, *New York Times.*

201 "After we're through, you can tell": Longgood, "Lawyer for the Defense," 26.

201 "was born with a constitutional pity": Ibid.

201 "I always remember that it isn't the man": Ibid.

201 "It is possible that he may have": Travis Fulton, "Not Responsible, Sisters Believe," *New York Journal-American,* January 23, 1957, 8.

202 "What we have": "Sisters Would Sell Home," *New York Journal-American,* January 24, 1957, 9.

202 "As I grew older, I began": Longgood, "Lawyer for the Defense," 26.

203 "He thinks he's a hero": "Bomber Visited by Brother; Plea of Insanity Due," *New York Journal-American,* January 27, 1957, 8.

204 "They followed me to France": J. T. Dalby, "The Case of Daniel McNaughton: Let's Get the Story Straight," *American Journal of Forensic Psychiatry* 27, no. 4 (2006), 23.

206 "[Bazelon] observed that most": Ralph Slovenko, *Psychiatry in Law/Law in Psychiatry* (New York: Taylor & Francis Group, 2009), xxiii.

208 "more revolutionary in its total effect": Ralph Slovenko, *Psychiatry and Criminal Culpability* (New York: John Wiley & Sons, 1995), 120.

208 "has removed massive barriers": Slovenko, *Psychiatry in Law,* 202.

208 "The prosecutor and the medical expert": Gregory Zilboorg, *Psychology of the Criminal Act and Punishment* (New York: Harcourt, Brace, 1954), 8.

208 "This was simply the first": "Police, Con Ed Clash over Who Delayed on Bomber Bagging," New York *Daily News,* January 25, 1957, 2.

208 "alert, cooperative, and eager to oblige": Report of psychiatric examination of George Metesky, March 1, 1957, indictment no. 321/1957.

209 "to get back at people": Ibid.

209 "We attempted to get him": George Carpozi Jr., "Why Bomber Was Called Insane," *New York Journal-American,* March 31, 1957, 8.

209 "a police production worthy": "Mad Bomber in Court with 20-Cop Guard," *World-Telegram and Sun,* January 31, 1957, 2.

210 "I went to go into the detention pen": Ibid.

210 "You are indicted for the crime": "Pleading by Bomber Put Off: 'Doesn't Understand Charge,'" *New York Journal-American,* February 1, 1957, 4.

210 "Okay, let's go": Ibid.

210 "He has delusions of grandeur": "Judge Orders Sanity Test for Mad Bomber," *New York Journal-American,* January 31, 1957.

211 "Gee whiz": Charles Roland, "'Bomber' Indicted for B'kln Blast," *New York Journal-American,* February 19, 1957, 1.

211 "This fellow is smarter than": "Metesky Hearing Postponed; Wait Full MD Report," *New York Journal-American,* February 20, 1957, 1.

212 "If the written report is not ready": "Court Calls Bomber In for Arraignment," *New York Journal-American,* February 28, 1957, 3.

212 "had been broken up by": "Coddling of Boy Gangs Denounced by Court," *New York World-Telegram,* April 12, 1946, 5.

212 "The judge looks very much like": "Mullen Says Judge Must Unlearn Bias," *New York World-Telegram,* September 30, 1948, 1.

214 "No institution, state or Federal, is justified": Alfred E. Clark, "Judge Streit Censures Institutions That Free Mad Killers Like Peakes," *New York Times,* July 29, 1952, 1.

215 "What the doctors say about sanity": Jack Roth, "Trial Is Ordered for 'Mad Bomber,'" *New York Times,* March 1, 1957, 31.

216 "It is my opinion": Associated Press, "The 'Mad Bomber' Must Stand Trial," *Kansas City Times,* March 1, 1957, 30.

216 "He's a sick man": Francis Segrue, "Tombs Rejects Bomber, He's Back in Bellevue," *New York Herald Tribune,* March 2, 1957, 5.

216–17 "She had better not": Jack Roth, "Jail for Bomber Leads to Dispute," *New York Times,* March 2, 1957, 23.

217 "I'm going to do what I think": Ibid.

217 "I remanded the defendant": "Judge Denies Clash over 'Bomber' Case," *New York Times,* March 4, 1957, 16.

217 "the growing cult of irresponsibility": Jerome Hall, "Mental Disease and Criminal Responsibility—M'Naghten Versus Durham and the American Law Institute's Tentative Draft," *Indiana Law Journal* 33, no. 2 (January 1, 1958), 213.

218 "The law is right there": Jack Roth, "Judge, Lawyer Clash at 'Bomber' Hearing," *New York Times,* March 23, 1957, 1.

218 "not interested in how long": Ibid.

219 "already determined the issue": Ibid.

219 "I'm anxious to proceed": Ibid.

219 "a rather bizarre conflict": Transcript of hearing before Judge Samuel S. Leibowitz, March 27, 1957, Kings County Court, *The People of New York v. George Metesky,* indictment no. 269/1957, courtesy of Municipal Archives.

219 "Out of courtesy and respect": Ibid.

220 "proceed in the manner provided by law": Ibid.

220 "plain English": George Trow, "Silver Seeks to Avert Fight over Bomber," *New York Post,* April 1, 1957, 32.

220 "Your motion is denied!": Jack Roth, "Bomber Ordered to Stand Trial," March 30, 1957, 21.

221 "To try an insane person": "Disregards Expert Opinions," *New York Journal-American,* April 4, 1957, 5.

221 "It's no use living": "Mad Bomber Ill, Says 'It's No Use Living,'" *Bridgeport Post* (Connecticut), April 11, 1957, 2.

222 "How many reports would you": Transcript of hearing before Judge Samuel S. Leibowitz, April 10, 1957, Kings County Court, *The People of New York v. George Metesky,* indictment no. 269/1957, courtesy of Municipal Archives.

222 "Of the thousands of schizophrenics": Ibid.

223 "That, Your Honor, is a question": Ibid.

223 "If these procedures are prolonged": Ibid.

224 "One would be less than human": " 'Bomber' Ordered to State Hospital," *New York Times*, April 19, 1957, 44.

SEVENTEEN: Matteawan

225 "had made peace with the world": "Metesky Moved into Matteawan," *New York Journal-American*, April 19, 1957, 3.

226 "Three weeks ago Metesky was able": " 'Bomber' Ordered to State Hospital," *New York Times*, April 19, 1957, 44.

227 "The Mutt and Jeff team": James, " 'Mad Bomber,' " 47.

227 "He just couldn't take it": Ibid.

227 "the isolation of dangerous": *The General Statutes of the State of New York for the Year 1888* (Albany: Weed, Parsons and Company, 1888), 6.

228 "He's still paranoid": "Mad Bomber Loses Weight at Matteawan," *New York Herald Tribune*, December 25, 1957, 20.

229 "If this is true": "Expert Asks Compensation for Bomber," *New York Journal-American*, April 7, 1957, 6.

229 "I'm perfectly all right": "Mad Bomber Loses Weight," 20.

229–30 "He was calm, smiling and condescending": Brussel, *Casebook*, 72.

Epilogue

232 "Everybody has a hunch occasionally": Brussel, *Casebook*, 72.

233 "I read about it in": Ibid., 76.

233 "I've heard a lot about you": Ibid., 77.

234 "The community is getting nervous": Ibid.

234 "Physically, this is a skinny kid": Ibid., 83.

234 "You solved the case by telephone": Ibid., 90.

235 "injected fear into a neighborhood": Gay Talese, "Air of Fear Grips Sedate East Side," *New York Times*, August 31, 1963, 29.

235 "Never before or since": Brussel, *Casebook*, 106.

235 "He confessed?": Ibid., 124.

235 "Describe this man to me": Ibid., 125.

235 "He isn't your man": Ibid.

236 "The case was officially closed": Ibid., 132.

236 "I suspected they would not consult me": Ibid., 137.

237 "We were desperate for clues": *Stranglehold: In the Shadow of the Boston Strangler*, strangleholdthemovie.com.

237 "I hope you can do your Mad Bomber trick": Brussel, *Casebook*, 138.

237 "unusual methods": Ibid., 137.

237 "The photographs we had been shown": Ibid., 146.

237 "Somewhere in this terrible saga": Ibid., 148.

238 "The ideas that had been milling about": Ibid., 151.

238 "What has happened to him": Ibid., 152.

238 "He was taking steps toward": Ibid., 154.

239 "Go ahead, Doctor": Ibid., 156.

239 "One more thing": Ibid., 157.

239 "He may want to tell of his success": Ibid., 158.

240 "Don't make a sound": F. Lee Bailey, *The Defense Never Rests* (New York: Stein & Day, 1971), 147.

240 "He had reached a point": Ibid., 148.

241 "He seemed more knowledgeable": F. Lee Bailey, interview with author, June 16, 2015.

242 "A man has to be paranoid": Mel Heimer, "My New York," *Titusville* (Pennsylvania.) *Herald,* August 1959, 6.

243 "While [Brussel] was for all intents and purposes": "Profiling: The FBI Legacy," *Forensic Psychology,* www.all-about-forensic-psychology.com/offender-profiling.html.

244 "the kind of society we had become": Robert K. Ressler and Tom Shachtman, *Whoever Fights Monsters: My Twenty Years Tracking Serial Killers for the FBI* (New York: St. Martin's Press, 1992), 153.

244 "Brussel did not really understand": Malcolm Gladwell, "Dangerous Mind: Criminal Profiling Made Easy," *New Yorker,* November 12, 2007, 36.

244 "By studying thousands of cases": Jim Clemente, author interview, June 10, 2015.

245 "What I try to do with a case": Mark Olshaker and John E. Douglas, *Mindhunter: Inside the FBI's Elite Serial Crimes Unit* (New York: Scribner, 1995), 151.

245 "It's the way you think": Thomas Harris, *Red Dragon* (New York: G. P. Putnam's Sons, 1981), 2.

245 "They make profiling seem like": Ressler and Shachtman, *Whoever Fights Monsters,* 271.

246 "Unless this article can fairly": *Berkson v. Time, Inc.,* Appellate Division of the Supreme Court of New York, 1959.

247 "You are a man now": Seymour Berkson letter to Bill Berkson, date unknown.

247 "It is a mad era": George E. Sokolsky, "Lying in a Hospital Bed a Time for Introspection," *Milwaukee Sentinel,* January 7, 1959, 26.

248 "As the day of the assassination": Robert A. Caro, *The Passage of Power* (New York: Alfred A. Knopf, 2012), 342.

249 "No one in management had the stomach": Hearst Jr., *Hearsts,* 304.

249 "Well, buddy": Ibid., 305.

249 "We think this will be a glorious": "A Beginning . . . Not an End," *New York Journal-American,* April 24, 1966, 14.

250 "I am *not* here to discuss": Associated Press, "New Man Heads Troubled Police Force," *Bee* (Danville, Virginia), June 28, 1962, 15.

251 "They were ready to go and demonstrate": James, "'Mad Bomber,'" *Rolling Stone,* 48.

251 "It is indeed a shameful situation": George Metesky letter to District Attorney Frank Hogan, November 24, 1963.

253 "inappropriate emotional reaction": Transcript of hearing, December 15, 1966, *George Metesky v. Dr. W. C. Johnston, Superintendent, Matteawan State Hospital,* Supreme Court of the State of New York, Dutchess County.

253 "When I seen the charge of the ward": George Metesky letter to Supreme Court of New York, Kings County, January 12, 1972.

254 "I was fearless": Kristin Booth Glen, interview with author, July 1, 2014.

255 "Matteawan will no longer be": "High Court Backs Commitment Curb," *New York Times,* May 30, 1973, 14.

255 "I think the judge is right": United Press International, "George Metesky a Free Man," *Naugatuck Daily News,* December 13, 1973, 9.

256 "I think it's best not to talk": "Follow-Up on the News," *New York Times,* April 7, 1974, 33.

256 "Free at last": Associated Press, "Mad Bomber Leaves Hospital a Free Man," *Naugatuck Daily News,* December 13, 1973, 9.

256 "I finally told her": Associated Press, "The Quiet Life Still Suits Man Who Made Noise," *Bridgeport* (Connecticut.) *Post,* January 26, 1975, 7.

256 "George was very faithful": James, "'Mad Bomber,'" 47.

256 "In a suit he looks like": Ibid.

257 "They never stop coming": United Press International, "Bomber Says Blast Shocking," *Bridgeport* (Connecticut) *Post,* January 10, 1976, 7.

INDEX

Triangle Shirtwaist Factory, 180
truce until January 10th
    cost of, 146
    end of, 150–151
    letter proposing, 141–142
Truman, Harry, 28
tuberculosis
    antibiotics and, 106, 227, 244
    as cause of grudge, 156
    near death from, 221–224, 226

U
Ubell, Earl, 188
Unabomber, 257
undiscovered bombs, locations of, 141,
    173

V
Valentine, Lewis, 53
vengeance, 101
Vietnam War, 80
Vollmer, August, 52
Volpi di Misurata, Giuseppe, 120
von Hohenlohe, Stephanie Julianne, 42

W
W (letter), handwriting analysis and,
    103–104
Wagner, Robert F. Jr., 67–70, 82
Wall Street bomb, 16–18

warning letters, 23, 57–58
Warren, Earl, 206
watch repairman, 54
Waterbury, 160–162
Waterbury Republican, 175–176
White, Stanford, 228
White Plains, 146–147, 152, 154
Whitmore, George Jr., 235–236
Whitney Museum, 120–121
Wilson, Woodrow, 17, 18
Workmen's Compensation Board
    compensation claims against, 153
    denial of claims by, 180–181
    O'Rourke and claims against, 196–197,
        229
    statute of limitations argument and,
        180, 197
World Journal Tribune, 249
World's Fair bomb, 18–20
World-Telegram and Sun, 150–151
writs of habeas corpus, 229,
    252–253

Y
Yippies, 250–251
Young, Joyce, 85–87
Young, Mary, 85–87

Z
Zilboorg, Gregory, 208
Zinno, Dominic, 49–50

Michael Weschler

Michael Cannell is the author of *The Limit: Life and Death on the 1961 Grand Prix Circuit* and *I.M. Pei: Mandarin of Modernism*. He was editor of *The New York Times'* House & Home section for seven years and has written for *The New Yorker, The New York Times Magazine, Sports Illustrated,* and many other publications. He lives in New York City.